Women with a Thirst for Destruction

Northwestern University Press
Studies in Russian Literature and Theory

Women with a Thirst for Destruction

THE BAD MOTHER IN RUSSIAN CULTURE

Jenny Kaminer

NORTHWESTERN UNIVERSITY PRESS / EVANSTON, ILLINOIS

Northwestern University Press
www.nupress.northwestern.edu

This book has been published with the support of the Andrew W. Mellon Foundation.

Printed in the United States of America

10 9 8 7 6 5 4 3 2 1

Library of Congress Cataloging-in-Publication Data

Kaminer, Jenny, author.
Women with a thirst for destruction : the bad mother in Russian culture / Jenny Kaminer.
pages cm. — (Northwestern University Press studies in Russian literature and theory)
ISBN 978-0-8101-2946-7 (cloth : alk. paper)
1. Mothers in literature. 2. Russian fiction—19th century—History and criticism. 3. Russian fiction—20th century—History and criticism. 4. Motherhood in popular culture—Russia (Federation) I. Title. II. Series: Studies in Russian literature and theory.
PG3096.M68K36 2014
891.7093520852—dc23

2013039162

∞ The paper used in this publication meets the minimum requirements of the American National Standard for Information Sciences—Permanence of Paper for Printed Library Materials, ANSI Z39.48-1992.

Contents

Acknowledgments

This project is over ten years in the making, and I am indebted both personally and intellectually to numerous individuals and institutions that have helped me along the way. My interest in gender in Russian culture was first awakened by Clare Cavanagh in an undergraduate course at the University of Wisconsin, and her encouragement, support, and astute questioning continued to guide me throughout my graduate career and beyond. Andrew Wachtel created an atmosphere of intellectual rigor and excitement, a small amount of which I modestly hope this book has captured.

Research for this project was supported by an American Council of Teachers of Russian (ACTR) Title VIII Advanced Research Fellowship, which allowed to me to conduct research in various libraries in both Moscow and St. Petersburg for six months in 2005. The members of the Foreign Historians' Congress provided invaluable fellowship and moral support during these exciting months.

I would like to thank my colleagues, both past and present, at Oberlin College (Amanda Blasko, Arlene Forman, Thomas Newlin, and Tim Scholl), the University of Sheffield, and the University of California–Davis for their support and mentorship. Susan E. Reid at the University of Sheffield read and provided insightful commentary on an early draft of the introduction, for which I am extremely grateful.

Part of chapter 1 originally appeared as "A Mother's Land: Arina Petrovna Golovlyova and the Economic Restructuring of the Golovlyov Family," in *Slavic and East European Journal* 53, no. 4 (2009): 545–65. Part of chapter 3 was first published as "The 'Angelic Little Image' Falls from Grace: *Adam's Rib* and the Reimagining of Maternity," in *Beyond Little Vera: Women's Bodies, Women's Welfare in Russia and Central/Eastern Europe,* ed. Angela Brintlinger and Natasha Kolchevska, Ohio Slavic Papers, vol. 7 (Columbus, Ohio, 2008): 55–71.

This project—as well as all the other important ones in my life—owes its biggest intellectual and emotional debt to my husband, Christoph

Gumb—my most compelling critic, faithful reader, astute proofreader, and technical support liaison. His contribution to this book is too large to quantify, as is my gratitude.

Women with a Thirst for Destruction

Introduction

A SINFUL MOTHER, according to Russian folk tradition, can portend the end of the world. At the end of the 1990s, several elderly women from the Starorusskii district in the Novgorod region of western Russia confirmed that the end of time was, in fact, drawing near, as evinced by changes that they observed in the local icon of the Mother of God. The women claimed that they witnessed an alteration in the Mother of God's expression—that she had "turned away from Christ"—and interpreted this as irrefutable evidence of the impending apocalypse. The Mother of God spurned Christ, they believed, because so many women now scorned their maternal obligations by having fewer children and hastening the depopulation of the Russian land. The disappearance of children led to the somber, joyless time in which they currently live, where "even the birds don't sing anymore." Both the signal and the cause of civilization's doom, then, could be traced back to the figure of the bad mother.[1]

In their vision of a transformed Mother of God coldly rejecting her Son, these women read the specific circumstances of post-Soviet society—a declining birthrate and the oft-acknowledged demographic crisis—in an iconic image of idealized maternity. In other words, their predictions of a worldwide cataclysm presaged by a bad mother reveal the interplay between the historical specificity of motherhood and a deeply embedded, ahistorical maternal mythology. This intersection of the temporal with the infinite in the women's judgment of the bad (non-)mothers in their provincial Russian milieu neatly fits Theodor H. Gaster's definition of myth as "any presentation of the actual in terms of the ideal," as "any expression of the concept that all things can be viewed at once under two aspects—on the one hand, temporal and immediate; on the other, eternal and transcendental."[2] In the women's description, the transfigured Mother of God icon represents the violation of the ideal of maternity in a specific historical context by actual women—those Soviet and post-Soviet non-mothers who have refused maternity for a myriad of (undoubtedly) complicated social, economic, and cultural factors.

The predictions of the old women from the Starorusskii district reveal the power invested in both symbolic and actual maternity by traditional Russian society. They also exhibit the blurring of boundaries between fantasy and reality in conceptions of motherhood and, by extension, the multifaceted value with which a bad mother may be endowed.

This study takes as its launching point the intersection between the historically specific and the iconic—the "immediate" and the "transcendental"—images of motherhood that characterizes the prognostications of the elderly women of the Starorusskii district. Does the women's faith in the Mother of God's ability to predict the future indicate the depth of their reverence for iconic motherhood? Or does their vision of the icon's "unmaternal" behavior reveal the diminishing of that reverence? Are the women projecting their despair at historically contingent bad motherhood onto the icon? Or is the ideal of motherhood altered by their experience of its reality? Although it is certainly impossible to penetrate the individual psychology of these women, this incident provides an evocative crystallization of the questions that I explore in this study. What, precisely, does it mean to be a bad mother in the context of a culture where, according to the philosopher Nikolai Berdiaev, "motherhood is the fundamental category"?[3] How do cultural, socioeconomic, and political factors influence definitions of positive and negative maternal behavior? How are these influences reflected in the cultural production of a given era? Can the bad mother be identified as a recurrent trope in Russian culture, one that encompasses several historical periods as well as multiple media and genres? If so, what are its salient characteristics? What continuities and discontinuities exist in the representation of this image by different authors, with different implied readerships, and in the highly disparate circumstances that characterize Russian, Soviet, and post-Soviet history? Does the figure of the bad mother violate the maternal ideal by exposing its contingency and variability? Or does it merely reaffirm the tenacity of the myth of the beneficent, self-sacrificing Russian mother (the genesis and characteristics of which will be discussed below)?

In exploring the answers to these questions, I do not attempt a survey of all the exemplars of bad motherhood in Russian culture. Instead, to elucidate this juncture between the "temporal" and the "transcendental" in representations of Russian maternity, I have narrowed the chronological focus of this study, concentrating on the image of the bad mother—one who shuns, subverts, or manipulates the maternal myth—in three crucial periods of Russian and Soviet history. In her analysis of cultural representations of motherhood in England and the United States, E. Ann Kaplan posits "three major economic/political/technological eruptions that affected the historical mother and produced corresponding changes in mother-discourses" in western Europe: the Industrial Revolution, World War I, and the electronic revolution following World War II.[4] In Russia, as Helena Goscilo has argued, "if . . . issues of gender gain greater currency during political or national crises," then "that pattern manifests itself specifically in an intensification of maternal metaphors."[5] I contend that the historic upheavals that most dramatically affected this "mother-discourse" in Russia and stimulated the subsequent "intensification of maternal metaphors" were the Emancipation of the serfs in 1861, the Russian Revolution of 1917, and the collapse of the Soviet Union in the early 1990s. The first chapter of this book, then, concentrates on works from the 1870s, the decade after the Emancipation and the Great Reforms, which also witnessed the rise of radical movements, culminating in the assassination of Tsar Alexander II in 1881. The reforms of the 1860s and 1870s—which included not only the liberation of some twenty million serfs but also the transformation of the legal system, changes in the educational system (including allowing women access to higher education), and the introduction of general conscription into the Russian army—triggered a wholesale reevaluation of all traditional institutions of Russian life, including the patriarchal family. In addition, the end of serfdom profoundly altered gentry life, necessitating a more intimate involvement in the daily tasks of child-rearing for some women while forcing others to seek employment outside of the home to prop up devastated household finances.

Next, chapter 2 examines works from the 1920s, the period immediately following the Russian Revolution. This decade experienced the effects of the 1918 changes in marriage and family laws designed to eliminate the authority of the Orthodox Church over domestic matters, while also hastening the "withering away" of the traditional family. In addition to this radical shift in official policy toward marriage, divorce, and procreation, the violence, deprivation, and displacement of several years of revolution and Civil War left most new citizens of the new Soviet state confronting a precarious and uncharted future. Finally, chapter 3 focuses on material from the 1990s, when the breakup of the Soviet Union and the accompanying social, cultural, and economic upheaval again caused a tectonic shift under the feet of Russians, now citizens of a vanished empire. In cultural works from all three of these periods, a "temporal," historically specific bad mother emerges to problematize the "eternal" image of the self-sacrificing, noble, and heroic maternal figure. Although certain aspects of motherhood in Russian and Soviet culture, as well as the myth of the Russian gentry childhood, have been previously explored by scholars, this study is the first to analyze the bad mother in both canonical and popular literature, and to track the development of this image from the nineteenth-century novel to late twentieth-century prose and film.[6] It is the first to identify and to analyze the bad mother as a recurrent but highly variable motif in Russian cultural works spanning several centuries.

The focus on these three historical periods also allows me to situate more effectively representations of motherhood in Russia within a broader European and cultural context. The central issue of Ann Taylor Allen's historical study of motherhood in western Europe from the late nineteenth to the twentieth century revolves around the varying individual and societal responses to what she terms "the maternal dilemma," which Allen defines as a striving to reconcile motherhood with women's autonomous individuality.[7] Does motherhood circumscribe a woman's contributions to both the private and the public sphere? Or is it possible to fulfill other functions alongside a maternal role? Early twentieth-century European feminist efforts to attain this elusive integration between motherhood and autonomy focused on the concept of "maternalism," an ideology that maintained that women deserved rights as citizens because of their contributions as mothers, that the qualities necessary for motherhood made women valuable to society as a whole and thus deserving of full participatory rights. The ultimate private function, motherhood was utilized as the means for gaining access to the public sphere and securing new rights (the right to vote in particular).[8] The notion that women's pursuit of civil rights should be based upon their maternal abilities was vehemently rejected by Western feminists later in the twentieth century. As Allen summarizes, "by 1970 . . . [the] shift in feminist debates . . . aggressively refused to acknowledge motherhood as a universal female vocation, moral mission, or duty of citizenship . . . the grandmothers' exalted ideal becomes the granddaughters' restrictive stereotype."[9] Simone de Beauvoir's declaration that the "one feminine function which is almost impossible to exercise in freedom . . . is maternity" exemplified the ambivalence about motherhood that characterized postwar European feminism.[10]

As even the most cursory acquaintance with Russian history and culture reveals, notions of "autonomy," "individuality," "public and private sphere" and "civil rights" (not to mention "feminism") possess quite different definitions and connotations in both the imperial Russian and the Soviet context.[11] Given this disparity, what, then, are the specifics of the Russian "maternal dilemma"? And, more importantly, what might the case of Russia reveal about the kind of maternal imagery that emerges during periods of transition and flux? The cultural production of a given era, by disseminating images of both good and bad motherhood, plays a pivotal role in reflecting, shaping, and fomenting the conflict between the individual and society that the maternal dilemma implies. I shed light on these questions by focusing on the interplay between the "immediate" and the "eternal"—between maternal mythology and historically contingent reality—in periods of exceptional societal shift. It is precisely during such periods of instability that, as in the incident of the old women of the Starorusskii region, the conflicts between iconic maternity and the actual behavior of mothers may come into the sharpest relief, as an analysis of the literature, popular fiction, and film that I analyze will show.

This study attempts to illuminate the symbolic value of maternity in Russian culture by analyzing the representations of those women who either violate the maternal ideal or expose its historical variability (or sometimes both). Although, in each decade under consideration, the image of the bad mother responds to different social realities, it also undermines or challenges certain common aspects of the dominant maternal myth. As discussed below, the ability to bring into harmony clashing elements within a family, and to mediate between that family and the outside world, constitutes a key tenet of the maternal archetype in Russia. The bad mother, then, refuses to assume this mediating function, allowing her own personality and desires to disturb familial balance. She also refuses to subordinate her own needs to those of her children, all the while extolling her own self-sacrificial virtues (as is the case in works from both the 1870s and the 1990s). In the works of contemporary author Liudmila Petrushevskaia (who will be discussed in chapter 3) in particular, the parasitical mother extends this aspect of the maternal myth to a grotesque extreme: self-sacrifice becomes smothering and tyrannical, transforming the devoted mother into a monster. Her mothers wield the maternal myth as a weapon in the ongoing war that defines familial relations in Petrushevskaia's works.

From the canonical nineteenth-century novel to late-twentieth-century prose and film, the bad mother, in all three periods discussed in this study, forces a reconsideration of the myth of the heroic, noble, and self-abnegating Russia mother. The multidisciplinary scope of this project—which includes classic novels and popular fiction, as well as film—allows me to identify recurring motifs in the images of negative maternity across genre and media, and to explore the elements of this image that have been the most tenacious and enduring. By focusing on the case of Russia, where maternity has been the repository of so much symbolic value, this study also sheds light on the nature of maternal imagery during periods of crisis. But first, it is necessary to identify the main characteristics of the iconic Russian mother against which the historically contingent bad mother has been defined, and to discuss briefly the evolution of Russian maternal mythology.

THE ICONIC RUSSIAN MOTHER

"The woman will be a good mother," writes Elisabeth Badinter in her history of modern maternity and the evolution of mother love, "to a greater or lesser extent as a direct consequence of the level of esteem the society bestows upon the maternal role."[12] This logic should render Russian mothers irreproachable, since the hallowed and unique position of the mother in Russian culture has been reaffirmed by religious figures, scholars, philosophers, writers, and political leaders for centuries. The worship of motherhood and the maternal principle has been a constant throughout Russian history, from the Christianization of Rus' to the present day.[13] Throughout the cataclysms of Russian history, the image of the mother retains its constancy and serves as the Russian woman's primary means of earning esteem in society.[14] The dynamic between mother and child provides the foundation for other social relationships, and any social phenomenon, if broken down into its constituent parts, will reveal a connection with motherhood.[15] The worship of motherhood even distinguishes Russian intellectual history from that of the West, according to one Russian scholar, because Russian philosophers never agreed with those Western thinkers—such as Schopenhauer, Nietzsche, Freud, and Weininger—who believed in the superiority of men and the weakness of women because of the latter's supposed existence primarily as child-bearers.[16] A woman accumulates value within the "Russian cosmos," according to Russian scholar Oleg Riabov, predominantly in a maternal guise.[17]

How did the maternal figure come to occupy such a prominent position in the "Russian cosmos"? The earliest clues undoubtedly lie in the pagan worship of a maternal divinity known as Moist Mother Earth (*mat' syra zemlia*) by the pre-Christian Slavs and Varangians. The cult of the Mother Goddess that flourished among these peoples viewed the earth not only as a maternal body that nourished her offspring, but also as the source of political authority and fertility. The "moistness" of Moist Mother Earth suggested her union with the waters of both the sky and the earth, as well as her pivotal role in the perpetuation of the cycle of life.[18] As Adele Marie Barker summarizes, "From earliest times when the earth was called by the pagan Russians 'mat' syra zemlia,' the damp mother earth, the image of woman has been associated with a life-giving force, with a physical and emotional nourishment which lay at the heart of man's ability to survive. The traits attributed to Moist Mother Earth—her generative powers and her ability to nurture life—became the foundation for the maternal archetype in Russia."[19] The veneration of Moist Mother Earth was eventually driven underground, but worship of her survived in the folk traditions of the Russian peasantry. After the Christianization of Rus' in 988, the characteristics of the pagan goddess merged with those of a new maternal divinity: Mary, Mother of God (*Bogoroditsa*). The worshipping of the Mother of God proved the most fruitful of the clergy's attempts to neutralize and control pagan cults. The persona of Mary combined with already existing and well-entrenched maternal influence in both the religious and the familial spheres.[20] The prominence of the maternal divinity in Russian Orthodox sentiment has been affirmed by religious thinkers and philosophers such as Nikolai Berdiaev, who observed that the Mother of God almost eclipses Christ himself in Russian religious belief. Berdiaev attributed great significance to the fact that, of the three elements of the Trinity, it is only the Mother of God that is given a "personal incarnation," symbolizing the people's much more immediate and visceral identification with her.[21] In medieval Rus', the personification of the revered maternal figure consisted of three parts: the Russian land, the church, and the Mother of God, which combined to form one maternal image.[22] A popular Russian peasant proverb underscores this tripartite imagery: "Your first mother is *Bogoroditsa;* your second mother is the earth; and your third mother is your own mother."[23] Seemingly, then, Christianity could not take root in Rus' without an acknowledgment of the people's powerful attachment to the maternal archetype and the channeling of this sentiment toward veneration of the Mother of God. This attachment endured throughout the centuries; as late as 1918, Orthodox writers were still arguing that, for the common lay people, Mary's importance had eclipsed that of Christ himself.[24] In his classic study of Russian religious belief, G. P. Fedotov summed it up succinctly when he declared that "the very core of the Russian religion [is] divine motherhood."[25]

A closer look at medieval Russian icons of the Mother of God highlights the centrality of the *Bogoroditsa* in Russian religious sentiment and also reveals certain salient features of the maternal mythology that this imagery helped to establish. If, in the Western church, the presence of the Mother of God was felt mainly through visions and apparitions, in Russia it was Marian icons that provided believers with the conduit for experiencing her closeness.[26] Russian Mother of God icons were distinguished from their Byzantine counterparts by two elements: a tendency toward a warmer, more tender depiction of the relationship between mother and child; and an emphasis on the *Bogoroditsa*'s intercessory function, which reveals that Mary's love for her son extends to all of humanity as well. The aloofness and solemnity of the Byzantine Mother of God are tempered by the *Bogoroditsa*'s display of maternal emotion, which came to be called *umilenie,* translated as "loving-kindness." If the "severe majesty" of the Byzantine icons emphasizes "the divinity of the Child-Christ," according to Leonid Ouspensky and Vladimir Lossky's classic study of Russian icons, then their Russian counterparts, by contrast, are "full of a natural human feeling—of mother-love and tenderness."[27]

All human emotions that are exhibited in icons are transformed by contact with divine grace. In the case of maternal sentiment, the transformation involves a broadening of motherly love to encompass all of mankind, to include all of those sinners for whom Christ sacrificed himself.[28] The *Bogoroditsa*'s personal grief becomes compassion for all of humanity, on behalf of whom she will intercede to the Heavenly Father. Devotional accounts recount how, before her death, Mary declared to the apostles that, once at the side of her Son in heaven, she would use her position to deliver personal pleas for the sake of the faithful.[29] This intercessory function is visible in an especially popular icon, the *Pokrov* (or "Virgin of the Veil"), which is typically elevated above the holy doors in an Orthodox church. It features two angels holding a veil that extends over the worshippers below, while Jesus delivers blessings responding to Mary's prayers for the sinners above it.[30] A literary illustration of the Mother of God's role as intercessor can be found in the apocryphal medieval text, "The Descent of the Virgin into Hell." At Mary's request, the Archangel Michael leads her on a tour of the grotesque sufferings of all of the sinners residing in hell, and she both weeps and provides momentary comfort for them. The sinners plead for her to intercede on their behalf, and Mary's protestations move Michael and the other angels to pray to the Heavenly Father for mercy. This gesture touches the Lord who, "seeing the intercession of the saints, became merciful for his Son's sake," and calls Christ to witness the prayers. The text ends with Christ granting the sinners a reprieve from their torments from "Good Thursday to Holy Pentecost," crediting "the intercession of my Mother who has wept much for you" for inspiring this act of mercy.[31]

Hence, the mythology of Russian motherhood—as determined first by the maternal divinity Moist Mother Earth and, more importantly, by the image of the Russian Mother of God (*Bogoroditsa*) portrayed mainly in medieval icons but also in various religious texts—stresses the tenderness, boundlessness, and mercifulness of maternal sentiment. Religious teachings exhorted women to minimize the gap between their own sinful, mortal selves and the ideal of the Mother of God through childbearing.[32] Both church doctrine and folk tradition perpetuated the idea that children were a blessing for a family and the only justification of a woman's presence in it. Accordingly, Orthodox doctrine encouraged reverence for mothers and strongly decried any signs of ingratitude toward them, with the demand to cherish and watch over one's mother already found among the earliest church didactic literature in 1076. Affirmations of the holiness of a mother's word and the wisdom of a mother's teachings and upbringing permeate church literature of the pre-Muscovite period.[33]

Significantly, the Orthodox incarnation of the Mother of God differed from that of the Western church precisely in this emphasis on her identity as a mother, rather than as a virgin.[34] Alluding to the pagan underpinnings of the Mary figure in Russia, Fedotov explains the linguistic foundation of the distinction between "Mother" and "Virgin": "The Mother of God was not casually chosen to replace the goddesses of birth. She was obviously the embodiment of motherhood, divine Motherhood itself . . . The most common name of Mary among Russian people is *Bogoroditsa,* the literal translation of the Greek *Theotokos:* not Blessed Virgin (or 'La Sainte Vierge'), not our Lady . . . not 'Liebe Frau,' but 'Mother of God.' "[35]

The Orthodox liturgy and the Russian pious tradition repeatedly emphasize Mary's maternity and fertility, rather than her virginity.[36] Simply put, the sanctified image of woman-as-mother has taken deeper root in the Russian national psyche than has the cult of the Virgin Mary.[37] One twentieth-century Russian thinker, the émigré philosopher I. A. Il'in, even argues that the Russian people's unique ability to recognize and worship this "divine mother" endows them with a kind of moral superiority: "A people capable of honoring the Bogoroditsa in this way prove that they have the ability to value the great mystery of motherhood, the secret of maternal love . . . The worship of the Bogoroditsa preserves in the national soul the foundation of love, tenderness, sacrifice, chastity, service, chivalry."[38] Hence, interestingly, Il'in claims that the Russians preserve in *themselves* precisely those positive qualities associated with the good mother—including love, tenderness, self-sacrifice, and modesty—through their veneration of the maternal.

In her role as intercessor, as discussed above, one of the Mother of God's salient functions is as a mediator between the earthly and divine realms.[39] The philosopher Sergei Bulgakov provides a vivid description of how the Mother of God fulfills this mediating role: "Like a merciful heart, like maternal mercy and pity, which does not judge but only grieves and forgives all, the Mother of God speaks out during the Final Judgment, where she pleads on behalf of the human race and represents the sinners . . . This is what comprises her mediatory significance [*posrednicheskoe znachenie*]: She brings to Her Son, the Savior of the world, the world that He has saved."[40] Acting as an intermediary, the *Bogoroditsa* protects believers not only from external enemies but also from the cruel judgment of God the Father.[41] This mediatory function also became associated with earthly female authority. In pre-Petrine Russia, the tsaritsa, even though confined to the *terem* (the female quarters in the homes of the elite), fulfilled the role of spiritual intercessor on behalf of the people to the tsar. The Mother of God figured prominently in prayers for tsaritsas from the sixteenth century onward, and the image, for example, of Catherine I (the wife of Peter the Great) as "dear mother-intercessor" (*matushka-zastupnitsa*) appeared frequently in both the public and private accounts of her contemporaries. As the Mother of God intervened on behalf of her sinful children, so the members of Peter the Great's circle appealed to Catherine to intercede with her husband on their behalf.[42]

The Mother of God's role as mediator extends into the dynamics of the Russian family, where the mother assumes responsibility for ensuring harmony. A strong taboo against mothers exhibiting any aggressive, destabilizing behavior exists in traditional Russian culture, and she bears culpability for any violence that occurs within a home (including if her husband beats her).[43] A mother must cement family ties and ensure closeness between siblings. When a mother becomes the senior woman (*bol'shukha*) of a household, she undertakes all duties involving commemoration of deceased relatives and ancestors, becoming the mediator between the dead and the living as well. Just as Marian icons were capable of uniting disparate groups of believers, of inspiring the formation of "one community through her person," so mothers, according to Russian maternal mythology, must neutralize chaos and discord within individual families as well as mediate between that family and the outside world.[44] The *Domostroi,* the pre-Petrine household advice manual, advised children not only to honor their parents lest they incur divine wrath, but reminded them of the intercessory function of a mother's prayers, which could shield them from harm.[45]

Illustrations of how and why a mother must fulfill this mediatory function can be found in both the Russian literary and philosophical traditions. The prominent nineteenth-century Slavophile A. S. Khomiakov, for example, believed that the family, founded on "self-denying egoism . . . brings sexual antagonisms into harmony."[46] A woman's ability to obtain a divorce, he believed, endangered this precarious balance. Divorce could lead to an irrevocable cleavage within society, where females and males would be eternally separated from one another. The collapse of family life symptomatized the menace of Western individualism—as opposed to Slavic communalism (*sobornost'*)—that the Petrine reforms had allowed to penetrate Slavic society, and that Khomiakov and the other Slavophiles vehemently opposed. According to Slavophile thinking, the Westernization initiated by Peter the Great in the early eighteenth century had already caused a fatal rift between the people, who preserved the ideal of the patriarchal family, and the elite, whose family ties were dissolving.[47] Khomiakov further argued that only a woman's role as a mother, and the presence of children, could protect her during the inevitable war of the sexes that would follow the division between husband and wife precipitated by divorce: "Children are the sole protection, sole and unbreakable, which saves the sex from the violence of male superiority." Hence, motherhood and the security of the patriarchal family neutralize the potentially destabilizing differences between men and women. Consequently, a woman who refuses to assume this harmonizing role "condemns [herself] to slavery."[48] The traditional family, in turn, helps to preserve the essential Slavic characteristics of the Russian people that are endangered by the incursion of corrupt Western values.

In her analysis of Tolstoy's *War and Peace,* Laura J. Olson describes how one of the work's heroines—the initially vivacious, flirtatious, and inconstant Natasha Rostova—briefly stimulates a disharmony similar to that envisioned by Khomiakov before finding salvation in the maternal realm. "After a moral fall in which she comes perilously close to attracting men in the manner of a femme fatale," Olson writes, "[Natasha] undergoes a transformation to a fertile matron, a mother."[49] In defining what she identifies as Tolstoy's new configuration of the family, Olson argues that part 1 of the "Epilogue" of the novel establishes "a bourgeois utopia within the context of the Russian aristocracy." This utopia is founded upon the principle of mother-as-harmonizer: "Conflict does not exist because the mother mediates all desire. The family members are protected from the ravages of Culture, of the outside world; their freedom from intervention by the state or by social pressure is ensured in this private sphere."[50] Thus, Natasha Rostova—who is transformed from a naive and frivolous young girl to a devoted and loving mother during the course of the novel—provides an example of how the abstract concept of the maternal figure as mediator is concretized in the daily life of a fictional family.

THE SELF-SACRIFICIAL MOTHER

In western Europe, a dramatic shift in ideas about the role and image of the mother occurred in the second half of the eighteenth century, a shift that would have a significant impact on the development of maternal mythology in Russia as well. After 1760, a mother's duties and the intimate details of her relationship with her children became an object of discourse. Women were advised to take a personal role in caring for their children and were strongly encouraged to breast-feed, devoting themselves exclusively to motherhood at the expense of all other pursuits. The new mother who emerged during this period was defined as one who wholly subordinates her own needs and desires for the sake of raising her children. From now on, the child would play the central role in the mother's life, and she would sacrifice herself in his service. This definition of the good mother persisted and strengthened, leading to the development of what Kaplan terms the "maternal sacrifice paradigm," which reached its peak in the nineteenth century.[51] One of the main theoreticians of this "new mother" was Jean-Jacques Rousseau, who, in his 1762 novel *Émile,* initiated the modern family founded on "mother love."[52] By the early nineteenth century, these Enlightenment ideas—those of Rousseau in particular—were already influencing Russian ideas about family life and stimulating a newfound focus on children. Russia might have proven fertile ground for Rousseau's ideas precisely because of the high value that the culture already placed on motherhood.[53]

In Russia, as will be discussed in detail in chapter 1, self-sacrifice also became a central tenet of the myth of the good mother. The "separate spheres" ideology, which emerged in the wake of the Industrial Revolution in Europe, exhorted women to act as moral guardians and bulwarks from the nefarious influence of the outside world. In English novels by writers such as Charles Dickens, William Thackeray, and Anthony Trollope, the "angels in the house"—docile, faithful, and unconditionally loving wives and mothers—provided comfort to husbands ravaged by the newly emergent capitalist marketplace. If the *Domostroi* deemed the male the ultimate master of the domestic domain, with the wife assigned an auxiliary role, the new cult of domesticity proclaimed the wife wholly responsible for transforming the home into a sanctuary capable of fulfilling all of the husband's needs and desires. As Barbara Engel deftly summarizes, the home was "no longer governed by the husband"; rather, it "was now to be governed *for* him."[54]

Both Rousseau's "new mother" and the Victorian "angel in the house" dovetailed rather neatly with existing maternal mythology in Russia.[55] The Russian variation on these European maternal myths merged self-abnegation with the mother's role as mediator. The educated classes actively read the advice manuals and other prescriptive literature stimulated by this ideology, which transformed the domestic sphere into a hallowed realm and placed the mother at the center of it.[56] In a pamphlet published in Moscow in 1869, for example, the critic Nikolai Solov'ev proclaims that a man should seek solace in a woman's moral purity rather than in petty vices: "In her . . . you will find all of the comfort that you vainly sought in bars, in hitting billiard cues and turning pale at the sound of lost money." Indeed, woman must make "the hearth shine with a new light and transform family life, which is full of conflict, squabbles, and banality, into a sanctuary where one can hide from societal ills and calamities."[57] As historian Richard Wortman has detailed, the image of the empress in Russia during this century—as in the other European empires of the period—also evolved to conform to this vision of woman as moral guardian. In a reaction against the values of the eighteenth century, embodied by the ambitious and ruthless Catherine the Great, the empress of the nineteenth century must "fit the new conceptions of the family and act as cherishing mother to her child. Her principal sphere was to become the home, rather than the court or state . . . She had to embody the purity and respectability of the regime, and, at the dynastic level, to act out the woman's nineteenth-century role as moral custodian of a society that otherwise could not afford morality."[58] Thus, the woman mediates between the individual family—whether it be royal, noble, or middle class—and the morally corrosive outside world, relying upon the "soul-healing power of female virtue."[59]

In Russia, not surprisingly, the maternal aspect of this virtue figured especially prominently. Unlike in the West, the Women's Question in Russia emerged in the context of a heightened emphasis on the mother's role as educator of future citizens.[60] In an article entitled "The Tasks of the Russian Mother," for example, published in the journal *Family and School* in 1874 (during the same period as the publication of M. E. Saltykov-Shchedrin's *The Golovlev Family* and L. N. Tolstoy's *Anna Karenina,* the two novels discussed in chapter 1), the author asserts that "only the influence of a good Russian woman can create a complete person." Although, in theory, a woman may work outside the home, she must never lose sight of her fundamental obligation to society: "A woman must . . . understand both the historical and social conditions for progress in her homeland and in society in general. In order to successfully complete the task that is her lot as a mother—raising an honorable citizen—she must renounce narrow-minded, bourgeois viewpoints. She must realize the full importance of the family for society as well as the full importance of her role." A woman who rejects or denounces motherhood (as the heroines of both novels discussed in chapter 1, Arina Petrovna Golovleva and Anna Karenina, do) is merely exhibiting symptoms of the "fever" of Russia's "transitional period"—undoubtedly a reference to the social upheaval characteristic of the years of the Great Reforms. Women cannot and should not escape their destinies as mothers, that is, as shapers of the fate of the nation.[61] Similarly, V. N. Zhuk's *Mother and Child* (1881)—the largest and most comprehensive child care manual published in imperial Russia—provided not only practical child-rearing advice but also aimed to instill in mothers an understanding of the historical and cultural significance of their task. The author assured his readers that, by properly raising healthy offspring, they "ensure the prosperity of the nation and contribute to the betterment of the human race."[62]

MOTHERS BETWEEN HEAVEN AND EARTH

In the early years of the twentieth century, the metaphysical element reappeared in Russian maternal imagery. Mothers once again mediated between the heavenly and earthly spheres, not only between the family and society at large.[63] According to Berdiaev, for example, no terrestrial boundaries limit a mother's love: "A woman is a potential mother not only to individual creatures but also to all of nature, to the entire fallen and helpless world."[64] He portrays maternal love as boundless, all-encompassing, and universal—similar to the maternal sentiment embodied in a Mother of God icon. Rozanov emphasizes a mother's infinite capacity for compassion and forgiveness: "Is there pity in the world? Beauty—yes. Meaning—yes. But pity? Can the stars have pity? A mother can pity—and so she will be higher than the stars."[65] Her unique ability to empathize elevates a mother to the cosmic realm.[66]

During this same period, the Orthodox Church also turned to women to safeguard the spiritual values they viewed as under assault by the social and cultural upheaval that had been intensifying in the aftermath of the Great Reforms of the 1860s and 1870s. Both clergymen and Orthodox writers focused on the positive influence that women could wield as a result of their supposedly more constant and fervent religious devotion and superior moral qualities. Hence, women were enlisted as spiritual emissaries, asked to act as a bulwark against the incursion of secular values and as guardians of the Orthodox faith.[67] Turn-of-the-century advice literature also reflected this romanticizing trend, emphasizing the sanctity of a mother's daily mission and her preternatural capacity for suffering. For example, the 1902 pamphlet *Mother and Child* proclaimed:

> Mother! What a sublime and sacred word it is! Mother suffers unimaginable pain in giving birth, feeds the child with her milk, helps him to take his first steps, and anticipates the minute wishes of this vulnerable being who does not know yet how to speak. She learns to understand his prattle, and instinctively sees into the very depth of his tiny innocent soul. She breathes for him, she lives for him! He is the beginning and the end of her dreams, he is the meaning of her entire life; for him she could fight any battle and make the greatest sacrifice.[68]

Thus, the mother possesses the ability not only to provide a child with necessary sustenance but also to penetrate his very soul. Motherhood, in turn, circumscribes a woman's physical, waking life as well as the metaphysical realm of her dreams.

The novel *Mother* (published in 1906) by Maxim Gorky—who would become an exemplary Soviet writer after the October Revolution and remain so until his death in 1936—also widens the traditional boundaries of motherly emotion and contributes to the development of maternal mythology in twentieth-century Russia. This novel serves, I contend, as a transitional work between the nineteenth century and the 1920s' texts discussed in chapter 2. *Mother* redefines the relationship between mother and son, with the latter now teaching and guiding the former. In the novel, the son acts as moral arbiter for the mother, instead of vice versa. He gradually instills in her his own revolutionary principles and inspires her self-denial for the socialist cause rather than for the individual family. Whereas in the beginning of the novel Pelagea Nilovna suffers senseless blows at the hands of her cruel husband, in *Mother*'s closing images she bravely endures a beating from policemen for the sake of revolution and righteousness. Her son's selfless commitment spurs the mother to an even greater level of self-abnegation, and his irreproachable example endows her previously empty sacrifice with significance.

Alongside her awakening to political consciousness, the mother also gradually transfers her maternal sentiment from her own son to all of the members of his revolutionary circle. As Katerina Clark observes: "As she changes, so does her sense of family change from one comprising merely Pavel and herself to one embracing the entire revolutionary group."[69] The mother's presence becomes indispensable, as revealed in the confession of one of the revolutionaries that "everybody needs you mother, everybody." Maternal love sustains the movement emotionally since, as the novel demonstrates, romantic attachments are incompatible with revolutionary ideals and commitments. Pelagea herself realizes the singularity of her role: "Can a mother help loving? She cannot. I love you all. You're all dear to me, and you all deserve to be loved. Who is to love you, if I don't?" Eventually, Pavel and his comrades meld together in her consciousness: "The image of her son, comprising all those who shared his fate, grew in her eyes, giving rise to thoughts of him that imperceptibly branched out in all directions."[70] Hence, Pelagea Nilovna still adheres to the nineteenth-century ideal of maternal self-sacrifice, privileging the needs of others above her own and affirming that "life is for our children. The earth is for them." Her attachment to her own son never wavers or diminishes: "For her, a woman and a mother . . . the body of her son was dearer than what is called the soul."[71] But, in her transference of motherly sentiment from the individual to the collective family, she anticipates the early Soviet mothers discussed in chapter 2.

MOTHERS OF A NEW WORLD

These fictional mothers from the 1920s, who were featured in Soviet magazines that reached a wide reading public, reflect a new morality of the family that emerged in the postrevolutionary period. This morality, as will be analyzed in greater detail in chapter 2, represents a departure from the reverence of the maternal archetype so well entrenched in Russian culture. It condones abandoning children so that women may contribute to the building of the new society, exhorting Russian mothers to turn away from their children—much like the Mother of God does in the vision of the women of the Starorusskii district—in order to help build the new state. The abandoning mother reigned only briefly as a positive role model, however—a casualty of the Stalinist Revolution of 1929. During the Stalinist regime's "stabilizing accommodation with middle class values," to borrow Vera S. Dunham's term, the abandoning mother was replaced by the mother who fulfilled her duties both to the state *and* to her individual family.[72] The 1936 Family Law codified a pro-natalist stance by outlawing abortions and providing bonuses for mothers of multiple children, as well as by making divorce much more difficult to obtain and instituting harsh penalties for fathers who refused to pay alimony or child support. While increasing the levels of both state and individual male accountability for families, in exchange this law compelled mothers to shoulder the double burden of both work and motherhood.

Accordingly, Soviet women's magazines now celebrated the joys of motherhood and featured stories of blissfully large families. Anton Makarenko—whose widely read and highly influential child care manual, *A Book for Parents* (1937), articulated the ideals of the Stalinist family—warned of the perils of raising only one child. Without siblings, according to Makarenko, a child could not develop the collectivist values necessary for a good Soviet citizen. Makarenko also targeted single mothers for particular opprobrium, deeming them incapable of successfully performing their maternal duties: "However good a person [a single] mother may have been, simple association with her alone could not give any positive results. Rather on the contrary: there is nothing more dangerous than the passive association of a good person, since this is the most favorable environment for the development of egoism."[73] Makarenko's vision of the true and effective Soviet family, then, demanded the presence of both parents as well as numerous children, marking a stark departure from the "abandoning mother" figure developed in works such as Fedor Gladkov's 1925 novel *Cement* (which will be analyzed in chapter 2). In the legal realm, the complete reversal of the early Bolshevik experiments with the "withering away" of the traditional family was completed by the passage of the next comprehensive family law in 1944, which eliminated the most radical elements of the 1918 and 1926 Family Codes (for example, by withdrawing recognition of de facto marriages and reintroducing the category of illegitimacy).[74]

In the postwar popular fiction that Dunham analyzes, she identifies a focus on the dilemma of the professional woman whose responsibilities leave her with little time to devote to family life. However, this woman is no longer portrayed as a fearless soldier in the battle for the glorious socialist future, as she had often been in the 1920s. Instead, the absence of the mother frequently causes guilt, and the behavior of partially abandoned children provides important insights into the tensions of postwar family life.[75] The fiction of the postwar period increasingly stressed motherhood, which assumed priority over a woman's professional obligations. Works by writers such as the Stalin Prize–winning author Vera Panova extolled the virtues of women who embodied traditional female qualities—kindness and devotion to family and home, for example—while simultaneously succeeding as workers and as citizens. The balance of this female imagery was tipped, however, in favor of the joys of motherhood.[76] Parenting advice literature of the postwar period even presented working mothers (ideally those with large families) as raising the best children, since their positive example instilled self-sufficiency and proper behavior in their offspring.[77] Thus, a woman's participation in the workforce enhanced her maternal effectiveness, and the regime expected that a woman excel in both the professional and the domestic spheres.[78] From the 1930s onward, the choice of Dasha Chumalova from Gladkov's *Cement* and other women like her from the fiction of the 1920s to abandon their children was no longer sanctioned. Women must now fulfill their duties both as workers and as reproducers, finding their ultimate satisfaction in the latter while never forgoing the former.[79]

"THE MOTHERLAND CALLS!"

During World War II, female imagery in general and maternal imagery in particular occupied a prominent place in political posters designed to inspire and steel the population during the ravages of war. I. Toidze's famous *The Motherland Calls!* (*Rodina-mat' zovet!*) poster (1941) incited citizens to sacrifice on behalf of the nation allegorized as a mother. With a defiant arm cast upward against a backdrop of bayonets, the female figure evokes both the new Soviet mother and an older, peasant milieu far removed from the transformations of industrialization.[80] On the other hand, the majority of artistic representations incorporating mothers portrayed them helplessly clinging to innocent babies and terrified children while under assault by fascists wielding menacing weapons.[81] Hence, the maternal archetype conveyed both strength and fragility as it inspired the valiant defense of the nation and sacrifice from its citizens and soldiers. Its utilization in wartime propaganda provided the link between the war and local loyalties, with an appeal to private emotions stimulating the call to public service.[82] After the war, the same archetype was deployed as part of what Susan E. Reid has termed the "iconography of normalization." "The figure of woman," Reid explains, "demobilized and restored to her supposedly natural, 'essentially feminine' preoccupation with her own appearance, family and home" was meant to aid the citizenry in recovering from the multiple traumas of the Stalinist terror and World War II. In other words, the iconic Russian mother was exhorted to turn back to her children in order to comfort the population and restore normalcy after a series of historical cataclysms.[83]

Maternal rhetoric during the Stalin period and beyond relied upon two familiar, well-established principles of the maternal archetype: self-sacrifice and the mother-as-mediator. "The word 'mother,'" G. N. Kaminskii, commissar of public health, proclaimed in 1936, "is the most respected, motherhood is the highest form of service to one's people and state."[84] Alongside such official proclamations of motherhood as women's ultimate societal contribution, their ability to work outside the home was touted as evidence that the Women's Question had finally been solved. In reality, however, this meant that duty and self-sacrifice—and the ability to work like a man but without concern for personal gain—defined the obligations of the Soviet woman. The infliction of such a double burden could succeed in the Soviet Union at least partially because of the familiarity of the image of the self-sacrificial mother, now glorified by Stalin.[85] Henceforth, Soviet women would assume the familiar self-abnegating role but, this time, on behalf of both their children—whom they must raise to love their country first and their parents second—*and* the state. This incitement to a dual sacrifice remained part of the official rhetoric until the emergence of the "back to the home" movement in the 1980s. When the loosening of media censorship during the glasnost period brought an array of social ills—such as drug abuse, prostitution, and crime—into the light for the first time, certain segments of Soviet society wondered if the emphasis on women's participation in the workforce had produced unintended and dire consequences. Instead of exhorting women to be both exemplary workers *and* outstanding mothers, as had been the case for multiple decades, the new, official motto was "realism." For the first time in Soviet history, women were ostensibly encouraged to *choose* between their obligations as mothers or as workers.[86]

After the collapse of plans to institute communal child-rearing, the mother's mediating function also reappeared. The state sought a special alliance with mothers to replace the "child colonies" that were too ineffective and too expensive to implement on a large scale.[87] Rather than mediating between the earthly and divine realms, or between the family and a morally impure society, from the Stalinist period onward the mother provides a direct conduit between the family and the Soviet regime. Instead of socialized child care, the plans for which were eventually abandoned due to lack of resources, mothers "were to act as mediators between the state and the child, with fathers, their role symbolically and materially appropriated by the state, banished to the margins of the new Soviet family."[88] Ironically, the symbolism of the maternal icon—its ability to impart comfort and represent continuity during periods of turmoil—was appropriated by the government during the period of immense suffering that mothers (alongside the rest of Soviet society) experienced during the 1930s and 1940s. As the promises that the Soviet government had made to its citizens remained unfulfilled, the symbolism of maternity was enlisted to fill the gap. As Elizabeth Waters deftly summarizes,

> In a society living under extraordinary pressure, in constant flux, the sense of continuity offered by the maternal image, its suggestion of intimacy and solace, had therapeutic possibilities. With the disappearance, one after the other, of those institutions mediating between the family and the govern-

> ment—political factions, voluntary organisations, (relatively) independent unions and press, and the zhenotdel (women's department)—the iconic conflation of mother and motherland, family and state served to humanise and legitimise the party.[89]

If the Mother of God icon could unite disparate worshipers into one community of believers, then the Soviet regime appropriated the maternal myth to unify the nation on an emotional level. The Communist Party itself adopted a maternal countenance, as exemplified in the following poetic verse by P. Kudriavtsev: "And we, like children, reach/For our Party-Mother, standing under her banner."[90] During the 1970s and 1980s, official Soviet rituals enlisted real-life mothers to carry out "ideological mediation" between the Soviet army and the civilian population. New recruits were escorted to their posts by a soldiers' mother, with the "mother bec[oming] a symbol, accumulating within herself all of the connotations of helplessness, suffering, weakness, and desecration at the hands of the enemy that the *Rodina-mat'* [Motherland] image contained during World War II."[91] Having descended from the lofty heights of turn-of-the-twentieth-century imagery, the iconic Russian mother, during the Stalin era and beyond, now fulfilled a more terrestrial and pragmatic purpose: enabling and legitimizing the Soviet government.

AFTER THE FALL

After the collapse of the Soviet Union, however, the state essentially retreated from the mother-child relationship. Mothers no longer receive the same level of state support—whether in the form of subsidized child care, child allowances, or child support enforcement provisions—that they did before 1991.[92] Surveys of the Russian press from the mid-1990s reveal that attitudes toward motherhood underwent a significant shift in the years after the demise of the Soviet Union. In particular, society now increasingly views motherhood as an individual choice, responsibility, and pleasure.[93] With the state no longer so strongly invested in the socialization of children, Russian women lament the absence of both male and governmental support, often noting that now no one besides themselves seems to need their children.[94] Ann Taylor Allen contends that personal gratification and psychological factors (as opposed to necessity or duty) first began to dominate in western European women's decision to bear children in the interwar period. A similar transformation of the "maternal dilemma" in Russia—at least in both official and popular discourse—would occur only roughly seventy years later.[95]

Anxiety about the mother's loss of moral authority, and the subsequent damage to Russian society, seems to accompany this transformation. Russian scholar Vera Ramikh claims, for example, that motherhood has been devalued in the national consciousness, as evinced by an increase in negative social phenomena such as child abandonment. The maternal myth, according to some observers of contemporary Russia, is dangerously weak and in danger of extinction. Anxiety about the falling birthrate (the Russian Federation experienced negative population growth for the first time in 1992) and the accompanying perceived loss of national vitality has stimulated an upsurge in nationalist sentiment that favors the immediate adoption of pronatalist measures to avert the annihilation of the Russian people. This new politicization of reproduction to save the endangered Russian gene pool calls on all women, as actual or potential mothers, to bear the responsibility for national survival.[96] In this climate of anxiety about the future of the Russian people and the mother's role in securing it, some journalists and writers, as will be analyzed in detail in chapter 3, wonder whether the contemporary Russian mother can reach the heights of maternal sentiment and behavior of the iconic one. Ramikh advocates a return to the cult of maternity, indicating a fear that the venerated Russian mother has receded into the past.[97] At the same time, contemporary female authors such as Liudmila Petrushevskaia (whose works will also be considered in chapter 3) appear determined to hasten these dire predictions by dismantling the image of the self-sacrificing and heroic Russian mother in their fictional works. At the beginning of the twenty-first century, then, the Russian maternal archetype seemingly stood at a crossroads, and the fear of its demise has elicited either apocalyptic forebodings or impassioned pleas for her to save Russia from its most destructive elements.

What, then, is the significance of the bad mother in the context of the development of maternal mythology discussed above? This study aims to show the contingency of this designation, its relationship to the social and political realities of each chosen period. Both of the nineteenth-century novels included in chapter 1, for example, respond directly to the "maternal sacrifice paradigm" so well developed and prominent in nineteenth-century European society, art, and literature. They also contribute to the debate about the status and fate of the Russian family that occupied writers and thinkers during the Great Reforms of the 1860s and 1870s. Communist ideology in the early years of the Soviet state still demanded sacrifice of mothers, but now for the sake of the collective rather than the individual family. It also briefly created a positive figure out of the abandoning mother, one who exhibits the proper attributes of a revolutionary by forsaking her children in order to battle for the socialist future. And the ruptures of the post-Soviet period have stimulated an intensified concern with the stability of the mother icon. The presence of the emotionally unavailable, indifferent mother in literature and the media is invested with ominous significance, with the bad mother symbolizing and foregrounding larger fissures within post-Soviet society as a whole.[98]

Chapter 1 details the development of the tenet of maternal self-sacrifice in the nineteenth century as well as its undermining by a confluence of factors around the middle of the century. It then focuses on two famous novels from the 1870s featuring female characters who, for contrasting reasons, reject the ideal of maternal self-abnegation: Saltykov-Shchedrin's *The Golovlev Family* (1875–80) and Tolstoy's *Anna Karenina* (1873–77). Both Arina Petrovna Golovleva and Anna Karenina replace self-sacrifice with self-interest, albeit of two distinct varieties, and this decision profoundly affects their individual fates as well as those of their children. Mothers occupied a crucial role in the debates over Russia's future that unfolded in the years after the Great Reforms of the 1860s, and the maternal figures in these novels shed important light on how two of the century's most important literary figures envisioned the outcome of these battles.

Chapter 2 identifies a new maternal figure that surfaced in the wake of the October Revolution of 1917, one that contradicts all earlier cultural ideals of Russian motherhood. The image of the abandoning mother in several works of popular fiction from the early 1920s and in Fedor Gladkov's seminal Soviet novel *Cement* (1925) reveals how a woman who turns away from her children, if she does so in service of the socialist cause, emerges as a positive role model. Or, as in a dramatized trial from the same period entitled *Trial of a Mother Who Abandoned Her Baby* (1924)—where the mother is judged for abandoning her son *without* a noble reason—as a lamentable but reversible phenomenon that underscores the benevolence and wisdom of the Soviet state. These two contrasting permutations of the abandoning mother appear at the intersection of multiple anxieties about the role that women were compelled to assume in the early years of the Soviet Union.

Chapter 3 explores the contrasting images of motherhood that emerged in the wake of the social, political, and economic instability that followed the collapse of the Soviet Union in 1991. In Russian media coverage of the Chechen conflicts of the 1990s, two disparate maternal figures assumed prominence: the heroic and noble member of the activist group the "Committee of Soldiers' Mothers," valiantly striving to save the sons of Russia from the brutality both of war and of the Russian army itself; and the Chechen female suicide bomber, undermining traditional maternal categories by committing acts of random violence. During the same period, cultural works such as the late-Soviet film *Adam's Rib* (1990) and Liudmila Petrushevskaia's story "Our Circle" and novel *The Time: Night* demonstrate how images of negative maternity challenged the notion that the iconic Russian mother could neutralize the volatility of the post-Soviet period.

Chapter One

Sacrifice Subverted: The Bad Mothers of M. E. Saltykov-Shchedrin and L. N. Tolstoy

THE VIOLATION OF the "sacred ideal of the family" absorbed Fyodor Dostoevsky's attention throughout his 1876 *A Writer's Diary*. In particular, he focused on trials involving the abuse or severe neglect of children, including the case of the nobleman Stanislav Kronenberg, who was accused of cruelly mistreating his seven-year-old daughter. Kronenberg's renowned defense lawyer, Vladimir Spasovich, argued for his client's acquittal based on the indisputable link between the power of the father and that of the state, claiming that the authority invested in the former insured the stability of the latter. Dostoevsky passionately disputed Spasovich's argument and the model of familial relations implicitly contained within it:

> We Russians are a young people . . . We love our sacred ideals, but only because they are, in fact, sacred. We do not uphold them simply as a means of supporting *l'Ordre* . . . We love the sacred ideal of the family when it is sacred in reality and not only because the state rests firmly upon it.[1]

Spasovich upheld a traditional, hierarchical view of the Russian family, while Dostoevsky seemingly advocated for a more progressive one that did not blindly reproduce the power dynamics of the autocracy.

This conflict between the writer and the lawyer encapsulates the shift in Russian familial relations that began roughly around the middle of the nineteenth century—in the wake of the emergence of the Women's Question after the Crimean War (1853–56) and the social tumult that followed the Emancipation of the serfs in 1861—a shift that would greatly influence discussions about the significance of motherhood in Russian society as well. The earlier model stressed the abnegation of the individual in favor of whoever ranked higher in the hierarchy of the family and, subsequently, the subsuming of the individual family under the power of the autocrat. The *Domostroi,* the sixteenth-century Russian household advice manual that firmly delineated domestic relations, elevated the "male head of household to a kind of kingship within the family."[2] The Russian judicial system reinforced this patriarchal structure, and imperial law buttressed the familial power dynamics that gave the father the same absolute authority over his wife and children that the state wielded over its citizens.[3] Indeed, it was not uncommon to refer to the father as the "tsar" of the family.[4] In an 1827 article on family law, for example, Ilarion Vasilev, an instructor in imperial law, writes: "The family is a representation of the State! . . . [The] father is the monarch, his wife and children are his subjects."[5] The legal definition of familial relations was formulated "in terms of authority, obedience, filial duty, and paternalistic obligation."[6] In other words, the constitution of the family was a microcosm of that of the state.

In the 1870s, as Dostoevsky explored the dynamics of sacrifice and suffering in relation to the family, rejecting the entrenched model of familial relations that the lawyer Spasovich upheld, the question of women, motherhood, and sacrifice was preoccupying two of the decade's other important literary figures: M. E. Saltykov-Shchedrin and L. N. Tolstoy.[7] This chapter first discusses the development of the tenet of maternal self-abnegation as well as its undermining by a confluence of factors around the middle of the nineteenth century. I then focus on two famous novels from the 1870s featuring female characters who, for contrasting reasons, reject the model of maternal self-sacrifice: Saltykov-Shchedrin's *The Golovlev Family* and Tolstoy's *Anna Karenina.* In both of these family novels, the mother who forsakes the "maternal sacrifice paradigm"—to borrow E. Ann Kaplan's term—contributes to the eventual disintegration of her family.[8] Both Arina Petrovna Golovleva and Anna Karenina replace self-sacrifice with self-interest, albeit of two distinct varieties, and this decision profoundly affects their individual fates as well as those of their children. In her study of motherhood in Augustan England, Toni Bowers observes the popularity of images of negative maternity during this period, noting that "these infamous, unloving mothers . . . represent one of early 18th-century British culture's most fascinating terrors." Bowers argues that this figure emerges at the intersection of the nascent "maternal dilemma" in Britain, that it reflects "the dissonance 18th-century culture increasingly perceived between two uneasily reconciled values: unique, coherent personal identity and sacrificial, self-effacing motherlove."[9] Roughly one and a half centuries later, the two fictional Russian mothers who provide the focus for this chapter reflect a similar unease about the clash between an extra-maternal identity and the demands of the myth of the self-sacrificial mother. The changes to the model of familial relations as well as the broader societal shifts that occurred in Russia during the Great Reforms of the 1860s and 1870s—including increased social mobility, urbanization, the relaxing of censorship, and the introduction of capitalist elements into the economy—rendered "self-effacing motherlove" problematic in the Russian context as well.

Although occupying opposite ends of the ideological spectrum, Tolstoy and Saltykov-Shchedrin both reflect this anxiety about the consequences of allowing fictional mothers to resolve their particular "maternal dilemmas" by choosing self-interest over self-sacrifice. Tolstoy ultimately affirms maternal mythology by portraying Anna Karenina's decision to turn away from her children as contributing to her alienation, despair, and, climactically, her suicide. Saltykov-Shchedrin, on the other hand, uses a similar image to unmask the emptiness of the Russian family, particularly after the maternal figure in the novel acts as a conduit for the introduction of market forces into familial dynamics.

THE TRADITIONAL FAMILY

What principles underscored the traditional model of the Russian family, and how was this model perpetuated? What shifts altered the landscape of Russian family life in the middle of the nineteenth century? And how did these changes affect the discourse of Russian motherhood? Dostoevsky's conclusions about the self-sufficiency and discreteness of the family, about its independence from the state, indirectly reject the hierarchical organization of family relations that had previously been so firmly entrenched. To reproduce this organization, a Russian noble child was taught to subordinate his own personality to those of the adults in his midst, while the adult's role, in turn, was circumscribed by the demands of hierarchy, service, and sacrifice for the state.[10] Dostoevsky's argument, however, denies the connection between the power of the state and that of the family.[11] Following this argumentation, the family is no longer sustained by the sacrifice of the individuals who comprise it. If the family and, by extension, the state, can survive and endure only at the cost of the suffering of a child, then, according to Dostoevsky, this price is too high to pay.

While Dostoevsky, in both his fictional works and *A Writer's Diary*, focuses most frequently on the torment of children, in reality the traditional structure of the Russian family demanded self-sacrifice above all from the mother. Female self-sacrifice buttressed the hierarchical system on which both the family and the state were founded. This readiness for self-abnegation was inculcated during childhood. Parents were advised by moralists "early on to teach their daughters to subjugate their own will to the will of others. This will assure them a happy life."[12] The upbringing of young girls was designed to impart willingness for self-sacrifice as both a wife and a mother.[13]

The emphasis on sacrifice continued into a woman's adult life. In her discussion of maternal education in Russia during the first half of the nineteenth century, Catriona Kelly points out that there existed "a consensus about the content of women's education, which should instill in its objects a code of self-restraint and self-sacrifice, a sense of women's privileged yet perilous situation as moral arbiters."[14] In 1804, one Russian educational expert summed up the culmination of this process with the following statement: "At twenty-five [a woman] must already live only for others."[15] In his 1866 examination of the female condition, French author Edouard Pompéry, in a pamphlet published and distributed in Russia, argued that a woman was endowed with the capacity for self-denial to compensate for the stronger, more masculine qualities that she lacks.[16] In her "primary role as a mother," he claimed, "a woman is absolute self-sacrifice; she no longer belongs to herself, instead giving herself up completely to her duty."[17] And women advised each other according to an identical ethos, employing the same vocabulary of self-abnegation: "You have still another sacred duty [besides being a wife]: you have dear little ones for whom you must sacrifice all your own pleasures," reads a letter from a woman to a friend published in an 1807 journal.[18]

The story "The Despotism of Maternal Love," published in the *Journal for Education* in 1859, presents a bad mother—one who manipulates the ideal of maternal self-abnegation—as an illustrative negative example. A widowed countess focuses her energies solely on the raising of her mild-mannered, meek son, Vol'demar, smothering him with her love. She imparts to him knowledge of her supposed sacrifice on his behalf, using it as a manipulative tool:

> [The mother] arrived at the conclusion that all of her actions were governed by love for him. Vol'demar could never challenge this weapon, because he clearly understood with what deep love his mother gave herself to him, living only for his present and future happiness. That's why in the end he always, without lengthy protest, gave in to her wishes, as unpleasant as that was for him . . . One had to marvel at the power that the countess wielded over her son as a result of her love for him. With the help of this love she subjugated him completely to her will.[19]

The "despotic" mother at the center of this fictional work wields the myth of the self-sacrificial mother as the ultimate weapon in subduing and controlling her son.

The mother's dominance continues unabated into the son's adult life. Although Vol'demar clearly prefers provincial life on the family's country estate, the mother forces him to move to the city. She tricks him into accepting a position as an assistant to an important diplomat in order to launch the career that she has unilaterally chosen for him. His mother's trickery throws Vol'demar into despair that eventually turns into a life-threatening illness. This turn of events causes his mother to suffer an attack of conscience where she wonders, for the first time, if she has, in fact, been acting in her son's best interest. The dramatic climax of the text occurs when she stumbles upon her son's diary, in which he debates the possibility of defying his mother's will. The obstacle to this defiance is, as usual, his knowledge of the sacrifices his mother has supposedly made on his behalf:

> Did my mother not live only for me? Did she not give up all the joys of life in order to live only for my sake? Were not all of her thoughts, wishes, goals directed at the strengthening of my happiness? . . . Maybe mother made mistakes sometimes, but her goal was always pure and lofty. She offered me the kind of great self-sacrifice that only a woman is capable of; aren't I, in turn, required to sacrifice myself for her? . . . The despotism of maternal love is already extending its hand to crush the last flower of happiness that was about to bloom on the soil of my soul. What awful, endless unhappiness mother is preparing for me![20]

The story contains a happy ending, however, as the mother's encounter with the "maternal sacrifice paradigm" in her son's diary motivates her renaissance. This reminder that a mother should sacrifice for her son, and not the other way around, leads her to repent her sins. The "scales fall off her eyes," and, weeping, she realizes the cruel "despotism of maternal love" with which she had tormented her son. In penance, she exiles herself with her own widowed mother, allowing Vol'demar to forge his own path in life, which includes marrying for love instead of for status as his mother had urged and living a quiet life on his estate, where he earns the affection and loyalty of all. The mother's earlier misuse of maternal mythology provides a cautionary tale for the journal's readership to heed.

This association of motherhood and sacrifice that Vol'demar's mother so wantonly manipulated began with the pain of childbirth, which endowed a woman with moral authority for the remainder of her children's lives. In an 1843 child-rearing manual, Konstantin Grum proclaimed that "it is impossible to calculate all the physical and spiritual suffering which women must endure at the time of pregnancy, childbirth, and nursing."[21] A son in particular, since he had little contact with his mother after being transferred to the male sphere at around age seven, tended to idealize his mother's sufferings on his behalf. He was "encouraged to see his mother as the embodiment of virtue. Her basic virtue, in his eyes, was usually martyrdom; prototypically, the pain she had endured at his birth."[22] In this association between the suffering of childbirth and morality, Russia paralleled Victorian culture in Europe and the United States, where opponents of the use of anesthesia in childbirth claimed that pain relief prohibited the development of "mother love" and imperiled the mother-child bond.[23]

Tolstoy's novella "Childhood" (1852) provides a vivid example of the influence a mother's suffering wields on the psyche of a son. As Andrew Wachtel has argued, the mother of Nikolai Irten'ev became the model upon which gentry autobiographers subsequently based their maternal figures. The template Irten'ev's "maman" originated was characterized by cultural refinement (knowledge of French and German, a well-developed musical talent) as well as kindness, a loving and uplifting smile, tempered religiosity, pity for the poor, and eternally fair and affectionate treatment of her serfs.[24] The mother's death is the climactic event of the work and heralds the end of the narrator's childhood. Her behavior leading up to her death exemplifies the self-sacrificial ideal. Her primary concern remains the fate of her children throughout her illness (her final words are "Oh Lord! The children, the children!"), and in her letters to her husband she affirms an inextricable link with her family that transcends earthly bounds:

> Will my love for you and the children end with my life? I understood that this was impossible. . . . My soul cannot live without my love for you. I know that it will exist eternally, if only because such a love could not have arisen if it was meant to someday disappear.

His mother's selfless suffering leaves its indelible imprint on Irten'ev: "Maman's eyes were open, but she did not see anything. Oh, I'll never forget that horrible look! There was so much suffering expressed in it!"[25] It leaves him preternaturally attuned to the egotistical elements in his own grief, to the insincerity that the contrast with his mother lays bare. He cannot reach the same level of self-abnegation as his mother had attained throughout her life and particularly in her final moments. The grief of others also does not seem pure or genuine. No one, apparently, can meet the standards of sincerity and purity that the memory of "maman" evokes. "Even after death," as historian Mary Cavender observes, "mothers retained their role as the symbol of the loving and warm domestic atmosphere."[26]

Irten'ev's mother's letter also reveals how a woman's identity was forged by living primarily for the sake of her children and husband. "Maman" could not imagine an end to her maternal love, even after death. A woman's actions on behalf of her children provided the narrative of her life with meaning, particularly in her final years. It was precisely this narrative that offered solace in the face of dashed hopes or disappointment.[27] Hence, a woman's existence was defined, organized, and bookmarked by self-sacrifice in favor of her children. The "cult of the perfect mother" that flourished among the

Russian gentry encouraged women to adhere to the saintly, self-denying ideal popularized by autobiographical and literary works.[28]

THE CHANGING FAMILY

By the late 1850s and early 1860s, the hierarchical model of the family and, by extension, the self-sacrificial mother who supported it, began to be challenged by a confluence of factors and events. The structure of the traditional family, and its impact on women in particular, became a focal point of debate among the educated classes. In the late 1850s, imperial family law—with its support of a patriarchal organization of domestic relations—became a target of fervent criticism. Historian William Wagner defines two contrasting definitions of the family that emerged in the legal debates of the post-Emancipation period: "While *the conservative, patriarchal, view* of the family embodied the principles of unlimited personalized authority and unequal ascriptive status on which the autocratic order rested, *the affective ideal* . . . contained conceptions of legality and individual rights which challenged this order" (emphasis added).[29]

By the 1870s, the "affective ideal" of the family, one no longer based on a rigid hierarchy but instead on mutual affection and respect, had become the underlying principle of most legal writing.[30] Liberal jurists argued that the abolition of serfdom in 1861 had changed social conditions and relationships so profoundly that it rendered earlier family law obsolete. Seeking to ameliorate some of Russia's perceived backwardness in comparison to the West, they aimed to instill the rule of law into domestic matters by, for example, making marriage and divorce the province of civil courts rather than of the Orthodox Church. Following the model of Catholic countries such as France and Italy, reformers sought to make marital separation legal. Women's rights—notably, the revision of family law—played the role of the "Trojan mare" in attempts by judicial reformers to instill legality into Russian society.[31] The church fervently resisted these changes, and the "crisis of the family" of post-reform Russia constituted a major factor of the "crisis of Orthodoxy" as well.[32]

The evolving structure of domestic life figured prominently in the ideological and philosophical discussions of the era as well. For example, M. L. Mikhailov, who articulated the call for women's education and became one of the earliest theorists of the Women's Question in Russia, referred to himself as a "champion of the family."[33] The family he envisioned, however, no longer accepted inequality as a foundational principle. Instead, he called for kinship relations grounded in the values of mutual respect and equality, rather than on a gendered hierarchy; in other words, the "affective ideal" that was simultaneously achieving prominence in legal debates.[34] Mikhailov served, perhaps, as a transitional figure between earlier visions of a reconstituted family and the Russian radicals' eventual call for its abolition. For him, the issue was not preventing women from becoming mothers, but, rather, helping them become better mothers by providing them with access to a more liberal education.[35] Similarly, although the issue of a woman's duty to her family versus her obligations to society as a whole was heatedly debated on the pages of the women's journal *Dawn* (published from 1859 to 1862), no call for the dissolution of the traditional family was made.[36] By 1863, however, what has been termed the "'free-love' tradition of the Russian intelligentsia" had begun, initiated by the proclamation *Young Russia,* which advocated the abolition of the family and the public rearing of children.[37] Hence, the emergence of the Women's Question (and the debates about the role of women in the family that it sparked), as well as that of the radical intelligentsia, who advocated rational egoism and the dissolution of the traditional family unit, problematized the firmly entrenched ideal of the mother as familial martyr.[38]

In other words, the family, rather than merely inculcating a sense of duty to society, was increasingly seen as obligated to contribute positively to the lives of the individuals who comprised it. The previously rigid hierarchy that placed the family squarely below the interests of the state began to shift. Since the sacrifice of the individual for the sake of the autocrat no longer seemed immutable, the ideology of maternal self-sacrifice was, in turn, also called into question. Not surprisingly, then, the proper definition of motherhood played a key role in the ideological debates of the Emancipation period and beyond. As the literature devoted to family improvement increased dramatically, both conservatives and radicals seemed determined to investigate the potential gaps between the maternal myth and reality. On the one hand, members of the radical intelligentsia such as Nikolai Chernyshevsky blamed mothers for improperly rearing their children, for not nurturing them adequately, and for acting as conservative agents who reproduced the hierarchical family dynamics now being questioned.[39] Conservatives, on the other hand, exhorted mothers to "embody the civilizing force, in its most positive sense." They encouraged women to act as a bulwark against the unsettling forces unleashed in the wake of the Great Reforms—such as the rise of populism and radical movements in the 1870s, and the modernization and industrialization of the economy, which caused substantial migration from the countryside to the city—that threatened both familial and societal stability.[40] Mothers, then, occupied a pivotal role in the battle for Russia's future that unfolded in the years after the Great Reforms. If "woman constituted a 'question' (as in 'zhenskii vopros')," as the literary scholar Jane T. Costlow summarizes, "it was one that originated in societal visions of her role as mother."[41] So what can the representation of negative maternity in two of the most important Russian novels of the period of the Great Reforms tell us about these "societal visions?" I will begin with *The Golovlev Family.*

A MOTHER'S LAND

Arina Petrovna Golovleva, the matriarch of *The Golovlev Family* (1875–80), M. E. Saltykov-Shchedrin's chronicle of the disintegration of a Russian noble family, has been called "perhaps the most notorious female proprietor in Russian literature."[42] She chooses economic self-interest over the mother's traditional role as self-sacrificer, and Saltykov-Shchedrin portrays her decision as contributing to the gradual dissolution of the Golovlev family. However, she also simultaneously pays homage to (and may perhaps sincerely believe in) the principles of maternal devotion and self-abnegation. Critics of the novel have tended to focus much more attention on the character of Arina Petrovna's son, Porfiry (also known as "Little Judas" [*Iudushka*]), than on Arina herself.[43] To the best of my knowledge, no study of the novel devoted exclusively to an analysis of Arina Petrovna exists. Most discussions of the character emphasize the oft-repeated biographical connection with Saltykov-Shchedrin's own mother, the despotic Olga Mikhailovna, but do not place Arina Petrovna within the larger context of maternal ideology of the nineteenth century, as the present analysis of the novel aims to do.[44]

Arina Petrovna's major challenge to this ideology lies in her single-minded passion for the accumulation of property and wealth. Her stewardship of the family estate was not, in and of itself, anomalous. As historian Michelle Marrese has detailed, "Russian noblewomen enjoyed one advantage virtually unknown to their counterparts in Western Europe: from the mid-eighteenth-century married women could own and dispose of property separately from their husbands," participating in roughly 40 percent of real estate transactions in nineteenth-century Russia. Interest in estate management and frugal, effective control of household finances also did not contradict Russian maternal mythology of the period. In nineteenth-century gentry autobiographies, mothers often maintain the family finances and are praised for their superior organizational skills and ability to manage the household.[45]

Arina Petrovna's transgression of this mythology, then, does not lie simply in her attention to property and finances. Rather, it stems from the degree to which she is motivated by self-interest despite repeated proclamations of self-sacrifice (and its accompanying moral authority), from how she evokes maternal mythology when it feeds her vanity and reinforces her position as the locus of familial power. It also derives from how she transforms the Golovlev family according to these principles of economic self-interest, as discussed below. Her desire for the uninterrupted expansion of the family estate, her "fever of acquisition," influences the psychology of the Golovlev family, both individually and collectively. Although Arina Petrovna improves the family's material conditions, her financial success corrupts the atmosphere of family life and hastens rather than prevents the decline of subsequent generations of Golovlevs.[46] Arina Petrovna transforms her family into one that resembles the prototypical "bourgeois family" envisioned by Marx and Engels, that is, one founded "on capital, on private gain." Borrowing Susan McReynolds's term, I argue that Arina Petrovna singlehandedly endows the members of her family with an "economic consciousness," defined as a "belief in exchange logic as the dominant principle governing human affairs and the relationship between God and humanity."[47] A close reading of the novel reveals how Arina Petrovna restructures the family according to principles of economic self-interest and how familial interactions take on the guise of economic transactions, with the omnipresent expectation of exchange. A. S. Bushmin has argued that Saltykov-Shchedrin's writings of the 1870s are characterized by the "dramas and tragedies" that arise as a result of "the collision of the principles of family and property."[48] In fact, these principles not only collide but also intermingle. In the novel, the family functions according to the same logic that underlies the sphere of property—facilitated by a mother who exploits the maternal self-abnegation glorified in Western art and literature of the nineteenth century.

Arina Petrovna's replacing of maternal self-sacrifice with self-interest also shapes the personalities and fates of her offspring. In a letter to E. I. Utin on January 2, 1881, Saltykov-Shchedrin wrote that, in *The Golovlev Family,* he aimed to "depict the bankruptcy of the principles on which contemporary society was based: 'the family,' 'property,' 'government.' He maintained that these institutions in actuality did not exist any more, that only their forms remained."[49] The maternal inheritance that Arina Petrovna bequeaths to her children ensures the perpetuation of a family existing only in form. Instead of raising the honorable citizens that the conservative rhetoric of the period prescribed her to do, Arina Petrovna imparts to her son Porfiry, the novel's primary villain, a tendency to privilege form at the expense of substance, helping to mold him into the ultimate hypocrite and a cruel father to his own sons.

Arina Petrovna's passion for money and land acquisition occurs against a backdrop of significant economic change in Russia. The period of time spanned in the novel (roughly twenty years, from 1856 to 1877/78) corresponds to the emergence of elements of a market economy within Russia. After the Crimean War, commercial and other enterprises began to expand due to increased government support, and the first private banks in Russia appeared. Legal restrictions on trade were abolished in 1863–65. The Great

Reforms of Tsar Alexander II (including the freeing of the serfs, the granting of significant autonomy to the universities and of limited self-government to rural and urban communities, and the relaxing of press censorship) contributed to the end of the incremental industrial growth that had characterized the Russian economy under serfdom. This process culminated in the 1890s with a rapid increase in industrial production under the stewardship of Minister of Finance Sergei Witte.[50]

The merchant class also attained a newfound political influence during this same period. The Emancipation of the serfs in 1861 unexpectedly bolstered the prestige as well as increasing the size of the merchant class; in Moscow, for example, the number of merchants more than doubled between 1852 and 1871.[51] At approximately the same time that the merchants' star was rising, however, the fortunes of the gentry were plummeting rapidly. The Emancipation of the serfs provoked what has been termed the "impoverishment of the nobility," precipitated by a sharp decline in gentry landownership in the second half of the nineteenth century.[52] As a whole, the pre-Emancipation landed nobility suffered from an extreme level of both agricultural and economic ignorance. Unlike Arina Petrovna, many members of the gentry never concerned themselves with thoughts of profit and, on the contrary, begrudged the transformation that market forces had wrought on their way of life. It was not until some thirty years after the publication of Saltykov-Shchedrin's novel that Russian agriculture was significantly affected by the spirit of gentry entrepreneurship.[53]

THE BURDEN OF MOTHERHOOD

At the very beginning of *The Golovlev Family,* Arina Petrovna's discomfort with the role of mother and her preference for "market forces" and the financial realm is described in detail:

> She was too independent by nature, too spinsterish, to see her children as anything other than a burden to her. She only breathed freely when she was alone with her business accounts and plans, or when no one interrupted her discussions with estate managers, village elders, house-keepers and so on. In her opinion, children were just one manifestation of what fate had decreed and against which she felt she had no right to protest; nevertheless, they did not touch one chord of her inner self, wholly preoccupied as she was with the minutiae of daily existence. There were four children—three sons and a daughter. She could not bring herself to talk about her eldest son and her daughter and was more or less indifferent towards her youngest son. Only for

> the middle son, Porfiry, did she have any feeling, although this was closer to fear than affection. (23)[54]

Her children constitute an inescapable fact of life that she fatalistically accepts but resists embracing. Arina Petrovna thrives exclusively in the realm of accounts, acquisition, and business dealings.[55]

She also remains immune to the biological connection that supposedly accompanies motherhood. For example, when her eldest son, Stepan, moves back to the family estate, Golovlevo, after squandering his inheritance, she essentially forgets about his presence: "She had completely lost sight of the fact that quite near her, in the estate office, lived a human being, her own flesh and blood" (63–64). The "ties of blood" that bind her to her offspring exert no influence over Arina Petrovna. In fact, she defines her sole maternal responsibility in the callous terminology of an uneven business transaction: she must "throw each of them a piece" (*vybrosit' im kusok*), that is, provide them with a parcel of land or some other material recompense, in return for which they will never return to Golovlevo again.[56] Arina Petrovna "was a woman of the highest principles: once having 'thrown them a piece,' she considered that she had no further obligations toward her repellent children" (27). Thus, she dispenses with the mother-child bond and its accompanying duties in this seemingly simple and mutually beneficial exchange.[57] Arina Petrovna cunningly manages to cut her losses while simultaneously buying her freedom from her "repellent" children and the burden of motherhood.

Stepan, however, violates this agreement by losing his "piece." In what has been called "the steepest economic decline in the novel," he is forced to sell the house in Moscow given to him by his mother in order to pay off his overwhelming debts.[58] The novel's opening scene, when Arina Petrovna receives this news, is significant for establishing a pattern of familial interactions and attitudes toward capital in the novel. It illustrates the violation of the sanctity of the mother-child relationship, supposedly predicated upon a mother's self-sacrifice, by its introduction into the market. Arina Petrovna identifies the gift of the estate to Stepan not as her exchange for freedom from motherhood but as a "parental blessing." This "blessing" carries with it a fair market value, and she curses her son for underselling it: "The rotten swine, letting a parental blessing go for eight thousand!" (20).[59]

This attribution of market value to a "parental blessing" (as well as Arina's frustrated urge to buy it back at a profit) reveals two aspects of the familial dynamic of the Golovlevs, as established by the matriarch and locus of power, Arina Petrovna. First, it links the family with a profit motive, underscoring the intermingling of the commercial with the familial and religious spheres in the Golovlev household. In short, nothing is sacred and everything is subject to pricing and selling. Second, it reveals that the self-sacrificial model that had previously characterized the maternal ideal no longer provides the foundation for the family chronicled in *The Golovlev Family*. The expectation of a return on the investment of maternal beneficence—evidence of Arina Petrovna's "economic consciousness"—has replaced the self-abnegation of mythologized motherhood.

An anticipation of some kind of reward—either liberation from the burden of motherhood, or acknowledgment of her selflessness by either God or by her children themselves—accompanies each of Arina Petrovna's acts of supposed generosity. For example, when she agrees to raise her two orphaned granddaughters, Annin'ka and Liubin'ka, after the death of her daughter, she presumes a heavenly reward: "Well, I'm putting something by for the orphans and at the same time I'm not charging them for their keep! I know God will repay me for being so generous" (27). This mercantile approach to piety reveals how Arina Petrovna's "economic consciousness" informs her understanding of family as well as of religion.

After a desperate Stepan escapes from Golovlevo, Arina Petrovna experiences momentary flickers of maternal emotion. In exchange for this rare kindness, however, she anticipates a display of devotion from her son, a tangible and appropriately theatrical acknowledgment of her charity: "Arina had hoped that he would kiss her hand" (67). Stepan fails to satisfy his mother's expectations. Instead, in what she interprets as a further affront to her maternal ego, he gradually wastes away and eventually dies. Arina Petrovna applies the same principle of exchange to her explanation of her son's death. Describing Stepan's demise in a letter to the novel's central villain, Porfiry, she claims that Stepan earned his fate: "Yesterday morning the Lord visited us with a new affliction. My son and your brother Stepan passed away . . . Let this be a lesson to all. Whoever neglects family ties must always expect such an end" (67). In an allusion to his squandering of the "parental blessing," she asserts a direct connection between his grim fate and a lack of respect for "familial bonds." This assertion is ironic, of course, given the narrator's earlier observation that Arina Petrovna had forgotten about Stepan due to her immunity to these same bonds. But it reveals Arina Petrovna's belief in divine retribution for her son's violation of the transaction that she had outlined: a "piece" of the family property in return for his absence from Golovlevo and her liberation from maternal obligation. Returning to the estate destitute, Stepan breaches this agreement and thus suffers the ultimate punishment. Arina Petrovna enlists God as the arbiter of the broken business deal between her and Stepan, assigning him the role of enforcer of the rules of familial capitalism (as determined by the matriarch herself). This again underscores how Arina Petrovna infuses an "economic consciousness" into the understanding both of religion and of family within the Golovlev household.

MATERNAL ILLUSIONS

Despite her indifference and even aversion to maternal sentiment, Arina Petrovna retains an awareness of the myth of the good mother and exploits this myth when she can profit by it and when it feeds her vanity. This gap between form and substance is identified in the opening pages of the novel: "Arina . . . had . . . grown completely unused to family life, although the word 'family' was always on her lips and although—to judge from appearances—she was solely and constantly motivated by concern for her family's welfare" (22). She nurtures the illusion that she fulfills her maternal obligations, single-handedly carrying the burden while all others remain content. "For whom am I saving all this money? For whom am I putting things by, not sleeping at nights, going hungry . . . for whom?" Arina Petrovna exclaims repeatedly, harboring the suspicion that hers has been an empty, unrewarded sacrifice (31).[60] She even evokes Christian imagery by pointing out that "I bore my cross when I was young" (56; *moloda byla—krest nesla*), endowing her supposed sacrifices with even greater significance.

Connected with this image of mother-as-hero is, of course, Arina Petrovna's acquisition of land, a process she recounts in epic fashion:

> More than once Arina had told her sons the saga of her first steps along the road to acquisition . . . "Perhaps you're thinking that your mother came by her wealth as a result of doing nothing? . . . No, my dears. You don't even get a pimple on your nose by doing nothing! After that first purchase I was laid up for six weeks with a fever." (52)

Through physical suffering, Arina Petrovna believes she has earned the moral capital she wields over her children. But rather than emphasizing the agonies of childbirth—"one of the most evocative images of maternal sacrifice"—she reminds her children of the physical hardships of land acquisition.[61] Thus, one aspect of the maternal myth—a mother enduring bodily torment for the sake of her children—is preserved, but with its essence somewhat comically and grotesquely replaced by a focus on the accumulation of wealth.

Arina Petrovna also frequently plays the "role" of the beneficent mother to fuel her vanity as well as to reinforce her position as the locus of familial power. This affectation is revealed in her reception of Porfiry and Stepan, when they return home for the family council:

> Bowed down by sorrow, Arina Petrovna gave her sons a solemn reception. Two maids supported her by the arms . . . She could barely drag one foot after the other—she had a great liking for *acting* the venerable mother in distress

> in front of her children, and at such times would laboriously shuffle along. (48; emphasis added)

Arina Petrovna's facade of solemnity and physical frailty projects the image of a mother heavy with the burdens of familial obligation, particularly the recent misfortunes of Stepan. This image sharply diverges, of course, from the reality of her indifference to Stepan's plight. Arina Petrovna slumps only from the anxiety caused by the underselling of her "blessing" and also from the unpleasantness of Stepan's unexpected, unsanctioned return. After Stepan's brief escape and shortly before his death, Arina Petrovna again exhibits her maternal vanity: "If you'd only stopped to think how you might have made people's tongues wag about your mother!" (66). This sudden concern with her image and reputation as a mother appears particularly self-serving in light of the desperation of her son's pathetic flight from the estate.

The surface of the maternal myth remains but masks only a void, as Arina Petrovna herself eventually recognizes. Her entire life, Arina Petrovna

> had been chasing shadows. All her life the word "family" had never left her lips. In the name of the family she had punished some and rewarded others; in the name of the family she had endured hardship, had suffered, had ruined her whole life. Now it suddenly turned out that the one thing she did *not* have was a family! (83)

These ruminations of Arina Petrovna's, as relayed by the narrator in indirect discourse, reveal how she has both internalized and transformed the sacrificial model of familial relations.[62] She has suffered privations, she claims, but she has also absorbed duties traditionally associated with the patriarch of a family, acting as executive authority and meting out justice according to her own whims and logic. The word "family" never leaves Arina Petrovna's lips, but she also expects liberation from motherhood. The disjuncture of these conflicting sentiments reveals the void at the core of *The Golovlev Family*.

MATERNAL LEGACIES

This hypocrisy also constitutes a central feature of Arina Petrovna's bequest to the next generation of Golovlevs. Intergenerational dynamics, according to the renowned economic historian Alexander Gerschenkron, form an individual's economic "time horizon," which he defines as "the distance at which men, in making economic decisions, are willing and able to look into the future and hence relates to their appraisal of the future as compared with the present." In the course of this discussion, he poses the following question about the Golovlev family: "What does the next generation actually inherit?"[63] The issue of a mother's particular bequest to subsequent generations occupied a prominent place in the Women's Question debates swirling in Russia at the time of the novel's publication. Arina Petrovna's maternal legacy to her son Porfiry, however, consists primarily in the privileging of form over substance, molding him into the consummate hypocrite. Critics have analyzed the nature of Porfiry's hypocrisy in detail. William Mills Todd III notes that "hypocrisy is Porfiry's great gift; the power to virtually hypnotize his victim by subverting family feeling and religion to his own ends." And Emil Draitser asserts a direct connection between Arina Petrovna's influence and the development of Porfiry's character, arguing that he evolved into an adept liar and sycophant—"the consummate hypocrite"—as a way to survive his mother's tyranny.[64]

However, none of these critics has analyzed how Porfiry ingratiates himself with Arina Petrovna by alluding specifically to the maternal moral authority that she claims to possess. In the following letter, for example, he blatantly appeals to her false sense of sacrifice: "Dearest Mamma, I know that you are shouldering a heavy burden on account of us, your unworthy children. I know that our behaviour often fails to justify your maternal concern for us" (30). And, in another letter, he even more explicitly alludes to the heavy burden she "selflessly" assumes after the death of her daughter and the adoption of Annin'ka and Liubin'ka:

> "You, dearest Mamma, have another cross to bear in the persons of two little orphans. Isn't it enough that you, our common benefactress, deny yourself in all things and, without sparing a thought for your health, devote all your strength to providing [for] your family . . . In my opinion, your only recourse, dear Mamma, in the present situation, is to recall as often as you can what Christ Himself had to endure." (30)

Porfiry's absurdly obsequious description of his mother's self-abnegation—particularly the reference to the suffering of Christ—reveals his awareness of the cult of the beneficent Russian mother. Porfiry attempts to craft a myth of the "good mother" that bears little resemblance to Golovlev reality by appealing to Arina Petrovna's vanity and thus, he hopes, improving his access to the financial resources that his mother controls. If Arina Petrovna utilizes the maternal myth to cement her authority and to fuel her ego, then Porfiry manipulates it for equally self-serving purposes.

In addition, Arina Petrovna bequeaths to Porfiry her absurd expectations for parent-child relations, which he exhibits in his own interactions with his two sons. For example, Porfiry's relationship with his son Petia is described in the following manner: "[Iudushka] knew that someone was mentioned *in his documents* as his son, to whom he had to send on certain dates a fixed sum (fixed by himself, that is), *in return* for which he was entitled to obedience and respect" (133; emphasis added). Like Arina Petrovna, Porfiry also views the parent-child relationship as merely a transaction, devoid of genuine emotion or substance. (His nickname, "Little Judas," evokes, of course, the paradigmatic example of betrayal in exchange for money.) Just as Arina Petrovna "threw a piece" to her children in exchange for their releasing her from any further maternal obligations, so Porfiry expects obeisance in return for his financial support.

Arina Petrovna believes that her son Stepan earned his grim fate because of a perceived lack of respect for familial bonds, and Porfiry also claims divine retribution for the scorn of blood ties. His brother Pavel, he speculates, has become ill because of his hatred for him (90). One of Porfiry's sons commits suicide because he was ungrateful and so receives punishment from God (135). The other son also dies tragically and prematurely, which Porfiry also attributes to a lack of respect and subsequent divine retribution (164). Pofiry, like his mother, assigns to God the role of arbiter punishing those family members who violate his own false exchange expectations. And the same "phantom" or nothingness that Arina Petrovna eventually identifies as characterizing the essence of the Golovlev family also permeates relations between Porfiry and his younger son, Petia: "Relations between father and son couldn't even be called strained: it was as if they didn't exist" (133). Thus, the "economic consciousness" that Porfiry inherits from his mother stimulates an absurd belief in divine punishment in exchange for the perceived neglect of illusory family bonds. For both mother and son, familial interactions assume the guise of economic transactions, with God the designated "invisible hand" that punishes any transgression of their exchange logic.

The correspondences between mother and son extend to the treatment that both of their respective "prodigal sons" receive. Both Stepan and Petia return to Golovlevo in defeat and are denied sympathy or parental support, leading indirectly to both of their deaths. Arina Petrovna is unaware of these parallels, of how her own traits have been absorbed and internalized by her children. During the family council, for example, she expresses surprise at Porfiry's lack of fraternal sentiment: "Can he really be such a bloodsucker as to turn his own brother out onto the street?" (57). She is later shocked that Porfiry exhibits another of her characteristics, cheapness. Arina Petrovna remains blind to her own corrosive maternal legacy, to the "economic consciousness" and its accompanying selfishness and miserliness that she passes down to the next generation.

Todd identifies food as a central symbol of this legacy, arguing that "the rottenness of the food Arina feeds her children becomes their moral essence."[65] And Darra Goldstein contends that the battles over food lay bare the struggle for power that constitutes the core of the Golovlev family: "Nourishment becomes the book's prevailing metaphor, a gastronomic conceit that chronicles the family's dyspepsia and eventual demise. Food and eating are used both symbolically and structurally to dramatize the gluttonous appetite for power that the family members share."[66] Indeed, the relation of the characters in the novel to food highlights how, in the Golovlev family, the material has subsumed the emotional or spiritual. Food, like the myth of the self-sacrificial mother, becomes a kind of currency manipulated first by Arina Petrovna and later by Porfiry. On the most basic level, Arina Petrovna's desire to save money prompts her to keep her children in a semi-starved state (24). Annin'ka remembers how, as children, she and her sister were fed sour milk by her grandmother (163). And, after Stepan's return, she feeds him just enough to keep him from dying of starvation (61). This abnegation of a mother's primary obligation to her children indicates that Arina Petrovna's economic instincts have superseded any maternal ones. In a perversion of a mother's traditional duties, Arina Petrovna fails to provide her children with any kind of nourishment, instead consuming them metaphorically.[67] Stepan, on his way back to Golovlevo, predicts that his mother will "chew him up": "From now on he would be all alone with that evil old woman . . . [who] would be the death of him, not by torturing him, but by consigning him to oblivion" (42). His father soon confirms this fear by warning that his mother will surely "devour him" (44; *s'est*).

Exhibiting another trait inherited from Arina Petrovna, Porfiry also denies his children figurative sustenance. When his eldest son, Volodia, swallows his pride to plead for money, Porfiry responds in the following manner:

> And by way of reply he [Volodia] was invariably offered some readymade maxim, which was like giving a stone to a starving man. It was a moot point whether Porfiry realized that he was offering stones and not bread. At any rate, he had nothing else, stones were all he was capable of offering. (137)

In response to Volodia's desperation, Porfiry can only offer meaningless phrases rather than the warm nourishment his son obviously needs. Starved literally and figuratively by his only parent, Volodia eventually commits suicide. The imagery of this passage evokes the New Testament, Matthew 7:9, when, during the Sermon on the Mount, Jesus asks: "Or what man is there of you, whom if his son ask bread, will he give him a stone?" The image of a hungry person receiving a stone instead of food could serve as a metaphor for all family relations within the Golovlev household.

Food also comprises a central element in the interrelations between Arina Petrovna and Porfiry. After Pavel dies and Porfiry assumes management of the estate, Arina Petrovna's appetite begins to decrease in protest (103). Eventually, she loses some of her earlier aggression and overt distrust of Porfiry and makes conciliatory gestures, but this softening is motivated at least partially by a desire to improve her diet: "His dear Mamma was almost constantly by his side—for the sake of a few tasty tidbits she had become a willing audience in her old age" (118). Arina Petrovna will endure Porfiry's vapid chatter for the sake of access to the all-important "piece" (*kusok*). Whereas she earlier possessed the power to throw each of her children a "piece" of land, the same term now signifies the "tidbits" that Arina Petrovna must await from Porfiry, whose hypocrisy, shallowness, and pomposity his mother tolerates in exchange for a full belly.[68]

In a rather dramatic shift from her fierce persona in the novel's opening chapter, Arina Petrovna begins to fear Porfiry because of the material comfort that he can now refuse her (130). Food acts as the primary currency of their relationship, and Porfiry's superior access to this currency endows him with a newfound power. "Now that she no longer holds the keys to the larder," as Goldstein explains, "Arina Petrovna is fearful of becoming precisely that which she fed to her son and her serfs: discards."[69] Porfiry initially begrudges his mother her requests for food, but he acquiesces out of fear of Arina Petrovna's maternal condemnation (117). In other words, he barters with his chief asset—food—to alleviate the anxiety that his mother provokes. Fear, it will be recalled, was also the only genuine emotion that her son evoked in Arina Petrovna in the opening of the novel (23). Thus, mutual fear and a craving for good food comprise the foundation of mother-son relations.

Before her deterioration and eventual death, Arina Petrovna experiences something akin to a maternal renaissance. She genuinely agonizes over the future of her granddaughters, for example, wondering if Pavel will leave them their fair inheritance before his death and how they will fare after leaving Golovlevo (98, 112). Arina Petrovna's transformation is so substantial that Porfiry even begins to look forward to her visits (123). Annin'ka draws a distinction between the two Arina Petrovnas, in the continuation of her reminiscences about being fed sour milk as a child: "But not recently, though . . . Recently she treated us very well. I mean when she was still rich" (163). Significantly, she bifurcates her grandmother's personal history according to the presence or absence of money. Indeed, even Arina Petrovna's softening, her exhibition of certain maternal sentiments that she had previously wholly lacked, does not elude the taint of the financial realm. When experiencing a wave of affection for Porfiry, she succumbs to yet another "fever of acquisition," but this time "no longer for herself—it was for the benefit of her favourite son" (77). Her newfound maternal instincts cannot be isolated from her economic ones, and Arina Petrovna, craving Porfiry's attention, longs to impress him in both arenas: "Arina Petrovna became overzealous, both as a mother and as mistress of a household wishing to demonstrate her great business acumen to her loving son" (77). Thus, motherly impulses are channeled and expressed through acquisitive ones. For the first time, Arina Petrovna longs for the affection of her offspring, not merely their fear and respect, as a reward for her business dealings.

Gerschenkron has characterized Arina Petrovna's management of the Golovlev estate in the following manner: "Along with the grand and bold policy of rational acquisition goes an attitude of avarice that is apprehensive and thoroughly irrational." One example of this is hoarding food until it begins to rot.[70] The onset of Arina Petrovna's maternal sentiments, like her economic reasoning, also betrays irrationality. In fact, her transformation is linked explicitly with the fading of her previously keen logical faculties: "From now on Arina Petrovna seemed to be living under a cloud . . . The more clouded her reason became, the more passionate grew her concern for the son who loved her" (77). Arina Petrovna's resurgent maternity appears to be a symptom of her diminishing grasp on reality. Once Arina Petrovna loses her earlier sharpness, she mistakes Porfiry's "form"—his obsequiousness and empty chatter—for "substance"—genuine sentiment. Arina Petrovna's fleeting reawakening to motherhood is tainted by its expression through her old "fever of acquisition" and by the mental fog that precedes it.

MATERNAL SPECTERS

After her death, his mother's presence continues to linger in Porfiry's consciousness; he even hallucinates and converses with her. The maternal and the financial realms continue to merge, even in this imaginary exchange, as Porfiry summons his mother to chastise her for depriving him of property. Warning that a "grave sin" hangs over her soul, he decides to quantify conclusively "what losses his dear Mamma had inflicted on him." For Porfiry, as for his mother, it is figures and accounts, not familial relations, which are truly "something holy" (246). His final encounter with his mother is with a specter, much like that which both mother and son eventually acknowledged comprised the essence of the Golovlev family.

The novel's ending, however, and the stirring of conscience that Porfiry experiences shortly before it, may be interpreted as an attempted reconciliation with his mother. The return of the dying Annin'ka to Golovlevo awakens Porfiry to the process of decay slowly consuming the estate and all of its residents (284).[71] This discovery triggers in him feelings of guilt toward his mother:

> "I'm the one who wronged Mamma, it was I who tormented the life out of her!" . . . and the longing to beg forgiveness grew stronger with every minute.

> He would not ask for it in the usual way, but by falling on her grave and growing numb as he sobbed his heart out in mortal anguish. (284)

A longing for rapprochement with Arina Petrovna accompanies Porfiry's first moments of compassion and humanity. This impulse prompts him to set out in the middle of the cold March night, clad only in his bathrobe, toward the direction of her grave. His frozen body is found near the road the next day, with his quest to plead for maternal forgiveness remaining incomplete.

In both the novel's opening and closing images, then, the sons of Arina Petrovna attempt reunion with her only to encounter death. For Stepan, the death is gradual, but he nonetheless senses its inevitability. The sight of the estate immediately evokes for him the image of a coffin, his only means of leaving Golovlevo (43). And Porfiry perishes in the frozen ground, a death symbolic of the lack of maternal warmth that characterized his life. Reconciliation with one's mother in *The Golovlev Family,* either voluntary or involuntary, is an inherently doomed mission.

I. B. Pavlova argues that, in his prose of the 1860s–80s, Saltykov-Shchedrin draws a parallel between the fate of the family and that of Russia as a nation.[72] According to the conservative rhetoric of the period, Russia's noble mothers bore the responsibility for nurturing the former to ensure the stability of the latter. Arina Petrovna shuns this responsibility of a mother to cultivate the Russian citizens of the future, choosing instead to develop the Golovlevo estate and her own proprietary ambitions. Her decision ensures the prosperity of Golovlevo but also the gradual dissolution of subsequent generations of Golovlevs.

"TOPPLING OLD IDOLS"

In his 1863 essay "Contemporary Specters," Saltykov-Shchedrin asserts that the most important function of the writer lies in exposing and defeating the phantoms upon which society has been falsely constructed. In an impassioned tone, he laments how difficult it is to not "burn with indignation, when life has been overtaken by forms that have lost all of their meaning, when there is an awareness of the inadequacy of these forms, but when bitter necessity nonetheless forces us to succumb to them, God knows why." These empty forms—including the family—have forced upon Russians the comic role of Don Quixote mistaking windmills for knights.[73] In *The Golovlev Family,* Saltykov-Shchedrin reduces maternal mythology to a kind of currency (much like food) manipulated for personal gain by both Arina Petrovna and her son Porfiry, thus unmasking the ideal of the self-sacrificial mother as precisely such a false knight.[74] By extension, the segment of Russian society that emphasized the importance of devoted motherhood to the future of the nation emerges as a misguided Don Quixote.

However, in *The Golovlev Family,* Saltykov-Shchedrin himself also attributes exaggerated importance to mothers, although he reveals their potential to accomplish negative rather than positive change. The character of Arina Petrovna debunks both the conservative valorization of the benevolent mother transmitting proper values to her children and progressive ideas about women's increased participation in spheres outside of the domestic one.[75] In order to accomplish his goal of exposing the emptiness and indefensibility of the Russian family, Saltykov-Shchedrin attacks the mother that occupies its sacred core, successfully satirizing the various models of maternal behavior being propagated in the ideological debates of the post-Emancipation era.

Simply put, a bad mother can influence society as significantly as a good one. The maternal figure in the novel functions as the intersection of multiple spheres—familial, religious, and financial—all of which are transformed by the introduction of elements of a market economy. Andrei Anikin attributes profound significance to the author's views on capitalism, speculating that "Saltykov's works, with their great influence on the Russian intelligentsia, perhaps helped to create the strongly anticapitalist mentality that prevailed among the intellectuals in the twenty or thirty years that led up to the Russian Revolution of 1917."[76] In *The Golovlev Family,* arguably Saltykov-Shchedrin's most important and influential fictional work, the mother acts as the conduit for the infusion of elements of a market economy into the family, the negative consequences of which undoubtedly reveal the author's "anticapitalist mentality." In the novel, the mother who bequeaths an "economic consciousness" to her offspring hastens the decline of a noble family. This new consciousness permeates two of the most important bastions of Russian society, family and religion, introducing spiritual and emotional values into the marketplace and rendering them subject to buying, selling, and exchanging. In keeping with his stated goal of "toppling old idols from their pedestals" in order to impel the restructuring of society, in *The Golovlev Family* Saltykov-Shchedrin reveals how neither the myth of the self-sacrificial mother nor the new economy—and especially not a combination of the two—can be entrusted with the salvation of the Russian nation, as symbolized by the fate of the Russian family.[77] I now turn to another seminal novel from the era of the Great Reforms that focuses on the challenges facing the Russian family, including the mother's role within it: Leo Tolstoy's *Anna Karenina.*

The heroine of *Anna Karenina,* like Arina Petrovna, also eschews the principles of traditional maternal self-sacrifice, although for markedly different motivations.[78] Anna privileges her emotional and sexual self-interest over her maternal obligations, contributing to her own deterioration and to an unclear fate for her two children. The seemingly irreconcilable conflict between her maternal attachment to her son, Serezha, and her increasingly desperate desire for Vronsky provide the novel with its tragic core, as several critics have noted.[79] Tolstoy presents communication between mothers as a privileged exchange, revelatory of what Jane Costlow has termed the "classless communality of mothering."[80] As Anna subsumes her motherly instincts, she is gradually excluded from this mode of communication, an exclusion that accompanies—and undoubtedly hastens—her descent into isolation and despair. Anna's decision to turn away from motherhood contributes to her alienation from maternity's "classless communality," which in turn helps create the cynical and solipsistic frame of mind that propels her to suicide. The novel charts Anna's devolution as a mother, depicting the conflicts between sincerity and falsehood, shrewdness and intuition, in her maternal sentiments—struggles that echo the novel's larger themes. The female characters in *Anna Karenina* confront the "maternal dilemma" in highly contrasting ways, and my reading of the novel also identifies the various models of motherhood that Tolstoy introduces in the work.

MATERNAL OR EROTIC?

The opening chapters of *Anna Karenina* are significant for establishing the dynamics of maternity in the novel as a whole. The first allusions to motherhood are narrated from the perspective of Stiva, who refers to his wife, Dolly, as "the mother of five living and two dead children" and "merely a good mother."[81] According to Stiva's logic, it follows from this statement that Dolly, out of a sense of fairness, must be lenient toward him and his infidelity. Dolly "was contented and happy in her children"; therefore, she should not fault him for seeking pleasure in the arms of a governess (6). Stiva's reasoning implies a disjuncture between sexuality and motherhood. This argumentation conforms to nineteenth-century European stereotypes about parental roles, according to which, as Amy Mandelker argues, fatherhood constricts a man's freedom to pursue his true destiny, while "maternity is considered the only fulfilling path in life for a woman, in whom maternal instinct presumably induces a state of selflessness and willing sacrifice."[82] Once she assumes a primarily maternal role, a woman should cede her sexual responsibilities to another woman (and, presumably, sublimate her own desires) while seeking fulfillment only in motherhood itself.

The conflict between Dolly and Stiva that opens the novel, prefiguring the later strife between Anna and her husband, unfolds at the cusp of what has been termed the "marriage crisis" in late imperial Russia.[83] Providing a stark indicator of the degree of domestic tension, the number of divorces in Russia increased significantly between 1850 and 1914, from a few dozen to a few thousand. Indeed, when including unsuccessful divorce petitions in the assessment, an even more striking picture of familial rupture in the post-Emancipation period emerges. This perceived crisis, playing out on a micro level in the Oblonsky household, figured prominently in public discourse of the time, prompting one church journal to proclaim ominously: "The breakdown of the family, despite the extreme difficulty of the divorce process, is one of the most serious social ills of the present time."[84] While relenting partially to increasing demand, the Orthodox Church—which viewed marriage as a sacrament and wholeheartedly resisted judicial reform and the secularization of family law—nonetheless erected formidable barriers to the obtainment of divorce. The process was complicated, lengthy, expensive, and frequently unsuccessful. The only acceptable grounds were abandonment/disappearance (including Siberian exile), sexual or mental incapacity, and adultery. At the time of the publication of Tolstoy's novel, the most common grounds for divorce were beginning to shift, with adultery overtaking disappearance by the 1880s and accounting for 90 percent of divorces by 1914. The difficulty of receiving a divorce could be overcome primarily through one route: collusion between the two parties involved. Since adultery could only be proven through the testimony of two eyewitnesses to the act of sexual intercourse, deception and bribery (for those who could afford it) during divorce proceedings abounded.[85]

For a woman wishing to leave her husband, as Dolly professes a desire to do at the beginning of *Anna Karenina,* the options were severely limited. Family law explicitly mandated "spousal cohabitation," a provision supported by the internal passport regime. Any travel beyond twenty miles from one's place of residence required proper documentation, and a married woman was inscribed on her husband's passport, having surrendered her own passport at the church on her wedding day. This regime left even women from the noble classes, such as Dolly, completely dependent on their husbands' cooperation, rendering them effectively incapable of free movement.[86]

Despite these daunting obstacles, Dolly attempts to prepare to leave Stiva at the beginning of part 1, chapter 4, and the reader views her through her husband's eyes as she does so: "Darya Aleksandrovna, in a bed jacket, and with her now scanty, once luxuriant and beautiful hair fastened up with hairpins on the nape of her neck, with a sunken, thin face and large, startled eyes, which looked prominent because of the thinness of her face" (13). The word "thin," repeated twice, and the image of the unnaturally prominent eyes paint Dolly as a fleshless, almost ghostlike figure lacking in the vitality of youth. Motherhood, implicitly, shoulders the blame for this physical transformation and the consequent waning of Dolly's sexual attractiveness. Dolly herself intuits this change in her husband's feelings: "She saw in him sympathy toward her but not love" (16).

This potential incompatibility of maternity and sexuality highlighted in the opening chapters continues with the arrival of Anna herself. Kitty, for example, views Anna as un- or pre-maternal: "Anna was not like a fashionable lady, nor the mother of a boy eight years old. In the elasticity of her movements, the freshness and the unflagging eagerness which persisted in her face, and broke out in her smile and her glance, she would have passed for a girl of twenty" (84). It appears impossible to reconcile Anna's motherhood with the enigmatic energy and attractiveness she exudes, to which Kitty and, of course, Vronsky fall victim. Kitty's observations, taken in the context of the split between maternity and sexuality established in the opening chapters, allude to the potential volatility of a mother who does not look like one.[87]

These early chapters present a struggle between two possible Annas, as the critic Edward Wasiolek has observed: "The settled matron past the turbulences of love, and the Anna of suppressed hunger for passion that attracts Vronsky at the first encounter." This struggle reaches its climax at the ball, where Anna longs to transcend the maternal category that excludes the erotic. A matron, or "aunt," Kitty imagines, would wear violet to a ball. Instead, Anna wears the black of the sexually aware woman, and the dress hints at the sensuality that lingers just underneath the facade of Anna's proper behavior and impeccable societal position.[88] Hence, Anna's internal struggle is indirectly tied to her maternal identity from the beginning of the novel, even before the consummation of her affair with Vronsky and the resulting conflict between son and lover.

Much later in the novel, Anna reveals that she has internalized the same cleavage between maternity and sexuality introduced through her brother. In part 7, Anna explains her decision to not have any more children to Dolly: "'You must consider, I am not his wife; he loves me as long as he loves me. And how am I to keep his love? Not like this?' She moved her white hands in a curve before her belly" (723). Anna refuses to sacrifice her beauty—without which, she believes, she cannot retain Vronsky's love—for the sake of bearing children. This issue of future offspring had become a volatile one between them: "The question of the possibility of having children had long been a subject of dispute and irritation to her. His desire to have children she interpreted as a proof he did not prize her beauty" (845).[89] Anna projects onto Vronsky a belief in the mutual exclusivity of sexual attractiveness and motherhood. As Caryl Emerson has observed, Anna denies the possibility that Vronsky's love may evolve or deepen. She fails to comprehend Vronsky's transition to a mature attachment no longer grounded exclusively in erotic attraction, instead clinging to an earlier and more rigid model predicated exclusively on his desire for her physical beauty.[90] Anna, in a sense, projects her brother's worldview onto Vronsky, negating the possibility for a mature love that reconciles the maternal and sexual categories to develop.[91]

MATERNAL COMMUNICATION

The opening chapters also establish the singularity of communication between mothers in *Anna Karenina.*[92] Anna relies on her profile as a mother to accomplish her goal of reconciling Stiva and Dolly. For example, Anna alludes to their common maternal experience by mentioning that Dolly's daughter Tania and her son Serezha are the same age. Dolly is sincerely touched when Anna remembers not only the names but also the illnesses of all of Dolly's children. Anna thereby establishes a connection and trust with Dolly by this subtle appeal to her sister-in-law's maternal consciousness. Significantly, their discussion of Stiva's infidelity, and Anna's lobbying on behalf of her brother, begins immediately after the encounter with Dolly's children (79). After this initial conversation, Anna isolates herself from any other company and spends the entire morning with Dolly and her children. Strategically, Anna interrupts this seclusion of two mothers only to send a note to Stiva asking him to come home for dinner (83).

Anna succeeds in her mission of hastening the reconciliation between husband and wife at least partially because of this appeal to maternal sentiment. Anna employs this tactic, however, to accomplish a morally ambiguous goal. She utters subtle untruths about Stiva that immediately ring false to the reader's ears. For example, Anna tells Dolly that Stiva himself cannot comprehend his own actions (82). However, Stiva's own ruminations, as relayed by the narrator in indirect discourse in the novel's opening chapters and directly during Stiva's dinner with Levin, render this statement implausible. Stiva understands fully the rationale behind his infidelity and wonders why his wife refuses to accept tacitly his logic. Anna also reassures Dolly that she remains "a divinity" for Stiva and that infidelity could never occur again (82–83). These assurances also contradict the information the reader receives earlier in the novel about Stiva's motivations and intentions. Hence, Anna taints the sanctity of maternal communication by introducing elements of falsehood into the exchange.

The first mother-to-mother conversation that Anna engages in, however, occurs prior to her arrival in Moscow, while on the train with Countess Vronskaia. On the platform in Moscow, Anna stresses the centrality of motherhood in the discussions between the women: "'Anna Arkadyevna,' the countess said . . . 'has a little son 8 years old, I believe, and she has never been parted from him before, and she keeps worrying over leaving him.' 'Yes, the countess and I have been talking all the time, I of my son and she of hers,' said Madame Karenina" (74). The two women seemingly form a quick bond on the basis of their common maternal experience. Like the later exchange with Dolly, this tête-à-tête alludes to a unique kinship and a special communication between mothers.

Countess Vronskaia's sincerity as a mother, however, had already been questioned several pages earlier: "Vronsky had never had a real family life. His mother had been in her youth a brilliant society woman, who had had during her married life, and especially afterward, many love affairs notorious in all society" (67). From this description, one may assume that Countess Vronskaia solved the "maternal dilemma" by choosing the enjoyments of society over sustained involvement with her children. She shunned traditional maternal self-sacrifice to engage in a string of love affairs. Consequently, Vronsky

> did not in his heart respect his mother, and without acknowledging it to himself, he did not love her, though in accordance with the ideas of the set in which he lived, and with his own education, he could not have conceived of any behavior to his mother not in the highest degree respectful and obedient, and the more externally obedient and respectful in his behavior, the less in his heart he respected and loved her. (72)

Vronsky's attitude toward his mother exhibits the same "form" versus "substance" division observed in the family dynamics of the Golovlev family. The empty gestures of respect and obedience that characterize mother-son relations only intensify Vronsky's inner indifference. This information colors the reader's perception of the exchange between Anna and Countess Vronskaia, casting the meeting of the two mothers in a somewhat false and superficial light. Hence, both of Anna's mother-to-mother encounters in part 1 of *Anna Karenina* are tainted: first by Countess Vronskaia's questionable maternal values, and then by the subtle untruths that Anna utters to accomplish her goal of convincing Dolly to reunite with her unfaithful husband.

In the first part of the novel, Anna encounters two divergent models of motherhood, as represented by Dolly and Countess Vronskaia. Dolly embodies active engagement with her children, suffering the attendant frustrations and disappointments as well as experiencing the joys. Gary Saul Morson has argued that Dolly "lives by constant attention to the prosaic details of daily life, especially those concerned with the most prosaic of institutions, the family."[93] Vronskaia, by contrast, preferred the pleasures of society life to the daily rigors of motherhood, and her son, as a result, "had never had a real family life" (67). The Countess, like Arina Petrovna Golovleva, presumably maximized the privileges afforded to noblewomen in the era of serfdom. After the abolition in 1861, however, many more upper-class mothers undoubtedly had no choice but to adhere more closely to Dolly's example. By the end of the nineteenth century, it had become increasingly unacceptable to view children as a "burden" that "one hastened to hand over to various uncles and nurses of the common people to raise," as one respondent in a custody case from the period phrased it.[94] These two contrasting visions of maternity also reinforce the split between motherhood and sexuality discussed above. To which model, then, does Anna herself more closely adhere in part 1 of the novel?

Initially, at least, Anna seems to reconcile these disparate trajectories, seamlessly making the transition from pre- to post-Emancipation noble motherhood.[95] While a guest at Dolly and Stiva's, her maternal emotions prompt her to dwell upon thoughts of Serezha:

> Toward ten o'clock, when she usually said good night to her son, and often before going to a ball put him to bed herself, she felt depressed at being so far from him; and whatever she was talking about, she kept returning to thoughts of her curly-headed Seryozha. (88)

This description portrays Anna as a caring, involved mother who participates in her son's daily life, à la Dolly. But at the same time, like Countess Vronskaia, Anna refuses to sacrifice the amusements of high society: she puts her son to bed *"before going to a ball."* Anna radiates youth and vivacity and still attends balls while apparently losing none of her maternal sincerity. She longs to linger on and share the motherly emotions that flood her memory (ibid.). Thus, Anna apparently bridges the divide between the Vronskaia and Dolly, the pre- and post-reform, models of motherhood by forgoing neither prosaic attention to her son's needs nor the pleasures of Petersburg society. Significantly, the arrival of Vronsky at the Oblonsky home interrupts Anna's reminiscences of her son. Her unexpectedly strong reaction to the sight of Vronsky—the mixture of "pleasure and dread" that he evokes—hints, perhaps, at the precariousness of this balance between devoted motherhood and carefree enjoyment (ibid.).

"THAT POWER WAS HER SON"

Upon her return home to St. Petersburg, an intensified focus on Serezha accompanies Anna's attempts to calm the emotions stirred by her encounters with Vronsky. Her response to her son's affectionate greeting at the beginning of part 1, chapter 33, however, betrays disappointment. The Serezha

Anna had envisioned fails to correspond with the real Serezha, and she must "descend" to reality from the lofty heights of her imagination to appreciate him in the present (124). Significantly, Anna views her son in the same light as her husband, who had earlier aroused such dissatisfaction when he greeted her on the train platform (part 1, chapter 30). The pallor of falsehood that colored Anna's conversation with Dolly now casts a slight shadow on her relationship with her son. Dolly had intuited an element of insincerity in Anna's household, and her presentiment of something amiss in the Karenins' family life now appears significant (78).

The sensual pleasure Anna experiences from Serezha's "nearness and his caresses," however, counteracts her initial disappointment (124). Her reaction echoes that of Stiva to his favorite child, Tania, in part 1, chapter 3: "and still stroking her little shoulder, he kissed her at the roots of her hair and the nape of her neck and let her go" (12). Unlike Stiva, however, Anna receives not only physical pleasure but also "moral soothing" from the embraces of her son (124). She relies on Serezha and on her role as a mother to contain the nascent sexual desire and sense of shame stirred by Vronsky. The harmonizing effects of domesticity—such as spending the entire evening with her son and putting him to bed—seemingly produce the desired result, neutralizing Anna's excitability after the Moscow trip and allowing her once again to feel "resolute and irreproachable," untainted by moral ambiguity (125).

Hence, in these first interactions with Serezha, Anna displays genuine warmth and attentiveness. The image of the devoted mother is colored, however, by the disjuncture between Anna's vision of her son and the reality of him, an indication that Anna departs from Dolly's model. These initial encounters allude to a battle between sincerity and insincerity, genuineness and falsehood within Anna's maternal identity. Her dependence on Serezha to counteract a growing attraction to Vronsky hints at the conflict between son and lover shortly to develop.

Later in the novel, Anna again turns to thoughts of her son in a search for calm amid the tumult caused by her relations with Vronsky. In part 3, chapter 25, on the morning after her confession of adultery to Karenin, Anna clings to the idea of Serezha as the antidote to her increasingly desperate dilemma:

> The recollection of her son suddenly roused Anna from the helpless condition in which she found herself. She recalled the partly sincere, though greatly exaggerated, *role of the mother living for her child,* which she had taken up of late years. (331; emphasis added)[96]

This description lays bare the element of pretense or exaggeration in Anna's maternal identity. Like Arina Petrovna had also done, she assumes the pose of the self-sacrificial mother, indicating an awareness of maternal mythology and the moral authority that accompanies it. The phrase "taken up" (*vziala na sebia*) also indicates something imported from without rather than developed organically from within. In the moral landscape of *Anna Karenina,* this trait is negatively marked.[97]

In the continuation of the above passage, Anna identifies her son as a source of power:

> . . . and she felt with joy that in the plight in which she found herself she had a power [*derzhava*], quite apart from her relation to her husband or to Vronsky. That power was her son. In whatever position she might be placed, she could not lose her son . . . She had an aim in life. And she must act; act to secure this relation to her son, so that he might not be taken from her . . . She must take her son and go away . . . The thought of immediate action binding her to her son, of going away somewhere with him, gave her this consolation. (331)[98]

For a moment, the abandonment of Serezha seems unfathomable to Anna. Henceforth, she will adhere to the self-sacrificial model, forgoing her romantic attachment to Vronsky in favor of her son. This revelation endows her life with meaning, clarity, and calm, and the "power" associated with Serezha may refer to the inner strength required to honor this maternal commitment.

Anna's resolve to privilege her motherly responsibilities weakens quickly, however. She does not escape with her son, despite this brief revelatory interlude. The association of her son with "power" also evokes a potentially less noble connotation since power, presumably, can be wielded to accomplish selfish goals. Indeed, Anna increasingly views Serezha as a pawn in the struggle with Karenin. For example, after receiving the letter from Karenin announcing his decision that their family situation will remain unchanged despite her recent confession, Anna suspects her husband of using the power of her maternal love to threaten and manipulate her:

> She recalled the words from the letter: "You can conjecture what awaits you and your son . . . " "That's a threat to take away my child, and most likely by their stupid law he can. But I know very well why he says it. He doesn't even believe in my love for my child, or he despises it . . . but he knows that I can't abandon my child, that there could be no life for me without my child." (335)

She projects her worldview, which connects Serezha with power, onto Karenin, attributing to him calculating motives and tactics. Anna articulates this accusation explicitly in part 4, chapter 4, after Karenin catches Vronsky in his home: "You take Seryozha to hurt me" (417). While contemplating the repercussions of divorce, Karenin himself acknowledges the possibility that his son may be co-opted in this manner, but he refuses to succumb:

"What would become of his son in case of divorce? . . . Keep him with him? He knew that would be an act of vengeance on his part, and that he did not want" (491). Indeed, in contrast to England and the United States, mothers enjoyed no particular favor in custody disputes in Russia, where the law placed the burden of providing a moral education for children on the shoulders of both parents equally. Custody cases were thus frequently decided according to officials' determination of the moral qualities of the mother and father, leaving the adulterous Anna at a distinct disadvantage.[99] Karenin, however, resists the temptation to employ his son as a weapon against Anna, casting doubt upon her earlier charges.

The climactic and emblematic use of the power associated with a child occurs, however, not with Serezha but with Annie, the daughter of Anna and Vronsky. In part 6, chapters 31 to 32, Anna writes a letter to Vronsky while he attends the elections, imploring him to return immediately due to Annie's serious illness. Anna greatly exaggerates her daughter's condition, however, solely to lure Vronsky home. Annie's illness provides no distraction for Anna from her all-consuming thoughts of Vronsky, merely providing a pretext for her plea for his return. Annie's complete recovery before Vronsky's arrival provokes annoyance rather than relief in Anna (756). A healthy child, who evokes less worry and sympathy, diminishes the power that Anna can wield over Vronsky. Anna's maternal sentiments recede completely, superseded by a desire to manipulate Vronsky. Hence, her daughter serves solely as a source of power in the battle Anna wages with her lover, and this incident represents, perhaps, the nadir of Anna-as-mother in the novel.

In light of Anna's earlier intuitiveness as a mother, her lack of feeling for Annie is particularly poignant. In part 2, chapter 27, for example, she immediately senses Serezha's discomfort around his father and responds appropriately:

> Aleksey Aleksandrovich was holding his son by the shoulder . . . and Seryozha was so miserably uncomfortable that Anna saw he was on the point of tears. Anna, who had flushed a little the instant her son came in, noticing that Seryozha was uncomfortable, got up hurriedly, took Aleksey Aleksandrovich's hand from her son's shoulder, and, kissing the boy, quickly led him out onto the terrace. (235)

Anna's maternal intuition reacts to her son's body language and silent unease. She reads his face and correctly determines his needs without an exchange of words. Serezha, consequently, feels most comfortable with his mother (ibid.). Anna and Serezha communicate without words, a mode of communication that the novel privileges, as exemplified most famously by the engagement scene between Kitty and Levin.

This link between mother and son remains even after Anna leaves Serezha to live with Vronsky, as witnessed in the scene where she secretly visits her son on his birthday. Although Anna plans every last detail of this furtive encounter, she cannot, despite her best efforts, prepare the necessary words to say to Serezha (604). But words prove irrelevant to their reunion, since Serezha intuitively understands his mother: "Seryozha knew all she wanted to say to him. He understood that she was unhappy and loved him . . . he saw she was miserable, and he felt for her." And Anna, in turn, correctly decodes the subtext of Serezha's words by reading his expression (610). Despite their separation, the mother-son bond between Anna and Serezha still transcends verbal communication, indicating a higher level of mutual understanding and sympathy. This undiminished link explains, at least in part, the unexpectedly strong reaction Anna experiences after her brief reunion with her son.[100]

MEMORY AND MATERNAL DECLINE

Within Anna's maternal identity, then, unfolds a struggle between intuition and calculation, sincerity and falsehood, attentiveness and disengagement. The novel presents Anna's devolution as a mother, a process that can be traced through observing the presence or absence of her children in Anna's memory. As Morson has argued, memory in *Anna Karenina* contains an ethical component. For example, Stiva's inability to remember the existence of his family encapsulates this connection between memory and morality.[101] The waxing and waning of Serezha in Anna's consciousness reinforces this similarity between brother and sister and illustrates the gradual subsuming of Anna's maternal emotions.

For instance, in part 3, chapter 15, on the morning after Anna's confession to Karenin, Serezha fades into the background of Anna's consciousness: "'Seryozha? What about Seryozha?' Anna asked . . . recollecting her son's existence for the first time that morning" (330–31). The reminder of the existence of a son startles and momentarily disorients Anna. Similarly, after she and Vronsky leave Russia for Italy, Serezha again retreats into the recesses of her mind: "Separation from the son she loved—even that did not cause her anguish in these early days. The baby girl—*his* child—was so sweet, and had so won Anna's heart, since she was all that was left her, that Anna rarely remembered her son" (527–28). Serezha now reminds Anna of her guilt before Karenin, whom she compares with a drowning man callously pushed away. Despite sensing the hurtfulness of her actions, Anna cannot escape happiness (527). A precondition for this happiness, however, is the submergence of thoughts of her son. Annie (temporarily) replaces Serezha in Anna's maternal consciousness, facilitating the joy Anna feels in spite of herself.

Later in the novel, in part 5, chapter 31, a battle wages between Vronsky and Serezha in Anna's memory. Lost in reminiscences of Serezha, she allows the image of Vronsky to fade momentarily. Just as Anna had spent an entire morning without remembering her son earlier in the novel, so she now forgets Vronsky. But Vronsky's face in a photograph, his familiar physical features, displaces the thoughts of her son, and she desperately demands her lover's presence (612). Thus, the balance in Anna's memory between lover and son tips back toward Vronsky, with the consequent ethical implications.

While Serezha occasionally threatens to dislodge Vronsky from his privileged position in Anna's thoughts, her daughter Annie, by contrast, leaves few observable traces on her mother's consciousness. Forgotten after her birth during the upheaval of Anna's illness, Annie survives solely due to the attention and care paid her by Karenin. The first "maternal" figure she encounters is, ironically, her mother's jilted husband. During her visit to Vronsky's estate, Dolly discovers the extent of Anna's disconnection from Annie's daily life. Anna cedes responsibility for her daughter's care first to Karenin and then to various hired caretakers. Her lack of basic knowledge about and interest in Annie contrasts starkly with the model of motherhood that Dolly embodies and that was, at least rhetorically, becoming the norm in late-nineteenth-century Russia. It also underscores her daughter's absence from Anna's memory, an absence connoting a moral lapse. Quite simply, Annie cannot inspire the same devoted and attentive love that Anna bestowed upon Serezha.[102] During Levin's visit, Anna proclaims that love transcends all quantification (790). The disparity between Anna's feelings for her son versus those for her daughter, however, betrays the falsehood of this statement. Anna's maternal love is finite, subject to moderation and modulation based on circumstances.

Anna, in turn, eventually wanes in her son's memory as well: "A year passed from the time that Seryozha saw his mother for the last time. Since then he had heard nothing about her . . . Those dreams and reminiscences of his mother that had made him ill after his meeting with her no longer occupied him" (821). By the last days of her life, Anna's relationship with Serezha had devolved into something akin to mutual amnesia. Her final hours are consumed almost entirely by thoughts of Vronsky and the supposed disappearance of his love for her; few memories of her earlier life surface amidst the obsession with her "betrayal" by her lover. In the final carriage ride before her suicide, however, a reminiscence of Serezha unexpectedly penetrates Anna's stream-of-consciousness monologue:

> Seryozha? . . . I thought too, that I loved him, and used to be touched by my own tenderness. But I have lived without him, I exchanged him [*promeni-ala*] for another love and did not regret the exchange [*promen*] as long as that other love satisfied me. (863)

For Anna, this uninvited memory lays bare the perceived superficiality of her earlier maternal identity. In the harsh light in which she now views all human relations, the sincere and tender aspects of her motherhood disappear as well. Significantly, she uses the verb "to exchange" to describe the swapping of Serezha's love for Vronsky's. As Arina Petrovna did, Anna now also employs the vocabulary of the marketplace to describe intimate relationships. Her choice of Vronsky over Serezha assumes the guise of a simple economic transaction from which she had hoped to profit, that is, receive satisfaction. Anna's worldview in her final moments betrays a cynical "economic consciousness," one that precludes the possibility of anything except selfishness in human relations (861). This belief in the transaction behind every human interaction renders absurd the self-sacrificial ideal of motherhood.

Anna's decisions regarding her own maternity eventually lead to her exclusion from the "classless communality of mothering."[103] As Vladimir Alexandrov points out, "Anna's abandonment of her son and her decision not to have any more children puts her at odds with the conception of women that the narrator articulates and that Dolly and Kitty embody."[104] In this state of isolation, Anna perceives humanity through a prism that is anathema to maternal sentiment of any kind. The struggle between sincerity and falsehood, intuition and calculation that characterized Anna's relationship with Serezha ceases. Her final memories, significantly, are of a pre-maternal self: "A feeling such as she had known when about to take the first plunge in bathing came upon her, and she crossed herself. That familiar gesture brought back into her soul a whole series of memories of her childhood and girlhood" (867). In these last moments before her suicide, Anna's maternal identity disintegrates completely.

Throughout her life, Arina Petrovna Golovleva viewed transaction and exchange as inherent to familial relations. By the end of her days, however, she had begun to question this philosophy, experiencing something resembling a maternal renaissance. By contrast, Anna Karenina, during her last moments, comes to view not only familial but all human relationships as founded solely on the principle of self-interest. As Arina Petrovna does from the very beginning, Anna Karenina, in the end, believes that sacrifice requires a reward. She expects this recompense not from her children, as Arina Petrovna had, but from Vronsky. For Anna, suicide becomes the logical response to a world structured according to the tenet of self-interest and disappointed exchange expectations. During Anna's last moments, family and her own motherhood retreat into the background of her consciousness. For Arina Petrovna, on the other hand, increasing introspection and doubt about the state of her family, as well as about her own efforts and supposed deprivations on its behalf, characterize the years leading up to her death.

Neither of these bad mothers completely lacks redemptive qualities.

Both Anna and Arina Petrovna exhibit moments of tenderness with their respective children, but elements of falsehood taint this sincerity. Both characters retain awareness of the myth of the good mother and the effect that motherhood produces. Arina Petrovna expects freedom from the burdens of maternity and acknowledgment of her acquisitive efforts on behalf of her family, while Anna attempts to counteract her attraction to Vronsky through her role as the "guiltless mother" and the moral authority with which it endows her. She also enlists the "power" of motherhood as a weapon in her later battles with Karenin and Vronsky.

Saltykov-Shchedrin reacted negatively to the publication of the first sections of *Anna Karenina.* In a letter to P. V. Annenkov dated March 9, 1875, he writes: "It's awful to think that novels can still be structured purely around sexual urges." Like many of his contemporaries, Saltykov-Shchedrin initially interpreted Tolstoy's work as merely an adultery novel from the upper classes. Despite this negative reception of *Anna Karenina,* he himself turned to writing a family chronicle soon afterward. Indeed, in an 1881 letter to Utin, Saltykov-Shchedrin confirms that the two novels are not so dissimilar, despite *The Golovlev Family*'s total lack of a love plot.[105] Although Tolstoy and Saltykov-Shchedrin occupied opposite poles on the ideological spectrum, both authors focused on the problematic nature of familial relations in Russia of the 1870s. Their respective family novels—*Anna Karenina* and *The Golovlev Family*—both diverge from the model of the happy gentry family that so frequently appeared in nostalgic accounts of childhood in Russian works from earlier in the century, including Tolstoy's own writings. The character of the bad mother—one who chooses an extra-maternal identity and rejects the "maternal sacrifice paradigm"—plays a central role in both of these authors' explorations of the dissolution and rupture of the Russian family. Despite the philosophical divisions that separated their authors, both novels assert a connection between the subversion of maternal self-sacrifice and the fracturing of the Russian family.

The novels ultimately diverge, however, in their contrasting responses to the "maternal dilemma." In keeping with Saltykov-Shchedrin's explicit goal of revealing the bankruptcy of Russian domestic life, *The Golovlev Family* offers no positive maternal role models and certainly does not present motherhood as endowing women with any transcendent qualities. *Anna Karenina,* by contrast, presents two characters—Dolly and Kitty—who both adhere to the positively marked model of committed motherhood. In exchange for their dedication to the domestic sphere, they are granted access to a privileged mode of communication—both to other mothers and to their own children (as evinced by Kitty's communion with her newborn son)—and Anna's exclusion from this mode constitutes part of her punishment for her affair with Vronsky. Saltykov-Shchedrin's bad mother, then, ultimately challenges the mythology of Russian motherhood while Tolstoy's underscores its power and the dire consequences faced by a woman who rejects it.

The clouds of domestic discord that had been gathering during the years that *Anna Karenina* and *The Golovlev Family* were published gathered strength in the remaining decades of tsarist Russia, and debates about the "sacred ideal of the family" that Dostoevsky had defended so passionately continued to preoccupy Russian society. The attempts of liberal jurists to instill the rule of law through the "Trojan mare" of women's rights provoked a severe reaction from conservatives, who warned that, without family relationships built on authority and obedience, the entire fabric of society would unwind.[106] Nonetheless, bowing partially to popular demand, in 1904 the Orthodox Church allowed the guilty party in a divorce case to remarry after a period of time, leading to a further rise in divorce applications. By the beginning of World War I, a tidal wave of divorce cases had overwhelmed the ecclesiastical administration. Frustration with the slowness, expense, and difficulty of the process inflamed popular dissatisfaction with the Orthodox Church and indirectly contributed to the eventual outbreak of revolution. "The family crisis," as Gregory L. Freeze persuasively argues, "was an integral component of the broader revolutionary process, fusing the quotidian and domestic with the larger meta-narrative of revolution."[107]

As it had for Saltykov-Shchedrin and Tolstoy in the 1870s, female deviance from traditional norms played an outsized role in anxiety about the dissolution of the family (and, by extension, the nation) in the final years before the collapse of autocracy in 1917. Amidst a heightened interest in sexual behavior following the Revolution of 1905, the neglect of maternal duties intersected with perversion in popular texts, which at times equated the "selfishness" of a woman's turn away from motherhood with a man's indulgence in masturbation. According to physicians and educators, mothers also bore the responsibility for the sexual continence of their sons, upon which "the quality of public life" depended. Mothers who could not raise sons capable of resisting the overpowering force of sexuality jeopardized the future of the Russian Empire. At the same time, as a growing number of women left the confines of domesticity for education and employment, medical and legal experts became increasingly preoccupied with the control of reproduction. With abortion rates steadily increasing since the 1890s, Russian criminologists meeting in St. Petersburg in 1914 debated the question of its decriminalization. Among opponents, panic about women's rapid transformation provoked fears about motherhood's eventual extinction. Without the support and intercession of the law, these experts maintained, motherhood as an institution faced an onslaught of modernizing forces that it could not withstand.[108]

Indeed, the profound changes in Russian life unleashed by the October Revolution of 1917 prompted the wholesale transformation of the iconic mother that had reigned supreme during the time of Tolstoy and Saltykov-Shchedrin. Just as family and the woman's role within it provided the locus for some of the most important ideological battles of the post-Emancipation era, so the proper definition of motherhood occupied a crucial place in the debates of the early Soviet period. The fictional mothers who provide the focus for the next chapter all reflect the attack mounted on the traditional mythology of Russian motherhood during the first decade of the Soviet state.

Chapter Two

"Her Life's Sacrifice": The Abandoning Mother as Positive Role Model in the Soviet 1920s

IN 1918, LESS THAN ONE YEAR after the October Revolution, a young Russian mother composed a letter to an acquaintance, a future writer for a Soviet women's magazine, describing and justifying her conscious decision to reject her biological son. This young mother, Raisa Vorsheva, explained that she preferred another child to her own, mentally deficient son. She pitied her child but did not love him, reserving genuine affection exclusively for Senia, the healthy and charming son of the building caretaker where she lives. Vorsheva viewed her own son, in fact, as an embodiment of the recently vanquished society of the past. Asserting her belief in "progress," Vorsheva contended that, in the future, a son such as hers would be impossible, since "people like my husband won't be able to marry, and young women like me will be able to work and won't have to sell themselves into marriage, like slaves."[1] Through eugenics and the liberation of women, then, the socialist utopia that hovered just over the horizon will eliminate the possibility of less-than-perfect citizens for its new state.

In 1926, although that utopia had yet to arrive, Vorsheva's fervent belief in a radically altered conception of motherhood for Soviet society reached a much larger audience. The addressee of her original 1918 letter, Il'ia Rents, had published her correspondence as part of an article in the September 1926 edition of the Soviet magazine *Women's Journal.* Readers of the magazine could discover the ideological underpinnings of Vorsheva's decision to turn away from her son. In her letter, Vorsheva issued a call for the piercing of the "halo" that surrounds "holy motherhood." The new socialist society had examined, she argued, other aspects of women's daily lives—such as marriage and love—while naively leaving only the "holy place" of maternity untouched. Specifically, she identified a mother's love for her own child above all others as a vestige of the past that demanded elimination. Comparing this exclusive form of love to "sexual fetishism," Vorsheva decried this aberrant phenomenon: "Of all the forms of sensuality, I find a woman's blind love for that piece of meat that is called 'her own' child to be the most unnatural and therefore the most repellent. There is nothing human, conscious or spiritual about this." She appealed to the reader to condemn the unthinking worship of motherly attachment: "Tell me, do you think it's normal and necessary to reverentially honor that blind maternal sentiment that has been preserved to this day, which deprives a mother of her right to *selection* and *consciousness* in her feelings toward her child, indulging her animal-like, sensual instincts towards him?"[2] Vorsheva's argument implied that a mother should retain the right to transfer her attachment to other children, that the properties of logic should replace raw emotion and biological connection in the allocation of motherly love. In other words, the darkness of "blind," instinctual maternity must be penetrated by the light of reason and conscious choice.

The publication of Rents's article caused a sensation among the magazine's readership, prompting Vorsheva to emerge from obscurity and write a letter defending her assertions and providing the continuation of her life's story. Her son, the reader learned, died after accidentally falling from a roof, but his mother found solace in the knowledge that this was "for the best." Vorsheva then activated the powers of maternal reasoning that she alluded to in her original letter and absconded with the caretaker's son, liberating him from what she deemed an abusive home life. She now works in an orphanage, dedicating herself to caring for abandoned children and to the raising of Senia. Vorsheva ended her letter to the magazine by claiming that the revolution has irrevocably reconfigured familial relations, that it has unmasked and challenged "one of the most frightening untruths of the old way of life—the rights of parents over their children—rights that stem not from a noble sense of obligation, but only from the so-called 'holy love' of a parent for his or her own child."[3] Vorsheva, in effect, relegated parental attachment to a biological child to the dust heap of history.

Rents, the author of the 1926 article that included Vorsheva's letter, wrote that he decided to publish Vorsheva's text because it seemed particularly relevant: "Yes, now is the time to publish it. Now, when tens of thousands of children die simply because they are not 'ours' but are 'someone else's,' when on the horizon looms the time when accidental and at times cruel parents will be deprived of the 'holy right of ownership' over small, living people. Now is the time to publish this cry of a mother, moaning under the burden of her 'holy aureole.'"[4] The publication of Vorsheva's letter elicited numerous and impassioned responses from the magazine's readership. One woman argued that Vorsheva's inability to love her own child rendered her an ineffective worker for society as a whole. Another affirmed that, while all children will be raised communally in the future, a mother will still never forget her own child among the "thousands of others." A third reader deemed Vorsheva "no better than a prostitute."[5]

As this volume of response indicates, Rents assumed correctly about the timeliness of the publication of Vorsheva's ideas. Indeed, Vorsheva's letter intersected with some of the central issues concerning motherhood during the postrevolutionary period: How has the relationship between mother and child been altered by the revolutionary upheaval? Who can most effectively raise a Soviet child—the builder of the bright socialist future—and to whom will this decision be entrusted? Has any biological connection between mother and child been severed or rendered irrelevant? How to handle the throngs of homeless children who were flooding Russian urban areas throughout the 1920s? Can the myth of the good mother, so firmly entrenched in Russian culture, be "pierced," as Vorsheva demanded and as the introduction of communal child-rearing required? Has the revolution given women the right or even the responsibility to abandon their children? And, given the altered social and legal norms, how can the abandoning mother be judged?[6]

In the early years of the Soviet state, the reenvisioning of motherhood preoccupied not only contributors to women's magazines but policymakers as well. The traditional structure of the family, and the mother's role within it, was challenged from the inception of the new society. One of the first pieces of legislation passed by the Bolshevik government, the Family Code of 1918, was designed to hasten what was termed the "withering away" (*otmiranie*) of the family. This new law negated the validity of religious marriages, giving legal status exclusively to civil marriages. It also allowed divorce at the request of either spouse, without any grounds, and eliminated the concept of illegitimate birth, granting equal rights to children regardless of their parents' marital status.[7] Communal child-rearing would replace the individual family unit, which was deemed an oppressive bourgeois relic, and children would eventually be "nationalized," as the wife of one prominent Bolshevik put it.[8] Consequently, traditional motherly sentiment and the mythology that accompanied it would need to be altered to dovetail with the needs and aspirations of the new society. Although practical constraints ultimately doomed experimentation with communal child-rearing to failure, family nonetheless continued "to function as a means of imagining the revolutionary future."[9]

This "revolutionary future" necessitated the rejection of previous cultural norms of motherhood and the creation of new ones. The Bolshevik regime aimed to build a new society populated by citizens transformed, in Leon Trotsky's words, into the "'improved' version of man." The reorganization of private life constituted a central element of this project to reconfigure and "complete the [individual's] physical and spiritual construction."[10] Another critical facet of this campaign involved the liquidation of organized religion and the purging of religious sentiment from the national consciousness. Accordingly, the iconic Russian mother, so rooted in religious symbolism, also demanded elimination. A poster from the early Soviet period graphically illustrates how previously sacred maternal imagery could be travestied. A pregnant Mother of God stands looking at a billboard advertising a film on abortion, with the caption reading: "Oh, why didn't I know about that before?"[11] The halo of "holy motherhood" did indeed require piercing, as the young mother Vorsheva had demanded. The fictional texts discussed in this chapter aimed to accomplish this goal. They presented to their respective readers an abandoning or bad mother—one who forsakes her biological children—as a role model, as long as a desire to serve society motivates her actions. If, as in the case of one of the texts analyzed, the mother abandons her child without such a worthy cause, then the author portrays her as helpless and incompetent without the intercession of the Soviet government. According to these works, the call of service to the Soviet state requires women to renounce traditional maternity and renders moot earlier categories of maternal guilt and innocence. These fictional texts also portray motherly sentiment as an obstruction to socialist progress, as part of a taint that women must surmount in order to participate fully in the new society. The various permutations of the abandoning mother explored in this chapter all illustrate the multifaceted attack mounted, during the Soviet 1920s, on the mythology of the noble and self-sacrificial Russian mother.

I first discuss works of short fiction that appeared in women's magazines in the early to mid-1920s. In these texts, two of the mothers transfer their maternal sentiments from their respective individual families to the larger family of workers. Both women retain the self-denying qualities of the traditional Russian mother, but they sacrifice now for society as a whole rather than for their own children. A third completely overcomes all maternal attachments, lightheartedly celebrating her son's upbringing by the state. I then turn to a dramatized trial entitled *Trial of a Mother Who Abandoned Her Baby* (Dr. B. Ginzburg, 1924). This play advocates not the elimination or transfer of maternal sentiment but, rather, its enlightening by the omniscient state. It presents the prosecuted mother as ignorant and pitiful in her inability to make wise choices for herself or her child. Her incompetence confirms that the state must intercede into the mother-child relationship, since mothers cannot be trusted to act appropriately on their own. Finally, I provide a close reading of Fedor Gladkov's novel *Cement* (1925)—which eventually became one of the paradigmatic literary works of socialist realism—whose heroine leaves her daughter to be raised in a communal home. The novel portrays abandonment as a painful but inevitable decision, one that facilitates the heroine's journey toward becoming the embodiment of the new Soviet woman.

In her letter, Vorsheva, the Soviet mother quoted above, defined attachment to one's biological offspring as a primitive, atavistic urge that should be conquered through reason. Similarly, all of the fictional works discussed in this chapter present maternal sentiment as something that must be overcome. Otherwise, it must be transferred to a worthier, less selfish object than one's own children (such as the revolution itself), or improved upon by an outside expert more knowledgeable than the mother herself (as seen in Ginzburg's play). In other words, motherhood either conflicts with revolutionary principles, deeming a woman a potential enemy of progress, or is too crucial to the new society to be delegated solely to the woman herself. Maternal sentiment, as portrayed in these fictional works, must be eliminated or enlightened, redirected or reimagined. The figure of the abandoning mother, as seen in these disparate texts from the early Soviet period, emerges at the intersection of multiple anxieties about the role that women were compelled to assume in the early years of postrevolutionary Soviet society.

WOMEN: VICTIMS OR ENEMIES?

The Family Code of 1918 was designed not only to impel the dissolution of the traditional family but also to establish a legal basis for equality between men and women.[12] This equality could only be attained, according to Bolshevik theorists, if women were freed from household labor, including child-rearing, and allowed to enter the workforce.[13] As early as 1899, Nadezhda Krupskaia (the wife of Vladimir Lenin), in her book *The Woman Worker*, argued that women should naturally advocate communal child-rearing: "The woman worker cannot fail to value all the benefits of socialized upbringing. Maternal instinct compels her to desire socialized upbringing."[14] The concrete implementation of these abstract ideals was discussed during the 1919 All-Russian Congress for the Protection of Childhood in Moscow, where participants enthusiastically affirmed the ability of the state to raise children successfully as well as socialized child-rearing's power to free women from their domestic shackles.[15] Thus, freedom from the daily tasks associated with rearing children would allow women to attain the equality promised by the Russian Revolution.

In 1921 Aleksandra Kollontai, another of the most prominent female Bolsheviks and head of the Zhenotdel (the department for work among women), issued her "Theses on Communist Morality in the Area of Marital Relations," where she outlined her ideas about the disappearance of the family and the emergence of communal child care. Like Vorsheva, she predicted the obsolescence of traditional parental bonds, which would eventually be superseded by the worker's collective.[16] "Just as housework withers away," Kollontai asserted, "so the obligation of parents to their children withers away." After giving birth, a woman will "return to the work she does for the large family-society."[17] A. G. Goikhbarg, author of the Family Code, exhorted parents to give up "their narrow and irrational love for their children" and believed that the state could "provide vastly better results than the private, individual, unscientific, and irrational approach of individually 'loving' but ignorant parents."[18] Freed by Communism from the burdens of both housework *and* motherhood, women will become equal citizens by working alongside men in the construction of the society of the future.

The campaign to liberate women from domestic bondage, however, was not inspired solely by noble motives to improve the lot of women. A suspicion that women's backwardness rendered them incapable of raising children properly underlay the idealistic discussions of communal child-rearing. Krupskaia, for example, who, in *The Woman Worker* had touted the benefits of the revolution for female workers, nonetheless criticized women for their inability to properly care for their own children.[19] Some Bolshevik thinkers believed that the ignorance and egoism of parents could hinder a child's development and deform their worldview.[20] At the All-Russian Congress for the Protection of Childhood, at least one delegate claimed that the state alone could ensure the proper development of future communists. Consequently, public rearing of children was desirable not because it enabled the full participation of women in the building of the new society, but because the Soviet state could accomplish the task of child-rearing much better than a mother could. Soviet hygienists displayed their antipathy for the irrational egotism of motherhood and encouraged women to engage in social activity that would free them from the impulse to privilege their own children over society as a whole.[21]

Throughout the 1920s, the Soviets waged a campaign for "obstetric enlightenment" that attempted to disabuse women of their traditional ways of child-bearing and rearing, teaching them instead to rely on the "proper and modern" techniques advocated by the state's medical establishment.[22] Through methods such as the consultation, visiting nurses, birth homes for infants, and various forms of propaganda, the Department for the Protection of Motherhood and Infancy aimed to replace the unreliability of women's "instinctual" ability to care for their own children with the certainty of scientific knowledge. Medical authorities maintained that high infant mortality rates were attributable not to poor conditions but to the incompetence and ignorance of Soviet mothers. In other words, the bad habits of mothers stood between Soviet society and the healthy new citizens needed to populate it. In line with this sentiment, propaganda of the period depicted women as incapable of performing even the most rudimentary child care tasks without the guidance of medical experts.[23] Other propaganda demonized the rural folk healer (or *babka*), illustrating the glaring contrast between the clean, bright, and healthy environment of the modern Soviet hospital and the unsanitary and ominous atmosphere of a birth attended by the *babka*. Soviet women who continued to give birth with the *babka*, according to the message these posters conveyed, invariably endangered the life of their child as well as themselves.[24] By clinging to traditional, rural ways, these mothers also imperiled the Soviet drive for progress and modernization and so posed a threat not only to themselves but to the entire collective.

Women, then, according to the Bolsheviks, were both the victims of centuries of oppression who could now be valiantly liberated and the embodiment of potentially conservative forces capable of derailing the whole revolutionary project.[25] The combination of idealism and suspicion that motivated discussions of communal child-rearing underscores this ambivalence. Women's child-bearing abilities were, in fact, part of what aroused this suspicion, and the elemental, egotistical, and unenlightened urge for motherhood helped to render a woman a *baba*. A potential obstacle to revolutionary progress, the *baba*, as Elizabeth Wood defines her, is an "illiterate, superstitious, and generally 'backward'" woman who represented the opposite end of the spectrum from the "comrade," the fully evolved and enlightened male member of Soviet society. Fear of the *baba*'s potentially pernicious and destabilizing influence on future citizens motivated the intrusion of the state into the mother-child relationship.[26] The fictional works discussed in this chapter all investigate how mothers attempted to avoid or overcome the *baba* taint associated with motherhood. Through abandonment of a child, can a woman transcend the supposed egotism of biological connection, as Vorsheva advocated? Can motherly attachment (like everything else marking a woman as a *baba*) be conquered, allowing a woman to reach a state of revolutionary enlightenment and become a full-fledged "comrade"?

HEROIC ABANDONMENT

These questions are explored in three works of short fiction—two stories and a poem—that appeared in the women's magazines *Female Worker* (*Rabotnitsa*) and *Female Worker and Peasant* (*Rabotnitsa i krest'ianka*) in 1923, 1925, and 1926, respectively. These magazines' intended audience was the politically undeveloped woman, and they aimed to instill specific values and templates for behavior to nascent new Soviet women across the republics.[27] In the 1920s, these women's magazines, unlike their Western counterparts, promoted the dissolution of gender differences and encouraged women to leave the domestic sphere in favor of a role in the public sphere alongside men.[28]

The short story "Mother," which appeared in *Female Worker* in December 1923, presents a mother abandoning the traditionally female sphere, including her children, to serve the revolutionary cause. The action of the story unfolds three years earlier, in 1920. In the story's opening line, the reader learns that Aunt Varia, the heroine, has successfully answered Kollontai's call to transfer maternal emotions from the individual to the collective. She has become "like a mother to all at the factory, especially to the young people." Like the mother of Pavel Vlassov in Maxim Gorky's 1906 novel of the same name, to which the story's title draws inevitable comparisons, she has become a communal maternal figure to her fellow builders of the socialist future.

Active in the Communist Party since 1913, Aunt Varia greets the arrival of the October Revolution as a "fully formed female revolutionary." Her tireless organizational work (endless meetings and commissions) leaves little time to devote to domestic life. Her four children placidly accept their mother's absence, however, and even boast to their friends about her political activism. Aunt Varia has transmitted her revolutionary values to her children, especially her oldest, fourteen-year-old Petia, who despite his youth considers himself a full-fledged Bolshevik. Mother and son, like in Gorky's *Mother*, are united in their devotion to the worker's cause. Unlike in Gorky, however, the relationship between the two does not evolve from discord to harmony; Aunt Varia and Petia hold consonant beliefs from the very beginning of the story. Even her youngest child, five-year-old Mot'ka, proudly declares: "Our mother is a Bolshevik!" Thus, due to her children's exceptionally tolerant stance, no tension develops between the mother's social obligations and her domestic ones. Aunt Varia even finds time to crusade against retrograde motherhood, defending those young women whose mothers berate them for their political activity. Varia embodies the mother of the future and serves as an example for other women in her community to emulate.[29]

When fighting against the "capitalist enemy" intensifies during the Civil War, Petia decides to join the army. Afraid to confess his intentions to his mother, he leaks word of his plan to others in the town. When Aunt Varia discovers her son's plot, she becomes consumed with worry. She has infected her son with an excessive amount of revolutionary zeal for his tender years. But a solution suddenly presents itself to Aunt Varia: she will head to the front herself as a "red nurse," insisting that Petia take care of the younger children, thus foiling his intentions. Initially reluctant, Petia eventually agrees to assume Aunt Varia's role as the maternal figure in the family:

> —"Dearest Petia, I'm headed to the front as a nurse . . . And them I'm leaving to you"—she gestured toward the children.
>
> —"You're going to the front?"

And Petia, without removing his coat, slumped helplessly on the chair. This turn of events he had not at all anticipated.

—"I know, Petia, that you wanted to go to the front yourself, right? I understand you . . . But you're still so young, you have plenty of time, son, so let me go . . . " Varvara Nikolaevna said rapidly as she caressed her son.

Suddenly, Petia impulsively embraced his mother.

—"Go on, mother dear, go on, and don't be afraid—I'll take care of them."[30]

Paradoxically, through abandonment of her children, Aunt Varia succeeds in fulfilling her obligations as both a mother and as a revolutionary. The story presents abandonment as a noble decision, one that potentially even saves the life of the impetuous Petia. In this idealized account of child abandonment for a heroic cause, the children Aunt Varia leaves behind suffer no negative consequences. They are fully evolved "comrades" already and so intuitively understand their mother's privileging of her social commitments over her maternal ones. In "Mother," the cause of revolution now requires of both mothers *and* children the self-sacrifice that traditional maternal mythology previously demanded of only the good mother.

"YOU'RE NOT A MOTHER, YOU'RE A MONSTER"

In "Mother," the heroine's devotion to Bolshevism at the expense of her children does not disturb familial harmony. "Family Matters," by contrast, a story that appeared in *Female Worker and Peasant* in October 1926, reveals the fissures within a family that a mother's dedication to the professional sphere causes. While Aunt Varia serves as a "red nurse," the heroine of "Family Matters," Anna Vlas'evna, works as a much-respected "red director" at the local factory. Her employees admire her exemplary work ethic (she always arrives earlier than anyone else to work) and feel affectionate toward her for her intuitive understanding of the worker's plight.[31]

In the domestic realm, however, Anna Vlas'evna encounters considerable difficulties. She lacks all talent for household tasks and, as the narrator sympathetically points out, she lives during times that demand a woman choose between public and private loyalties: "Were these really the years when there was enough time for both the entire family of workers and one's own family?" As a result, her three children grow up neglected, a fact that does, at times, trouble Anna Vlas'evna: "Occasionally Anna Vlas'evna would think: 'Those kids are abandoned.' But then she'd wave her hand and say to herself: 'Eh, let them look at their mother, then they'll learn how to live. And the most important thing now is to cast off the yoke of oppression'" (12).

She believes that setting an example for her children is more important than active involvement in their daily lives, and that the needs of society as a whole supersede their individual ones. Consequently, she deposits her children in an orphanage. Anna Vlas'evna reverses this decision almost immediately, however, but not because of any sympathy for her children's plight. Rather, she worries that they receive places in the orphanage only because of her professional status, thus potentially denying access to needier others (ibid.).

Her children, unlike Aunt Varia's, feel no pride at their mother's accomplishments and object to her disregard of them: "They don't love their mother, she's a stranger to them, they hardly ever even see her—no chance of receiving a mother's care or caress . . . That which she gave to her work and to other people the children believed was rightfully theirs and had been stolen from them. And they harbored resentment and hurt toward their mother." Anna Vlas'evna's children fail to forgive her sacrifice of their individual present for the collective future. But she finds comfort in the knowledge that, in postrevolutionary Soviet society, genetic bonds no longer determine the boundaries of "family":

> Anna Vlas'evna thought about how she had let her own children slip by; how, while she was out agitating, alien, hostile people had grown up right next to her . . .
>
> —"Well, that's okay," she comforted herself, "that family that's taking shelter in the barracks, that's assembling every day in front of the machines—that's my family too." (13)

Anna Vlas'evna, then, has successfully overcome the primitive, egotistical form of motherhood that privileges one's own children above all others. Like Aunt Varia, she fulfills Kollontai's exhortation to become a "mother to all," thus satisfying the new society's criteria for good motherhood, despite her neglect and abandonment of her biological children.

During the course of the story, however, Anna Vlas'evna does make one concession to maternal loyalty, the fallout from which confirms decisively her commitment to the collective over her own children. Her proud and willful oldest daughter, Valia, refuses to work as a manual laborer at her mother's factory, insisting instead on a position in the office. Anna Vlas'evna reluctantly agrees, but her spotless reputation among the workers immediately receives a stain. When discussing her decision, a note of doubt creeps into the workers' voices, and Anna Vlas'evna soon notices their disapproval of her actions on her daughter's behalf (14).[32] Anna Vlas'evna corrects this lapse in judgment by insisting that her daughter's name be added to the list of laid-off workers. After she ensures Valia's unhappy fate, the chaos in Anna Vlas'evna's life instantaneously subsides: "Anna Vlas'evna sighed with relief.

How carefree, how secure she felt. And it seemed to her that the backs of the workers straightened out approvingly, that their voices became cheerier, and that the entire factory became more positively inclined toward the red director Anna Vlas'evna" (14).

When faced with a choice between her daughter's individual happiness and maintaining her moral authority with her workers, Anna Vlas'evna unapologetically chooses the latter. Loyalty to one's own offspring is a remnant of the bourgeois past, and the ideal Soviet woman, as Anna Vlas'evna exemplifies, rejects all such frivolous trappings. At home, she explains the rationale behind her actions to Valia, who responds, predictably, with insults rather than understanding: "'You're not a mother, you're a monster!' cried Valia." The divide between mother and family remains impenetrable. The story ends with Anna Vlas'evna confirming the incompatibility of maternity with participation in the building of the new society: "I should never have given birth to all of you . . . Obviously you can't be everywhere at once, and it's no use trying to chase after two rabbits . . . I made a mistake in starting up all of this family business. The factory and the party are dearer to me than my own family. I can't think or act otherwise" (15). Anna Vlas'evna has become a "comrade," dedicating herself exclusively to her factory and to the Communist Party. Her brief experiment with maternal loyalty fails, and the reader presumes that Anna Vlas'evna's effective abandonment of her children in favor of the "worker's collective" will continue unabated.

Both Aunt Varia and Anna Vlas'evna forgo their maternal obligations in order to devote themselves exclusively to the Bolshevik cause. For the former, her children's enlightened stance facilitates this decision, while for the latter, her family's expectation of traditional maternal attention leads to a permanent rift between mother and children. Both authors portray their respective mothers as positive figures and present their decisions vis-à-vis their children as admirable ones. Both stories impart the lesson that children must adjust to the new Soviet reality (and the sacrifices this demands from their mothers), deeming them heroic if they succeed, backward if they fail. Neither woman lacks traditional maternal qualities, such as a readiness for self-sacrifice. Rather, both have successfully transferred those qualities from the individual to the collective family, to the worthier and nobler object of revolution and the construction of the new society.

A MOTHER TO NONE

In January 1925, *Female Worker* published a poem valorizing the defeat of traditional maternal sentiment and celebrating a mother's effective abandonment of her child. P. Kudriashev, the author of "Mother and Son," begins by describing the mother's conflict between her family and her other responsibilities, a plight similar to that of Aunt Varia and Anna Vlas'evna: "She's no time to look after her son/Or to bring him up/By day she's at the factory behind a machine/And then it's a meeting and off to bed." The routine of work and social activism leaves this "new woman" no time to devote to the raising of her son. In the poem's second stanza, the reader discovers, however, that this predicament causes the mother no distress: "And in the morning to the workshop again/So it is every day, every year/But her breast doesn't yearn for her dear one/Her little son won't perish!"[33] The third line of this stanza alludes to the severing of the biological connection between mother and child. The mother's breast does not long for her son; both the literal and the figurative bonds between mother and son have been dissolved.

Unlike the two short stories discussed above, "Mother and Son" presents a solution to the Soviet mother's dilemma, one which facilitates this disappearance of maternal attachment: the ceding of responsibility for the raising of her son to the state. The reader learns, in the third stanza, that the Soviet government now offers an organized solution to the predicament of the "new woman": "He's with the pioneer group/Which is better than either mother or father/They give him good examples/And prepare a steadfast fighter." The state-sponsored alternative to the traditional family, the pioneer youth group, even serves the needs of the child better than his own parents could. The son now leads an idyllic life, as the fourth stanza describes: "There the child is cheerful and happy/With clever games and singing/And there all have the same goal:/To forge the worker's collective." The poem presents the government-organized and controlled environment of the pioneer group as more desirable than the child's own home. The boy in the poem presumably spends the majority of his time there, thus learning how to "forge the worker's collective" while his absent mother works simultaneously for the same goal. The separation of mother from child is, according to the poem, a precondition for the realization of this Bolshevik vision. The poem ends with further confirmation that the mother has conquered all maternal sentiment: "And that's where her little son is/For the second year now./At the factory his mother the delegate/Laughs to all: 'He won't perish!'" The factory has replaced the home as the center of this mother's universe, and she suffers no misgivings about the fate of her son. The Soviet state will raise him to be an ideal citizen, and maternal love remains irrelevant to the achievement of this result. This poetic paean to the abandoning mother portrays maternal sentiment as already obsolete, no longer an obstacle to the successful building of the society of the future.

Unlike the heroines of "Mother" and "Family Matters," the mother in the poem "Mother and Son" exhibits no traditional maternal characteristics. She has become not a "mother to all" but, rather, a mother to none. The three works of popular fiction discussed, then, present increasingly extreme visions of the renunciation of maternity. In the story "Mother," like in Gorky's novel, the bond between mother and son remains, but it has been channeled toward and subordinated to the higher calling of service to society. Both Aunt Varia and her children willingly accept and even embrace this sacrifice. In "Family Matters" and "Mother and Son," by contrast, the respective mothers acknowledge no responsibility toward their biological children. They forsake all ties to their individual families in favor of the larger "family" of workers. But, as Aunt Varia's departure from her family to become a "red nurse" presumably saves the life of her son, so the mother's abandonment of her son in the poem improves his lot as well. He now leads a joyous existence under the care of the pioneer youth group. Both works present abandonment as an admirable, even heroic decision. While in "Mother" and "Mother and Son," the mothers' actions cause no internal familial conflict, in "Family Matters" Anna Vlas'evna encounters hostility and eventual estrangement from her children. All three works present traditional motherly emotion for one's individual children as outmoded at best, absurdly laughable at worst. Maternal attachment obstructs socialist progress and so must either be redirected at the "worker's collective," as seen in "Mother" and "Family Matters," or eliminated completely, as seen in the poem "Mother and Son."[34]

MOTHERHOOD ON TRIAL

While these fictional works valorize child abandonment and the defeat of maternal attachment to biological children, another work from the same period aims to enlighten the dark ignorance of a naively abandoning mother. The agitational drama *Trial of a Mother Who Abandoned Her Baby* reveals that, in the Soviet 1920s, idealistic notions of communal child-rearing and the society of the future coexisted with the practical concerns of the present.[35] As Vorsheva identified attachment to one's own offspring as primitive, so doctors labeled traditional mothering practices—the use of midwives in particular—as unenlightened and even dangerous. A woman's irrationality and lack of knowledge demanded the intercession of professional experts, since children were simply too important to the future of the state to be left solely to the care of mothers.[36] *Trial of a Mother* exemplifies the propaganda of the period that sought to rationalize the perceived unreliability of maternal behavior, to transform motherhood from a subjective, intuitive function into a highly specialized craft that could best be learned from trained Soviet health professionals.[37] The prosecuted mother in the agitational trial is a tabula rasa upon which the Soviet government must inscribe the appropriate knowledge and erase the destructive imprint of sexually opportunistic men and irresponsible, ignorant old women. The mother, along with her child, must be saved from herself by the benevolent, omniscient state.

Trial of a Mother was written at the request of the Health Commissariat in 1924 by Dr. B. S. Ginzburg, a doctor in the Department for the Protection of Motherhood and Infancy.[38] It was the first published trial of a mother, and its unusually large print run of 100,000 indicates that it may have been designated an exemplar of the genre.[39] The authors of agitational trials were typically specialists in fields such as public health, agronomy, or industry, rather than professional writers. The genre itself was highly conventionalized and formulaic, typically containing a homogenous master narrative that usually compelled a similarly uniform performance style.[40] The defendants in these mock trials were most likely accused of some kind of a moral or social infraction rather than an actual criminal offense. But, despite the fictional nature of the crime being prosecuted, the trials nevertheless strove for verisimilitude in the re-creation of the Soviet courtroom environment.[41]

Through the staging of a fictional trial—and the repetition of what Julie A. Cassiday has identified as the pattern of "confession, repentance, and reintegration into society"—Bolshevik values were supposedly inculcated. Through audience participation and frequent discussion periods after performances, viewers were encouraged to apply the lessons of the mock trial to their daily lives. "The melodrama of unmasking the internal, hidden enemies of Soviet power," Cassiday observes, "created a legal justification for the new regime and compelled viewers to apply the verdict they watched on the stage to their own lives."[42] Female audience members were frequently presented with especially vivid representations of the "unmasking" of women who were obstructing socialist progress. The authors of the mock trials, like those of a great deal of the propaganda generated in the early years of the Soviet Union, deemed female characters the most backward and needy of enlightenment in order to neutralize their potential threat to the revolution. If women could be properly educated, however, then they could ensure the transmission of the proper social values to subsequent generations as well. One of the purposes of the agitation trial featuring a female defendant was, in fact, to persuade women to admit their own backwardness and need for guidance from the proper Soviet authorities.[43]

The preface to *Trial of a Mother* identifies child abandonment as an example of precisely the type of primitive female behavior that must first be unmasked and then eliminated:

> Abandonment! A cursed, terrible legacy of the past. An expression of that slave-like abjection that can even cause [a mother] to forget her responsibility towards her own child! An indicator of the low level of consciousness, of the centuries-old enslavement of woman, who was taught to look at both herself and at her child as an object.[44]

Child abandonment lays bare a woman's underdeveloped consciousness, unmasking her true *baba* nature. The Soviet government will, of course, combat this scourge. The triumph of Bolshevik values, the author asserts, will effectively preclude the possibility of abandonment. Along the path to this outcome, however, the transgressing mother must inspire not only pity but also hatred (4). The arousal of these feelings of loathing and shame constitutes one of the goals of *Trial of a Mother.* Hence, unlike in the works of short fiction discussed above, where the abandoning mother, motivated by her commitment to society, stirs admiration, in the agitational trial she symbolizes a dark past that must be defeated.

The defendant in the trial is Daria Nikolaevna Tikhonova, a twenty-year-old worker from the provinces who has been living in Moscow for two years. The charges against the accused are brought by the director of the Department for the Protection of Motherhood and Infancy, who received Tikhonova's abandoned one-month-old baby from the police. During the reading of the charges, Tikhonova's refusal to meet with the administration of the department is foregrounded (8). Tikhonova rejects the assistance of the state, and the court views this decision with as much severity as the act of abandonment itself. Thus, the prosecution accuses the mother both of ill-treating her child *and* of ignoring the services offered her by the Soviet government.

In the defendant's first encounter with the prosecutor and defender, she insists that a desire to improve her son's lot motivated her decision to abandon him:

> DEFENDER: Tell me, Citizen Tikhonova, did you know that by abandoning your child you were dooming him to certain death?
>
> TIKHONOVA: No, I just wanted to do the best thing for him. He would have died with me anyway.
>
> PROSECUTOR: Did a doctor tell you that he would die under your care?
>
> TIKHONOVA: No, it was granny Semenova . . . she knows about this kind of thing. (9)

This initial exchange establishes the defendant as guileless rather than calculating, hopeless rather than selfish. It also introduces one of the play's central conflicts: medical science versus the ignorant *baba* who peddles false and dangerous information to uninformed young mothers. Tikhonova accepts the advice not of a doctor but of one such *baba,* her landlady Semenova. This reference to Semenova also alludes to how Tikhonova falls sway to outside influence when making critical decisions, especially those involving her child.

The testimony of various witnesses gradually reveals the factors contributing to Tikhonova's abandonment of her son. These accounts paint a picture of the defendant as a woman lacking control over her own life. Tikhonova herself recounts how she naively acquiesced to the questionable demands of her child's father, whom she met at evening courses. She unsuspectingly agrees first to move into his apartment and next into his room:

> TIKHONOVA: As soon as I moved in there, he started pestering me to marry him. I was scared to make the decision by myself, but then I agreed, and we starting living together. He convinced me to quit my job and the courses. (13)

The father of the child, Obmenin, succeeds in isolating Tikhonova from the outside world and all productive activity. Although the lack of savvy and self-confidence of a young girl from the provinces can certainly be understood, later testimony reveals that more knowledgeable acquaintances had tried to warn Tikhonova. Kalugin, a friend from her courses, explains his futile efforts to enlighten her: "I told her not to move in with Obmenin, but she didn't listen. I told her more than once to not believe his tall tales, that he was already married. She didn't listen to me and paid for it bitterly" (17). Tikhonova's decision to trust Obmenin rather than Kalugin underscores the faultiness of her logical faculties and instincts for self-preservation.

After she becomes pregnant, these instincts recede even further. When a predictably enraged Obmenin demands she appeal to a midwife for an abortion, Tikhonova offers no resistance. Only the midwife's refusal to perform the procedure on a four-month-old fetus prevents Tikhonova from ending her pregnancy (13). Her testimony provides no insights into the expectant mother's own feelings about the possibility of abortion; she dispassionately and obediently follows Obmenin's directives. Obmenin eventually abandons the pregnant Tikhonova and—unaware of her right under Soviet law to sue the father of her child for support, even if they are not married—she suffers destitution and privation. The callous testimony of Obmenin, who denies a sexual involvement with the accused and even attempts to portray her as promiscuous, further confirms the tragic error of Tikhonova's choices (15–16).

After Obmenin departs, Tikhonova allows another nefarious outsider to influence her decisions about her own motherhood: her landlady, Irina Petrovna Semenova. Her testimony establishes Semenova as an uneducated, abrasive woman who has transplanted her peasant habits from the village to the city. In the estimation of Soviet health professionals, rural women—with their superstitions, adherence to tradition, and lack of education—were deemed the most incompetent in their mothering practices.[45] It was Semenova who convinced Tikhonova to deliver the baby at home rather than under a doctor's supervision, as she explains in response to the prosecutor's query about the circumstances of the birth:

SEMENOVA: She wanted to go to a shelter, but we talked her out of it . . . I'm a specialist in this area. Back in the village I took care of these things, and here, in the city, I delivered the neighbor's kid, and all of my daughters' kids too. (22)

After the birth of the baby, Semenova tells Tikhonova that she has "bad milk," advising her to feed the baby cow's milk and porridge. The young mother accepts this advice, and the health of the baby, Vasia, predictably deteriorates. Finally, Tikhonova acquiesces to Semenova's most extreme advice, abandoning her baby:

TIKHONOVA: Semenova was badgering me: "Give him up, give him up to a shelter, he'll die with you anyways." . . . What could I do? I had nowhere to turn, and he wouldn't let me work. It's true that, because of Vasia, I couldn't work for her like before, and she got mad and grumbled. (22)

Tikhonova thus unmasks the selfish motivation behind Semenova's advice. In order to ensure Tikhonova's availability as a household helper, she successfully convinces the young woman that no option besides abandonment remains.

The testimonies of Obmenin and Semenova that the prosecutor elicits reveal the formula for the creation of an abandoning mother: cruel treatment by an opportunistic boyfriend plus manipulation by a selfish, backward *baba.* Tikhonova demonstrates very little will of her own during the crucial moments of her pregnancy and after the birth of her son. All important decisions about her own maternity—from whether or not to have an abortion, to where to deliver the baby and how to feed him, to whether or not to abandon the child—she cedes to one of these two individuals, mainly Semenova. In his closing speech, the defender contends that Tikhonova submitted to the heinous commands of Semenova in a mentally clouded, somnambulant state (36). Tikhonova herself insists that her actions lacked conscious choice: "Could a mother consciously harm her own child? But unconsciously, it's true that I did it, like that comrade said (*indicating the defender*)" (39).

Despite this "unconscious" decision to relinquish her maternal obligations, Tikhonova demonstrates sincere tenderness for her son. She recounts how she secretly trailed the police officer who found the baby, locating the children's home where he was deposited. A worker from the home describes Tikhonova's daily visits and her eagerness to help Vasia, irrespective of her own impoverished state: "Once I let slip that we were low on diapers . . . She came in the night and brought her last sheet and tore it up to make diapers for Vasia. She even wanted to tear up her own shirt" (14). Tikhonova thus displays one of the key qualities traditionally associated with the good mother: a readiness to sacrifice one's own needs for the welfare of the child. The defender argues that Tikhonova unquestionably loves her son and that her actions are inspired by concern for his welfare (37). Hence, Tikhonova possesses enough physical maturity to conceive, deliver, and bond with a baby but, as her defender points out, her critical faculties are those of a child (35). So how, then, can Soviet society handle such immature and unthinking motherhood? How can this abandoning mother, who, the prosecutor argues, represents hundreds and even thousands of women, be judged? (ibid.).

The solution lies in the molding of this raw maternal sentiment by the enlightened organs of the Soviet state. Lengthy testimony by a doctor-expert details the dire consequences of leaving mothers to their own devices. For example, he cites statistics indicating that 95 percent of Soviet women give birth with the assistance of superstitious village women like Semenova (25). He asserts that the care of Soviet children is, in fact, more plagued by superstition than any other sphere (28). Mothers fail at even the most fundamental tasks of child-rearing, again introducing statistics that show how Soviet mothers are not capable of properly feeding their infants (27). The darkness of this ignorance must be penetrated by the light of knowledge. The strengthening of state institutions devoted to motherhood provides the only solution to primitive maternity and its inevitable result: a high infant mortality rate. As the doctor summarizes, simply being a mother is not enough; one must be a sensible mother (27). The state will supply the necessary element of enlightenment to transform maternity from an instinctual and potentially dangerous phenomenon to an informed and rational one that benefits Soviet society as a whole.

In laying out the charges against Tikhonova, the prosecutor emphasizes her inexcusable ignorance of the legal protections for mothers that the omniscient state had instituted. For example, he faults her for not realizing that she could sue Obmenin for child support:

> PROSECUTOR: Does she not know that in Soviet Russia there is no such thing as legitimate or illegitimate children . . . Our law protecting the interests of mothers and their children allows a pregnant woman, long before she gives birth, to file an official claim that so-and-so is the father of her future child . . . As you can see, the legislation is designed to alleviate the situation of children and their mothers. Did Citizen Tikhonova take advantage of this? As you can see, she did not. (33–34)

The prosecutor presents Tikhonova's unawareness of Soviet law as a crime equal in gravity to that of abandonment itself. The accused herself admits that, if she had possessed this knowledge, the crime would not have occurred (39). Hence, she confirms the need for the law and the state to insert themselves into the mother-child relationship, protecting the vulnerable mother from unscrupulous men and the innocent child from the mother herself.

The court finds Tikhonova guilty of the charge of abandonment but—citing her proletarian background, the hardships she endured, and her sincere repentance—orders that Vasia be returned to her care (40).[46] The true villains in the case, Semenova and Obmenin, will be prosecuted, demonstrating the beneficence and wisdom of Soviet justice. At least one published account of a performance of the play indicates that the audience became quite emotionally involved in the trial's outcome: a review in the July 1924 edition of *Female Worker* describes how an audience of 3,000 factory workers screamed for Tikhonova's acquittal.[47] *Trial of a Mother* offered the following lessons for those and other audience members, women in particular, to apply to their own lives: mothers, when left to their own devices, cannot be trusted to make beneficial decisions for their children. Reproduction was simply too important—and the new scientific expertise too compelling—to be entrusted to the unstable whims of female experience and intuition.[48] The life of the fictional character Tikhonova provides a cautionary tale about the dangers of untutored maternal sentiment. It also affirms the integral role of the state in molding, educating, and controlling the lives of Soviet mothers.

DASHA CHUMALOVA: NEW SOVIET MOTHER

Another work of fiction from the 1920s—one that reached a much larger audience than those discussed above—also focuses on altered mother-child relations under the new regime, abandonment, and the role of the state in child care. Serialized in the journal *Red Virgin Soil* in 1925, Fedor Gladkov's *Cement* is one of the earliest works of Soviet fiction to feature an exemplar of the new Soviet woman and to explore how the 1917 Revolution transformed Russian womanhood and the institution of the family. It would eventually serve as a prototype for the socialist realist novel, with its plot and positive heroes repeatedly imitated in later Soviet fiction.[49] During the course of the novel, the female heroine, Dasha Chumalova, undertakes a journey toward the goal of revolutionary enlightenment—she becomes a "comrade"—but this necessitates the subsuming of her motherly emotions. Gladkov presents child abandonment as a necessary, if admittedly painful, prerequisite to the new woman's full participation in the construction of the society of the future. As Anna Karenina's did, Dasha's maternal sentiments for her daughter, Nurka, whom she deposits in a children's home, also gradually deteriorate throughout the text. Dasha—like the heroine of "Family Matters," who discovered that genetic bonds no longer circumscribed the boundaries of family—eventually transfers her maternal sentiments to an object from the larger "family of workers." The novel also associates children with chaos and the untamed forces of nature that obstruct revolutionary progress. This characterization reinforces and legitimizes Dasha's decision to abandon her daughter in her quest to become a "comrade."

The novel opens with the homecoming of Dasha's husband, Gleb Chumalov, after three years of fighting in the Civil War. He encounters a decaying landscape, with the previously thriving cement factory reduced to a weed-ridden, useless heap. Agriculture has overrun industry, as symbolized by the intermingling of animals and machinery: "Concrete and stone. Coal and cement . . . Filigree-towers of the electric conveyor. Smoke-stacks higher than the mountains. Net-work of cables. And, right next to it all, stalls and live-stock?"[50] The hero's task appears obvious: he must restore industrial civilization's supremacy over agriculture and the ignorant townspeople who have failed to keep it at bay.

Rural life's inappropriate incursion into the industrial sphere is symbolized not only by livestock but also by children. In the description of the town Gleb encounters upon his return, the narration draws a parallel between goats and children: "In the square, beyond the wall, a mob of dirty children were playing, and paunchy, snake-eyed goats roamed, nibbling at bushes or acacia shoots." The roaming children behave like animals and represent a threat to the renaissance of the factory, just like the goats. The narrator observes an affinity between the two groups: "Like giddy maidens, the goats scream and laugh with the children" (2). These comparisons suggest that both the animals and the children are remnants of the past that have penetrated inappropriately into the present. Nature and, by extension, the children who represent it, must be reconquered. As Eliot Borenstein has argued, Soviet fiction of the 1920s draws a connection between both nature and the family as enemies.[51] The decrepit cement factory under assault by both goats and children pointedly illustrates these two overlapping planes of battle.

In the next chapter of the novel, when Gleb visits the town's children's home, goats and children are again explicitly equated:

> The children were straying about like the goats at the factory, fighting with each other, crying. Some groups were turning over the soil, digging greedily and hurriedly like thieves, glancing fearfully behind them. They would dig and dig and then turn and tear the booty from each other's grasp. The one who was stronger and cleverer would roll clear of the heap of little bodies and run aside with his loot, gnawing greedily, chewing and choking, tearing at it with his hands as well as with his mouth. Near the fence some children were swarming over the muck heap. (34)

In this description, children have been reduced to animal-like behavior, with a Darwinian survival of the fittest determining who will live and who will perish. Demoted to a lower rung on the evolutionary ladder, they have been expelled from the family in the same way that the goats must be chased out of the factory.[52]

As these images of previously thriving industry overrun by goats and children foreshadow, Gleb returns to a family as unrecognizable and stagnant as the rundown factory. His wife, Dasha, refuses to resume her former domestic role, with her attention and responsibility focused wholly on the community and on the construction of socialism.[53] Most fundamentally, she informs him that their young daughter, Nurka, now resides in the town children's home. The fate of Nurka concretizes the implicit suggestion that children, like animals, hinder progress and so must be exiled. The decrepit factory and his denuded hearth blend together in Gleb's consciousness: "His wife, Dasha, who had passed by him, strange and distant, wounding him to the heart . . . the empty house . . . the empty factory with its dusty cobwebs . . . all was strange to him" (23). Neither the factory nor the family of the past exist any longer, but Gleb vows to fight to resurrect the former (25). The novel links the fates of both from its opening images, so can the prerevolutionary family be reborn as well?[54]

This question is explored through the prism of the maternal identity of Gleb's wife, Dasha. Before the revolution, we learn that Dasha cared selflessly for Nurka and created an ideal home, a "young bride [who] bloomed as did the geraniums in the window-box" (5). In his longing for the now aloof and cold Dasha, Gleb alludes to her previously tender motherly emotions: "He waited for her voice and for her love. He expected her to come to him and gently, as of old, to press his head to her bosom, whispering like a mother, like a friend." Gleb conflates sexual and maternal love, implying that Dasha's immense motherly kindness sustained her husband as well. Before the revolution, Dasha, with the tenderness and boundlessness of her maternal sentiment, embodied the iconic Russian mother. Now, however, "Dasha was silent, cold, near and . . . a stranger," revealing, presumably, the narrowing of this previously infinite maternal emotion (32).

In fact, Dasha has apparently overcome the supposedly primitive attachment to her own child above all others and now nurtures numerous children. As Thea Margaret Durfee notes, "the message . . . is that Dasha has given up her own daughter only to become a mother to all children, even to the cosmos itself."[55] The residents of the children's home "Krupskaia," it becomes clear, turn to her for emotional sustenance:

> The children danced around, staring at Gleb and hungrily waiting for Dasha's voice and hand. The girls, with their hair cut like boys, kept stretching out

> their hands towards Dasha, clasping violets. Each wanted to be the first to put the flowers into her hands. . . . "Aunt Dasha! . . . Aunt Dasha!" . . . Dasha laughed and patted the children's little heads; they were evidently accustomed to this caress and were waiting for it as for their ration of food. (37)

The children require nourishment from Dasha as much as from food. She has become what Lenin's wife Nadezhda Krupskaia (who served as deputy minister in the Commissariat of Education from 1929 to 1939, and for whom the children's home in the novel is named) would later term a "collective mother," or one who channels parental attachment to a loftier and worthier goal. In an article titled "The Collective Mother," published in the journal *About Our Children* in 1930, Krupskaia contends that "parental feelings do not have to degenerate into proprietary ones" as is the case in capitalist countries, where parents selfishly obsessed with the welfare of only their biological children resemble "dogs licking their puppies." In the more highly evolved socialist society, Krupskaia argues, parental emotions can be raised to a "higher level"; they can be expressed through "especially attentive, caring relations to all children, not just to one's own . . . they can be 'sublimated.' "[56] Dasha has apparently achieved this sublimation of maternal attachment, declaring to Gleb that their daughter merits no special consideration: "In what way is Nurka any better than the others? She has had her hard times too" (35). Dasha's maternal identity now thrives exclusively in the communal environment of the children's home, as Gleb himself observes: "Dasha, hand in hand with Nurka, was truly a mother, and more so here than at home" (37).

"THE BIRTH OF STRENGTH"

This steely new Soviet woman does, however, occasionally agonize over the fate of her daughter. Unlike the mother in the poem "Mother and Son," who laughs off any concern about her son abandoned to state care, Dasha wonders about her complicity in Nurka's uncertain fate. After encountering a group of wretched homeless children on the street, Dasha compares Nurka's existence in the supposedly ideal, state-controlled environment with their animal-like one:

> Nurka was in the Children's Home, but was she happier than these naked little beasts? Dasha had once seen Nurka with the other children digging in the rubbish heap behind the dining-room of the Food Commissariat. It seemed to her then that her daughter was already dead, and that she, Dasha, was no longer her mother; that Nurka had been abandoned to hunger and suffering

> through Dasha's fault. It seemed that her occasional caresses in the Children's Home were not the fondling of a mother, but of a sterile blooming. She had carried the little girl in her arms right to the Children's Home and her heart was ravaged with pain. (120)

This passage alludes to a cleavage within Dasha's maternal identity, to previously tender emotions now as dead as Nurka herself seems. What factors contributed to this disappearance of Dasha's attachment to Nurka, to the weakening of the bond between mother and child? The answer lies in the brutality Dasha endures during the Civil War and Gleb's absence. The chapter in which she finally recounts for Gleb the events of this period is called "The Birth of Strength," and it reveals how the emergence of an emboldened and independent Dasha accompanies the recession of the maternal Dasha. In other words, the growth of this "strength" occurs alongside the death of motherly affection.

By the time Gleb returns home from the Civil War, Dasha is fully prepared to serve as her husband's mentor, as Durfee has convincingly argued. Dasha has already advanced along the trajectory that would later become typical for the socialist realist hero, which entailed transcending the "initial, elemental state marked by impulsive, 'spontaneous' actions and emotions (*stikhiinost'*)" toward the "careful deliberation and consideration of his actions and complete political awareness (*soznatel'nost'*)."[57] Or, to put it in other terms, Dasha has transcended the irrationality and primitiveness of the *baba* and so can exemplify a female "comrade." Elaborating on this conclusion, I argue that the recession of Dasha's maternal identity accompanies her journey from "spontaneity" to "consciousness." Dasha's ordeals during the Civil War stimulate her evolution into the ideal Soviet woman, but this state of revolutionary enlightenment, of "consciousness," excludes the possibility of maternal attachment to her daughter. Implicitly, then, Nurka is connected with this "elemental state" of "spontaneity" and hence an obstacle to the building of the socialist future.

When Gleb first leaves to join the fighting, the bond between mother and daughter remains unbreakable, as encapsulated by the image of Nurka on Dasha's breast: "in this tear-drowned agony, she lay in her lonely bed, with Nurka at her heart" (158). United in their grief, the two endure isolation, fear, and vulnerability in tandem. When Dasha is summoned to her husband's cause, however, she leaves Nurka to a neighbor's care in order to serve as a "Green Wife."[58] Preparing for the inevitability of interrogation and even torture and death, Dasha's transformation begins: "And this year steeled Dasha with experience, cunning and strength. How that came to her she did not know. The other women shared in her strength and she became their leader" (163). But Nurka still occupies the foreground in her thoughts, and, after her kidnapping by Whites, Dasha worries only that they "might try to force her through Nurka. She could not stand that" (ibid.).

After Dasha's rape by White soldiers, however, the first indicators that the ties between mother and daughter are weakening appear. Lying "half-naked and half-dead," Dasha hallucinates Nurka's image: "Twice she seemed to see Nurka; the child was stamping with her little feet, dancing the wild Hopak dance, tipsily. Dasha stretched her hand towards her." During her most vulnerable and painful moment, Dasha seemingly finds solace in images of her daughter. But Nurka's presence quickly disappears from Dasha's thoughts: "Then Nurka came no more into her mind. She saw no more of her as though Nurka were the extinguished image of a dream" (166). Nurka no longer plays the central role in her mother's consciousness. Her specter flickers briefly but then recedes even further during the moments Dasha believes are her last before the Whites execute her: "Nurka was forgotten, as though she had never existed; then suddenly her image flew past her, with little hand outstretched and one short outcry: 'Oh!' This shook her like a blow of the whip in the cellar. Then Nurka disappeared again and was forgotten like a dream long past" (167). Nurka, like the children who overrun the decrepit cement factory, belongs to the "spontaneous" past and cannot penetrate her mother's increasingly "conscious" present: "And even when death was grinning in Dasha's face, Dasha could not forget her child. Then Nurka disappeared, dissolved into her blood with the rest of the past; and when one day Dasha was being marched up to the noose of death, it was without thinking of Nurka, who appeared at the last moment only like a far-away ghost" (245).

The extraordinary suffering Dasha endures creates a temporal separation between mother and daughter. Nurka belongs now to an unreachably innocent time, to a dreamlike existence that Dasha cannot resurrect. These experiences harden her irrevocably, and "after this Dasha never shuddered again; and always her eyebrows were knit in a deep frown." The desiccation of Dasha's previously warm and nourishing home follows immediately: "She never got home until midnight, and her room became stained with damp, and full of cobwebs; and dust settled in the corners. The flowers at the windows faded and dried up" (169). Dasha, burnt and hardened by revolutionary fire, attains "consciousness" but can no longer sustain maternal warmth.[59]

Nonetheless, Dasha senses keenly her responsibility for Nurka's deterioration and eventual death. She affirms a child's need for love from an individual rather than a collective mother:

> Dasha knew better than all the doctors in the world why Nurka was fading out like a little star at dawn. It is not only the mother's milk which a child

> needs; it is nourished also by the heart and the tenderness of its mother. The child fades and withers if the mother does not breathe upon its little head, if she does not warm it with her blood, and does not surround its sleep with her care and presence. (244)

The events that Dasha terms simply "life" and cannot identify conclusively—"revolution, struggle, work, Party"—create an unbridgeable chasm between the maternal Dasha and the builder of the socialist future. The new Soviet woman, as Dasha exemplifies, sacrifices her maternal identity and the life of her child on the altar of revolution.[60] Significantly, in the descriptions of her decline, Nurka loses her childlike state and ages unnaturally and prematurely: "Now she saw Nurka alive, with the face of an old woman and with sunken eyes made sad by death; and once again, as long before, she felt not strong enough to *step over* her body. And she saw: Nurka was her life's sacrifice; and this sacrifice was unbearable for her" (245; emphasis added).

Nurka, a symbol of the past and enemy of progress, ceases to be a child before finally perishing. In order for Dasha to participate fully in the construction of Soviet society, she must cross the threshold—"step over"—from her maternal sentiments toward her social obligations. The suffering she endures during the Civil War period facilitates this transition.[61] As Vera S. Dunham observes, "Dasha weeps, flings herself down on mother earth, and tears it with her nails. Yet she personifies the new morality by making herself free."[62] But, unlike the heroines of the short fiction discussed above, Dasha suffers as a result of the sacrifice of her daughter, mourning the loss of her unrecoverable motherly tenderness as well.[63]

The death of Nurka represents the irreversible demise of Gleb's prerevolutionary family; unlike the cement factory, his domestic life can never be resurrected. The new society allows no time to honor the tragedy of the death of a child, however. After Dasha informs Gleb that Nurka died during his absence, grief momentarily unites estranged husband and wife:

> Gleb felt at first as though he had received a terrible blow in the chest. When this passed, his heart felt swollen to bursting and he had a sickly feeling in his entrails, as one feels when falling from a height. . . . Dasha stood leaning with her back to the wall, and Gleb saw her eyes, suffering, quivering and full of tears.

But the coarse coughing sounds that the Communist leader Gromada emits immediately shatter this private moment. Gromada, symbolizing Bolshevik society, interrupts Gleb and Dasha's quiet grief, allowing them no inviolable space in which to mourn. The vulgar present intrudes on the remembrance of the past's young representative (262).

A CHILD-WOMAN

The fate of another character, Polia Mekhova, also sheds light on how the dynamics of maternity and childhood are developed in the novel. Although Polia holds the important position of secretary of the Women's Section of the party, she is repeatedly associated with the realm of childhood rather than that of adulthood. In the reader's first introduction to her, for example, she is depicted as having "on her upper lip a light down like a boy's," "dimpled cheeks plump and rosy as a schoolgirl's," and "eyes [that] were round and clear, like a child's" (45–46). And later in the novel, during the chapter entitled "The Party Cleansing," the narration describes how "Polia stood before the table, looking very small, like a young girl" (275).[64]

Polia eventually becomes a romantic interest for Gleb, and he stresses her childlike qualities when contrasting her with Dasha: "There was Dasha, so fine, so near, difficult to understand and to overcome. And Polia was a weak child, all fire, trembling with emotion and impulse." Earlier in the same scene, Polia is observed "chattering like a little girl" (151). Polia lacks the impenetrability of Dasha, the layers of complexity typical of the adult personality. Instead, she exhibits emotion and vulnerability in a naive and direct manner. Gleb continues to observe Polia's childlike demeanor when he contemplates a sexual relationship with her:

> She stood before Gleb, so simple, frank, so lost in her bewilderment, so trustful and so near . . . He had only to embrace her, to take her into his arms, and she would snuggle up to him like a child and become so close to him; and his caress would appease her, and she would laugh once more as she had not long ago. (213)

Once again foregrounding Polia's simplicity and weakness, Gleb fantasizes about a paternal influence on her, about easing her childlike anxiety through physical contact.[65]

These repeated descriptions of Polia as a child reinforce her symbolic connection with the children who overran the cement factory and, of course, with Nurka. Anxiety frequently consumes Polia, as if she intuits the precariousness of children's (and, by extension, her own) place in the new society. She confesses her fear to Gleb, pleading for his understanding: "What's the matter with me, Comrade Gleb? . . . It's as though I were infected with the plague. I feel the earth trembling underneath my feet . . . It's as though a vile crowd were jeering at me and I'm ashamed because I cannot protect myself" (211). Polia senses that her excessive emotionality and childlike nature have led to her estrangement, comparing herself to someone stricken with the plague and therefore irreversibly driven out of the collective. She fears alienation from the "family of workers" in the same way that children such as Nurka were exiled from the individual family unit. Polia also affirms her link with the past by lamenting her survival into the present: "'Why didn't I die then, in those days? Dead in the streets of Moscow? Or in the Army? Why did I have to live to know these torturing, shameful days, dear Comrades?'" (266). Polia, like the children in the rundown cement factory, represents a relic from the past enduring into the present, a leftover without an assured place in the new society.

Polia's rape by the Communist Badin violently ends her childlike state. Bursting into her room one night as if emerging from the nightmares that continuously torment her, Badin actualizes Polia's fears, and she views his assault as unavoidable and long awaited:

> "What do you want, Badin? What do you want?"
>
> She had not time even to lower her hands. With his frightful weight he fell on to the bed, pressing her to the pillows.
>
> "Be quiet, little Polia . . . Be quiet, quiet . . ."
>
> She was suffocated beneath the intolerable weight of this perspiring flesh and the dizzy odour of alcohol. She did not resist, crushed in the shadows; she could not resist: how could she when this was inevitable and unalterable? (249)

The novel's earlier descriptions of Polia as childlike endow the rape with additional brutality. And the description of the immediate aftermath of the attack suggests that she was a virgin: "She lay motionless on the couch, all naked and crushed. Her chemise was pressed like a damp bundle above her breasts and smelt of sweat and of another nauseating odour which she had never known before" (250). Badin's rape of Polia can be interpreted as a symbolic assault against the state of childhood in which she inappropriately lingers. If children pose a potential threat to the success of the new society, then Badin's violence, like the exile of Nurka to a children's home, reveals the extreme measures that this society will take to eliminate that threat.

Forcibly deprived of her physical innocence, Polia's other fear is realized when she is thrown out of the "family of workers," that is, expelled from the party. On the brink of physical and mental breakdown, she appeals to Dasha for help. Dasha's first advice to Polia conveys the message that childish vulnerability and sentimentality must be conquered: "Our hearts must be of stone, Comrade Mekhova. Let our heart burst, if it must, but we don't want a heart of tears—not a heart of cotton-wool! One's heart must be like flint. . . . You may rely upon me; I have strength for a long time to come yet" (266). After the death of Nurka, no remnants of the past remain for Dasha, no "soft" elements prevent the complete hardening and strengthening of her heart. Now a woman of steel, she can sustain Polia in a maternal way through the transmission of her new strength.

Dasha eventually agrees to live with the stricken Polia, assuming an explicit rather than implicit maternal role, as she informs Gleb: "We're going to live together. Comrade Mekhova has got a screw loose—she's got to be repaired and put into working order again" (289). Polia takes the place of the dead Nurka, and Dasha again proves herself a "collective mother" by nurturing an orphan from the family of workers.[66] But the vocabulary Dasha employs to describe her new role reflects how motherhood has been refashioned to suit the needs of the new society. She will "repair" Polia like a malfunctioning machine, restoring her to optimal productivity and ensuring that she can once again toil for the worker's collective. The new Soviet woman possesses a hardened heart, as Dasha explains, and this renders her a sober, unsentimental mother. Dasha's emotionless mothering signifies, along with Badin's rape, another attempt to destroy Polia's childlike state and the impediment to progress that it represents.

AN "INHUMAN SACRIFICE"

Durfee cites *Cement* as evidence that "the Bolsheviks never really rejected the importance of motherhood." Gladkov endowed Dasha, she argues, "with strong maternal overtones, at the same time that he liberated her from a traditional domestic environment."[67] Dasha does, as mentioned earlier, exhibit certain characteristics of a "collective mother." As Vorsheva advocated, Dasha successfully reallocates her maternal sentiment outside the narrow confines of the individual family. She nurtures the children who live in the communal home and assumes a maternal role in the life of the unfortunate Polia. Both of these actions, however, are enabled by the abandonment and eventual death of Dasha's own biological daughter. If the novel stresses the significance of motherhood, then it is an altered vision of maternity, one predicated upon a mother's negligence of her traditional responsibilities. Dasha evolves successfully toward the goal of "comrade," but the defeat of her maternal attachment to Nurka precedes and perhaps even hastens this evolution.

In the penultimate chapter of the novel, a character observes the corpse of a recently deceased newborn child washed up along the shore:

> A red handkerchief was tied around its head, there were socks on its feet, and one could not see its little hands as it had a white cloth tied around it. The corpse was quite new and the little milk-white face was peaceful, quite lifelike, as though asleep . . . The warmth of its mother's hand was almost still

> upon it as could be seen by this scarf, the carefully tied white cloth, and the tiny socks upon its chubby feet . . . From where came this little child, so inhumanly sacrificed . . . ? From a wrecked ship? Thrown into the sea by a frenzied mother? (301–2)

The red handkerchief, of course, symbolizes Communist society and parallels the one that Dasha dons. Despite the symbolic red color that he wears, however, the infant will not reap the benefits of the utopian society that this color represents. Excluded from the future, the child's body is left to languish "against the debris and the seaweed" (301). The image of this small corpse poignantly and pointedly encapsulates the fate of children in the novel as a whole.

One of the novel's characters speculates that the infant may have died at his own mother's hands, but the guilt of this anonymous child's mother is impossible to determine conclusively.[68] The causal link between the death of Nurka and Dasha's decision to place her in a communal home, however, is less ambiguous. Dasha knowingly abandons Nurka, offering her as an "inhuman sacrifice," just like the dead baby who washes up on the banks of the sea. Dasha acknowledges that a child needs the love of an individual rather than a "collective mother," but her Civil War sufferings and societal commitments render her incapable of delivering this love.

The novel's representation of children legitimizes Dasha's choices. *Cement* presents children as obstacles to progress, as primitive remnants of a past that must be overcome. The rape of the fragile Polia symbolizes childhood's violent conquest. And the demands of the present leave no time or space to mourn the death of a child. The heroine of *Cement,* the exemplar of the new Soviet woman, successfully achieves revolutionary enlightenment and becomes a "comrade." She avoids the *baba* taint of motherhood by sublimating her maternal emotions and abandoning her daughter. If Dasha represents the new Soviet woman, then the novel *Cement* reveals the incompatibility of traditional maternal bonds and the new society for which that woman toils and sacrifices.

Popular responses to the widely read novel's reimagining of femininity and domestic relations varied. According to a study published in 1928, for example, *Cement* elicited significantly more positive responses from male than from female readers: working-class women rated the novel favorably only 26 percent of the time, compared with 50 percent of men. These same female respondents reacted particularly negatively toward the character of Dasha, commenting, for example, that "the working woman can learn nothing from Dasha's behavior" and that "a woman should not follow Dasha's example."[69] At the same time, a questionnaire distributed to factory workers in the mid-1920s revealed more sympathetic responses, with some respondents affirming their belief that "Dasha's attitude toward her personal life [is] perfectly correct."[70] Although no definitive, quantitative measurement of the success of Soviet attempts to promote new cultural models of motherhood—such as those discussed in this chapter—exists, these varied responses testify to the challenges of disseminating such profoundly transformed notions of womanhood.

Nonetheless, the fictional mother who abandons her children in the Soviet 1920s, as portrayed in the texts discussed above, is not meant to inspire antipathy or condemnation. Rather, the authors characterize abandonment as a wholly justifiable, even heroic, response to the exigencies of the historical period. Or, in the case of the agitational trial—where the mother is judged for abandoning her son without a noble reason—as a lamentable but reversible phenomenon that highlights the munificence and expertise of the Soviet state. In creating a new morality for the postrevolutionary period, these authors now present as an ideal the same maternal actions that would have elicited a negative judgment from the nineteenth-century readers of *Anna Karenina* or *The Golovlev Family.* Whether glorifying a mother who forsakes her children to serve society or demonstrating the danger of a mother left to her own devices, these texts illustrate how the Soviet state inserted itself into the mother-child relationship and assumed a position of primacy. The interests of the state either supersede those of the child, or the state is portrayed as more qualified to make the decisions traditionally the prerogative of the biological mother. In either case, the "halo of holy motherhood," as at least one Soviet mother from the 1920s had advocated, is undeniably pierced.

Moreover, the contrasting and highly incompatible versions of the abandoning mother that emerge from the fictional texts examined in this chapter—the bold and steely revolutionary who forgoes motherhood for the sake of service to the collective, versus the naive and vulnerable young woman whose maternal identity cannot properly evolve without the assistance of the state—neatly encapsulate the contradictory position of women in the early years of the Soviet Union. Was woman a victim in need of salvation, an ally whose strength could be harnessed, or a potential enemy to be thwarted? The propaganda generated in the early years of the Soviet state offered conflicting answers to this question, and the fictional abandoning mothers discussed here reflect this inconsistency.

The abandoning mother as a positive figure would be replaced by very different maternal ideals in subsequent decades, such as the "heroine mother" who gave birth to many children. From a legal standpoint, the official stance toward abandonment altered in 1934, when mothers were deemed criminally responsible for relinquishing their children and abandonment began to be categorized as a crime equivalent to murder.[71] The presence of this figure in the works discussed here, however, represents a unique and radical, if brief, chapter in the history of the Russian "maternal dilemma." These texts ignore the complexity of the balance between motherhood and autonomy, treating the "dilemma" as if it simply did not exist. They convey the moral that a woman may leave her children behind in pursuit of a loftier goal, whether or not the decision causes any negative consequences for either the mother or the child. For the remaining decades of the Soviet Union, women were offered no such option, and they assumed not merely a "single" burden but what has been termed a "triple" burden, with motherhood and household responsibilities coexisting alongside professional commitments.[72]

THE STALIN YEARS

Of the two exemplars of the variation on the bad mother motif discussed in this chapter, the one represented by Tikhonova would enjoy a longer life span. The intrusion of the state into the mother-child relationship intensified after Stalin consolidated power in 1929, most notably with the pro-natalist 1936 Family Law that instituted rewards for mothers of multiple children, complicated the process for obtaining a divorce, and outlawed abortion. The official propaganda that emerged both immediately before and after the passage of this law frequently portrayed women as weak and indecisive, unable to resist the pernicious influence of devious men who coerced them into unwanted and unnecessary abortions. The moral hierarchy of *Trial of a Mother* reappeared, with the selfish, pleasure-seeking, and abortion-advocating male counterpoised to the innocent, selfless, and undeniably maternal female.[73] All women naturally desired motherhood, and the government would intercede to ensure that they could fulfill this destiny by prohibiting abortion and defending them against unscrupulous men. It would mercifully remove the burden of choice from an expectant mother's shoulders. As historian Sheila Fitzpatrick aptly summarizes, "In the inevitable conflict between women's interests, construed as altruistic and pro-family, and men's interests, read as selfish and individualistic, the state was unquestionably in the women's corner."[74] In other words, Stalin-era family law aimed to remove all obstacles to the realization of a woman's maternal destiny, including men. The disparate punishments meted out to men for encouraging illegal abortions (imprisonment) versus to women for seeking them (monetary fines) underscored this view of women as passive victims of male immorality, in the mold of Tikhonova.[75] At the same time, the prohibition on abortion supposedly highlighted the superiority of the Stalinist revolution to the October one. In the wake of 1917, the country's material poverty compelled abortion as a necessary evil, whereas Stalin's ascension to power ostensibly guaranteed security and abundance for all Soviet citizens, thus rendering abortion superfluous.[76] Hence, government intervention in reproductive decision-making not only compensated for a woman's naturally weak and vulnerable nature but also affirmed the success of Stalinism.

As the Dasha Chumalova model of Russian motherhood receded into the background during the Stalin period, the pagan roots of the maternal archetype resurfaced. In popular songs, poems, and visual culture of the 1930s, a fertile, markedly feminine body replaced the "neutered female image" of the earlier decade.[77] While actual agricultural productivity declined in the wake of the violent campaign for collectivization of the early 1930s, a "pathos of fertility," as Hans Guenther terms it, emerged to fill the void.[78] Mothers once again assumed their symbolic association with the land and nation, as Soviet nationalism increased during the second half of the 1930s.[79] The word *rodina* (motherland) returned to prominence—a process that culminated during World War II with I. Toidze's famous *The Motherland Calls!* poster.[80]

The overt physical manifestations of a woman's child-bearing abilities returned from the margins to the center of the cultural imaginary.[81] Alexander Deineka's 1932 painting *The Mother* encapsulates this shift in maternal representation from the 1920s to the Stalin era. Painted in warm, earthy hues, it depicts a small child sleepily perched in a mother's arms, basking in the glow of her adoring and reassuring gaze. The mother stands naked, with her back to the viewer, and the silhouette of her bare breast—symbolizing fecundity and nurturance—appears in the lower left of the canvas. Deineka foregrounds the intimacy and exclusivity of the mother-child bond, as well as its timelessness—the painting lacks any details (such as clothing or furnishings) that could situate it within an identifiable historical era.[82] The sentiments evoked in *The Mother* contrast sharply with those exhibited in the works discussed in this chapter, which stress both the communality and the historical specificity of the relationship between mothers and children. It is hard to conceive of an image more distant from that evoked only seven years earlier, in the poem "Mother and Son," which lightheartedly celebrated the impermanence of those same mother-child bonds. In the words of a critic from 1938, "for the new [Soviet] woman . . . motherhood has ceased to be a calamity and has become a source of joy and communal pride."[83]

Alongside this celebration of a woman's fundamentally maternal nature, the myth of the Great Family was also introduced into Soviet culture during the Stalin period. With Stalin serving as the symbolic father of the nation, this myth cast Soviet citizens in the role of obedient, humble, and unflaggingly loyal children. By the mid-1930s, a hierarchical axis of power had replaced the earlier, fraternal ideal of the First Five-Year Plan (1928–32).[84] Many literary heroes of the decade surmounted the trials of orphanhood to discover their true destiny in the larger, patriarchal family of Soviet society, with the sage and beneficent father Stalin at its helm.[85] The mythology of "the happy Great Family" united "the young people, the earth mother, and the wise father."[86] Images of joyous mothers and children abounded, with Stalin hovering benevolently over the scene and leaving no doubt as to "whose holy spirit has done the ideological inseminating."[87] This symbolic union relegated actual fathers to the periphery of the Soviet family, where they could pose no challenge to Stalin's preeminence—a marginalization that would problematize familial relations throughout the Soviet period and beyond.[88]

In summary, then, the maternal body as well as the nation troped as mother both returned to rhetorical prominence during the Stalin years. Simultaneously, this era—characterized by housing shortages and arbitrary state violence—created increasingly difficult daily burdens for actual mothers. If official rhetoric under Stalin reinstated a secular "halo of holy motherhood," celebrating the ease with which maternal and professional commitments could be reconciled, the reality of most mothers' lives consisted of a much more mundane struggle for their own and their family's survival amid a climate of scarcity, mass arrests, and unrelenting fear. The mothers depicted in the unofficial Soviet literature of the Stalin era, during the late 1930s in particular, reflect this cruel reality rather than the facile happiness of the Great Family with its infinitely fertile and joyous mother. The image of Dasha Chumalova and others like her attained an unintended irony in light of the forced separation of mothers and children that occurred on a massive scale during the Stalinist Terror and World War II. Two important literary works of the 1930s—Anna Akhmatova's famous poem "Requiem" and Lidia Chukovskaia's novella *Sof'ia Petrovna*—both utilize a maternal figure to illuminate the ordeals women endured during those darkest of years in Soviet history. Through their respective reconceptualizations of the "mater dolorosa," Akhmatova and Chukovskaia poignantly employ mothers as "the most effective measure of the devastation of Stalinist society."[89]

SOF'IA PETROVNA

Chukovskaia's *Sof'ia Petrovna,* although written in 1939–40, remained unpublished in the Soviet Union until the Perestroika period of the 1980s. At the beginning of the text, its titular heroine embodies the effortless and uplifting synthesis of motherhood and professional accomplishment so touted during the Stalin period. After her husband's death, Sof'ia quickly acquires the training necessary to support her young son, finding such satisfaction in her job as a typist that she cannot imagine how she had lived without it for so long. Her son, Kolia—handsome, intelligent, kind, and assured of a bright future—testifies to her success as a mother. Blithely unburdened by any critical awareness of the dark clouds of repression and violence gathering over Soviet society of the 1930s, Sof'ia seems to have stepped directly out of a propaganda poster celebrating Stalin's success in supposedly "solving" the Women's Question.[90]

The Terror of the late 1930s gradually encroaches upon Sof'ia's contented existence, however, eventually subsuming her completely. After the inexplicable arrest of her upstanding son, Sof'ia swiftly encounters the indifference and brutality of the Soviet state. While clinging to an almost childlike belief in the justice of the system, she futilely attempts to navigate the bureaucratic labyrinth in search of information about Kolia. Sof'ia adheres to the self-sacrificial model of motherhood, neglecting her own comfort and health and believing in a mother's salvational powers. She even attributes Kolia's arrest to his leaving the maternal sphere of influence, imposing a simplistic logic of motherly power onto the chaos of the Great Terror.

Sof'ia's journey into the prison underworld leads her to confront an alternative, almost exclusively female, society that flourished during the Stalin years—the prison line:

> Sof'ia Petrovna learned quite a bit during those two weeks . . . She learned that, leaving the house after a short sleep, on the street, on the staircase, in the corridor, in the hall . . . there would already be women, women, women, old and young, in kerchiefs and in hats, with infants and with three-year-olds and without kids—children crying from exhaustion and silent, scared, terse women. Just as, during her childhood, after a trip to the woods she would close her eyes and see berries, berries, berries, now when she closed her eyes she saw faces, faces, faces . . .[91]

These women, predominantly mothers, occupy a parallel space to the "official" world Sof'ia inhabited before her son's arrest. This description highlights their ubiquity—government buildings are bursting from the throngs of women—as well as the seemingly unending nature of the women's quests. Despite her similar plight, however, Sof'ia remains isolated from this community of fellow sufferers, feeling no solidarity with them because they are the "wives and mothers of poisoners, spies and murderers" (46). Sof'ia does not extrapolate a wider phenomenon of unjust persecution from her innocent son's predicament. Rather, she clings to her facile acceptance of Soviet propaganda and thus imagines herself superior to the other mothers, rejecting any measure of comfort that this fellowship may have afforded her.

Sof'ia's workplace quickly succumbs to the prevalent climate of paranoia and denunciation, forcing her to leave her post. After the suicide of her only friend and Kolia's transfer to an unknown labor camp to serve a ten-year sentence, her isolation is complete. In the work's final chapters, Sof'ia's sanity gradually deteriorates as she writes naive letters to Stalin and succumbs to the fantasy that Kolia receives a pardon, joyously awaiting his imminent return. The novella's concluding scene contains the symbolic severing of ties between Sof'ia and her son. Kolia's long-awaited letter finally arrives, and in it he begs his mother to intercede on his behalf with the authorities. Fear, however, compels Sof'ia to burn the letter. The reader understands that Kolia's desperate pleas will remain unanswered. Sof'ia rejects the mother's traditional intercessory function, and, simultaneously, her maternal identity disintegrates. Chukovskaia's novella reveals the ultimate impossibility of maternal ties for a woman who had seemed to embody the ideal qualities of Soviet womanhood, with its twin pillars of motherhood and work. The climate created by the Great Terror deprives Sof'ia of both of these sources of fulfillment, upon which a woman's success in Soviet society had been predicated. *Sof'ia Petrovna* demonstrates how both the myth of the self-sacrificial mother and that of the mighty Soviet mother cannot withstand the pressures of a regime of terror. The anxiety of interpretation engendered by Sof'ia's burning of Kolia's letter—does she act to protect herself or her son? Is it a selfish or a selfless act?—remains unresolved. At the same time that official rhetoric proclaimed motherhood not a "calamity" but a "source of joy" for Soviet women, motherhood itself—or any other familial relationship to a repressed individual—was considered a crime deserving of arrest, exile, or worse.

A SOVIET "MATER DOLOROSA"

Anna Akhmatova's poetic cycle "Requiem," written during approximately the same years as *Sof'ia Petrovna*—1935–40—and widely acknowledged as one of the greatest works of twentieth-century Russian poetry, develops many of the same motifs of maternal transformation, loss, and suffering as Chukovskaia's novella.[92] It draws upon Akhmatova's actual experiences (after the arrest of her son, Lev Gumilev) with the same nightmarish labyrinth of prison lines, female anguish, and interminable waiting encountered by Chukovskaia's fictional heroine. Whereas Sof'ia represents the multitudes of average Soviet women who silently endured the depravities of the Stalinist terror, Akhmatova's poetic work aims to describe the indescribable, to commemorate and give definitive voice to the maternal torment of those years. The work's opening section, "Instead of a Foreword" (written in prose), establishes this poetic mission by describing a conversation in a Leningrad prison line, where the author spent seventeen months. In a whisper, a nameless, physically ravaged woman asks Akhmatova if she can describe what she sees there, and the poet replies that she can. While Sof'ia's callow belief in Soviet propaganda isolated her from other grieving mothers, it is Akhmatova's poetic gift that sets her apart from the crowds of women who languished outside prison gates during the Stalin years. With "Requiem," Akhmatova combines the poet's mission to speak for the masses with the mother's traditional role as mediator, as she bears witness to a specifically female suffering that might otherwise have remained unarticulated.

"Requiem" alternates between intensely intimate descriptions of the speaker's own personal tragedy, including direct addresses to her son, with more sweeping observations on the fate of her fellow women and the Russian nation as a whole. The scope of the tragedy encompasses the natural world—even "the mountains bend before this grief/the great river does not flow"—while the great land of "Rus'" is reduced to "squirm[ing] under bloody boots."[93] As it did for Sof'ia, the arrest of her son bifurcates the speaker's personal history, and two discrete personas take shape during the cycle: the "carefree sinner of Tsarskoe Selo" and the "mater dolorosa." Akhmatova's lyric persona addresses her younger self in stanza 4, wishing to bridge the temporal gap to "show . . . how your life will turn out: you will stand outside the Crosses Prison/three hundredth in the line with your prison parcel" (283). The burden of motherhood during a regime of terror renders vapid and absurd her earlier, hedonistic existence.

This stanza also highlights one of the central tensions of "Requiem": between exceptionality and anonymity. During her lighthearted youth, the speaker enjoyed a privileged status within a circle of friends that prized her wit and talent. Her prison vigils, however, have transformed her into merely another nameless woman, distinguished neither by fame nor by charm. Akhmatova undermines the possibility of meaningful recognition in "Instead of a Foreword," when she describes how someone "who of course had never heard of my name" had "identified" (*opoznal*) her, placing the verb in ironic quotation marks (281). The work "Requiem" itself, however, prevents Akhmatova—and, by extension, the other women—from slipping into collective anonymity. Indeed, the cycle's final section, "Epilogue," explicitly connects Akhmatova's poetic legacy with the experiences that inspired "Requiem" and with the women who shared them. If her countrymen wish to erect a monument to her, she demands that they build it not "near the sea where I was born . . . /nor in the Tsar's Garden . . . /but here, where I stood three hundred hours/and they never unbolted the door for me" (288). Such a memorial would concretize the inextricable link between Akhmatova's dual role as mother and as poet. By extension, it would also elevate her fellow suffering mothers—those whom she wanted "to name . . . but they took away/the list"—from the depths of anonymity to the heights of an immortal benevolence (287).

"Requiem" also endows maternal grief with unique nobility by evoking the death of Christ and the exceptional suffering of his mother, Mary. While official Soviet culture of the 1930s foregrounded the pre-Christian, pagan maternal archetype, Akhmatova, by contrast, draws upon the paradigmatic, biblical "mater dolorosa." Section 10 of the work, entitled "Crucifixion," creates a hierarchy of suffering, with the mother occupying the highest spot: "Mary Magdalene smote her breast and wept,/the disciple whom He loved turned to stone,/but where the Mother stood in silence/nobody even dared look" (286). The precise contours of Mary's anguish remain unexpressed, as she forgoes the histrionics of Mary Magdalene and the numbness of Christ's disciple. The magnitude of her grief surpasses the valor of the bystanders, none of whom can summon the courage to gaze at her directly. Hers is an unarticulated, primordial suffering that transcends the limits of language and human fortitude. While *Sof'ia Petrovna* demonstrates the impotence of maternal myths when confronted with the Stalinist terror, "Requiem" situates maternal suffering during the same period within a specifically Christian context, forging a direct link between the Soviet "mater dolorosa" and her biblical counterpart.[94]

The all-female prison line provides the most prominent point of intersection between *Sof'ia Petrovna* and "Requiem." Akhmatova, however, dedicates her poetic gift to memorializing and describing precisely those anonymous throngs of women from whom Chukovskaia's fictional heroine attempted to distance herself. "Requiem" deems the line the most important location of the poet's life, and the work is bookmarked by evocations of those women who persevered in their futile missions despite both "the cruel cold" and "the July heat" (287). "Requiem" concludes by affirming the poet's task of commemoration and by valorizing the heroic heights to which motherhood can inspire a woman. *Sof'ia Petrovna,* by contrast, ends with the severing of ties between mother and son, as symbolized by Sof'ia's burning of Kolia's letter. Both fictional texts ultimately reveal the hollowness of the dominant Soviet mythology of joyous motherhood effortlessly coupled with paid labor. Chukovskaia debunks the relevance of maternal myths in the face of mass repression, violence, and paranoia, while Akhmatova creates a new myth for the Stalinist terror, one that relies heavily upon Christian imagery of maternal suffering. Both *Sof'ia Petrovna* and "Requiem" utilize the plight of the mother of an unjustly imprisoned son to unmask the chasm between official rhetoric and tragic reality that characterized Soviet life during the 1930s and beyond.

The cracks in the mythology of the indefatigable Soviet mother-worker first revealed in the unofficial literature discussed above continued to surface during the remaining decades of the Soviet Union. The myth of the Great Family was dismantled in the wake of Stalin's death in 1953, as part of the disavowal of the cult of personality initiated during Nikita Khrushchev's Thaw.[95] Soviet women regained the legal right to obtain an abortion in 1955, but official propaganda relentlessly stressed the steep personal price of exercising this right. Although the change in law returned to women the "burden" of reproductive choice, the state continued to invoke the specter of Tikhonova—the naive victim incapable of effective, independent decision-making—in deterring women from seeking abortions. Health pamphlets warned that the complexity of choosing to use contraception or to terminate a pregnancy necessitated professional, medical advice; it was simply too overwhelming for women to make these decisions on their own. Pro-natalist propaganda instilled a fear of abortion's devastating consequences: infertility, premature aging, sexual dysfunction, and marital discord, not to mention the emotional distress of interfering with a woman's immutable desire for motherhood. "Antiabortion rhetoric" during the Khrushchev years, as historian Amy E. Randall points out, "characterized women as victims who had to 'survive the severity of abortion.'"[96] Men, who were now portrayed as having an innate need for fatherhood, no longer posed the main obstacle to a woman realizing her maternal destiny, as they supposedly had after abortion was outlawed in 1936. Rather, it was a woman's inability to act in her own best interest that the state would counteract.

By the 1970s, demographic pressures further exposed the seams in the ideal of the Soviet worker-mother. Dire projections about falling birthrates and labor shortages prompted demographers and other officials to deemphasize women's professional accomplishment while raising the prestige of family life.[97] Articles in the official press enjoined women to privilege motherhood above all other pursuits. Many films from the decade focused on "the double-life of the Soviet woman, straddling the often conflicting worlds of public and private production," no longer ignoring the problem as they had during the Stalin era.[98] In the same period, author I. Grekova's 1979 novella *Ship of Widows* also pointed to the gap between maternal myth and reality in post–World War II Soviet society. Set in a communal apartment inhabited exclusively by widows, the work details the stultifying effects of the "slavish" (as it is repeatedly termed) maternal love heaped on Vadim, the spoiled and callow only son of one of the apartment's denizens, Anfisa. *Ship of Widows* strips the devoted Russian mother of most of her nobility, revealing the toxic and suffocating effects of her desperate affections. The solipsistic Vadim only begins to acknowledge Anfisa's sacrifices on his behalf in her last months of life, after a stroke deprives her of the ability to appreciate his transformation. As it had for Porfiry Golovlev, Vadim's realization of the magnitude of his guilt before his mother occurs only after her death. Whereas Porfiry's attempt at posthumous maternal reconciliation indirectly leads to his own demise, Vadim's awakening to culpability prefigures the beginning of his new, presumably more meaningful life. Nonetheless, *Ship of Widows* presents a decidedly ambiguous picture of the ultimate worth of decades of Anfisa's maternal toil. In a sense, the work anticipates the warped maternal figures who populate the work of Liudmila Petrushevskaia, discussed in chapter 3.[99]

With the loosening of censorship during Mikhail Gorbachev's glasnost period in the 1980s, a mother could embody the moral bankruptcy of the regime rather than the success of the Soviet project, as witnessed in the blockbuster 1988 film *Little Vera,* directed by Vasily Pichul. The titular heroine, Vera (whose name in Russian, ironically, means "faith"), rebels against her stultifying life in a provincial Russian town through sexual encounters, one of which leads indirectly to the death of her father and to her own self-destruction. During the course of the film, Vera discovers that her parents chose to have her solely in the hopes of landing a more spacious apartment. Thus, material considerations—not the natural expression of an innate desire or civic obligation—motivate the choice for motherhood. The film reveals how the joyous children depicted in images of Stalin's Great Family—the generation of Vera's parents—can bequeath no comparable happiness to their own offspring.[100]

In the next chapter, I turn to the final years of the Soviet Union and the first decade of the post-Soviet period, when anxiety about the demise of iconic Russian motherhood preoccupied many contemporary observers and writers, and when the vulnerability of the idealized maternal figure reflected the dislocations of a society experiencing unprecedented cultural, social, and economic upheaval.

Chapter Three

"Mother-Destroyers": The Bad Mother in the Late-Soviet and Post-Soviet Era

DURING THE MOSCOW THEATER HOSTAGE CRISIS of October 2002 (also known as the Nord-Ost Siege), the image of the vengeful mother, dressed all in black and with a bomb-belt strapped around her waist, captured the attention of the Russian media. Although these so-called Chechen "black widows" had participated in earlier acts of terror, the seizing of nearly 900 hostages in the theater in the center of the Russian capital was their most high-profile and brazen act to date.[1] The accounts of hostages who survived the siege (and the mysterious poisonous gas released by Russian special forces that killed 129 of them) differed in their characterizations of the eighteen women, describing them as anywhere from sympathetic to wantonly cruel. A young former hostage, for example, recalls being approached by one of the female terrorists who "smiled and asked whether I have a mama and a papa, and how I'm feeling."[2] And a musician from the Nord-Ost orchestra describes the empathy he and other hostages felt for the women and their cause: "They were closer to us in that moment than anyone from the outside. We talked with them . . . we understood that no one needs this war in Chechnya, not the hostages, not the terrorists. They told us: 'We just need some kind of peace.' And we agreed with them."[3] One eyewitness had contrasting reactions to two of the women, observing that one of them was "cheerful and charming" while another was "simply a boor."[4] Another account, by contrast, contains no ambiguity in its representation of the Chechen women, describing the cruelty of one particular subgroup of women (all sisters of the same militant) who forbade the hostages from moving even slightly in their seats for many hours.[5]

Despite this lack of consensus about the collective character of the black widows or about the amount of empathy they inspired in their hostages, their identity as mothers, for at least several Russian observers, seemed to hold the key to the successful resolution of the crisis. A psychologist analyzing the phenomenon of female terrorism, for example, offered the following advice: "We have to remember that a woman is a mother, the defender of the hearth, one who nurtures with kindness, with words, with beautiful actions . . . Who knows, maybe if simple women, perhaps even *multi-child mothers,* had gone into the theater, maybe they could have persuaded the fighters and secured the release of the children from the theater" (emphasis added).[6] Another psychologist (a specialist in group psychology) argues that female terrorists are more desperate and thus more dangerous than their male counterparts. The only possible way to neutralize this volatility, he claims, is through the intervention of other Chechen women and the maternal instinct that they embody: "The only thing that can hold any value for the female terrorist are the lives of women and children from her tribe . . . I would convince as many Chechen women and children as possible residing in the capital to come to the theater. And to give those Chechen women the chance to negotiate with the female terrorists."[7] Thus, for both of these Russian medical professionals, mothers (present or future) are both the instigators of and the potential antidote to female terrorism. The first psychologist, significantly, even suggests that "multi-child mothers" may be the most effective in stabilizing the violent impulses of their fellow women; in other words, a woman's moral persuasiveness increases according to the number of children she has birthed. And the "black widows," some of whom were not the mothers but rather the widows or sisters of fallen Chechen fighters, could not escape their maternity. Regardless of their particular family situations, it is their conscience as mothers that must be appealed to and activated. The advice of a Russian journalist from 1863 that "all women should be considered mothers before all else" is still heeded 140 years later.[8]

Motherhood, according to one Russian scholar writing in the 1990s, ensures a balance between potentially destabilizing elements and prevents society from descending into chaos during crises, such as those exemplified by the Nord-Ost Siege. During such periods of uncertainty, "the mother-child relationship becomes almost the only social cell where basic values are preserved and transmitted."[9] A society's self-destructive impulses, then, can only be tempered by a mother's transmission of civilizing values.[10] Motherhood is a stabilizing force that counterbalances the dynamism of social and economic tumult and political change, such as Russia experienced during the transition from Communism and throughout the 1990s. To alleviate the social ills that this period produced, governmental support for the institution of motherhood should be strengthened. Rather than building more prisons, for example, Vera Ramikh argues that the Russian government should invest in motherhood, the foundation of Russian society, to conquer the problems of the post-Soviet period.

The journalists and observers of the Nord-Ost crisis who fixated on the maternity of the female Chechens revealed, perhaps, a similar impulse to impose order on chaos through the valorization of a mother's powers. This chapter explores how the belief in a mother's ability both to save and to destroy Russian society reached a new intensity in the post-Soviet period. These seemingly disparate tendencies can be observed in the emergence of heightened maternal imagery during media coverage of the Chechen conflicts of the 1990s and in the drawing of a symbolic connection between the decline of motherhood and the collapse of Russian society. The bad mothers in the literature and film of the late-Soviet and post-Soviet period discussed here, however—in the works of Liudmila Petrushevskaia and in V. Krishtofovich's 1990 film *Adam's Rib*—simultaneously question these notions of a mother's exalted abilities. For Ramikh, the cooperation of literature and the mass media was essential in enlisting motherhood as a solution to social problems.[11] Literature must help to educate mothers so that they can wield their full power as potential saviors of Russian society. The fictional bad mother—one who either partially or wholly replaces nobility and self-sacrifice with physical or psychological violence against her children—undermines this vision of maternal salvation.

Two contrasting images of motherhood emerged from the popular media accounts of the Chechen conflicts (1994–96 and 1999–2009): the heroic and beneficent member of the activist group Committee of Soldiers' Mothers, attempting to save the sons of Russia from the brutality both of war and of the Russian army itself; and the Chechen female suicide bomber, subverting traditional maternal categories with her recourse to indiscriminate violence. These two conflicting maternal figures—the noble mother versus the violent one—also reoccur in other journalism from the period, with apocalyptic forebodings directly linking criminal motherhood to the decay of Russian society. To make the transition from maternal imagery in these nonfictional accounts to that found in literature and film, I employ some of the concepts introduced by the novelist Leonid Bezhin who, in a 1992 article, analyzed the phenomenon of the masochistic mother from both a literary and a socio-historical perspective.

A MOTHER'S CLEAN HANDS

The notion that mothers could somehow ameliorate the violence of the Chechen conflict did not originate with the Nord-Ost Siege. On June 10, 1996, a delegation of women (comprised of Russian members of Parliament, soldiers' mothers, social activists, and journalists) flew to war-ravaged Ingushetia, in the North Caucasus region. The goal of this trip was to hold parliamentary hearings (under the auspices of the Committee on Women, Family and Youth of the Russian Parliament) devoted to the topic "women for peace in their society." A journalist from the newspaper *Female Muscovite* (*Moskvichka*) ("a newspaper for women") accompanied the group and, in July 1996, the paper included a special section devoted to coverage of the event.

Although the women who participated in the trip were not exclusively mothers, the press coverage elided the non-maternal identity of those present. For example, one headline read: "Citizens, be alert, an assault force of mothers has landed." And another declared that the "accursed questions" raised by the Chechen conflict—"why? for what?"—tortured all "honest Russians" but were felt most acutely by mothers. A majority of the articles expressed the utopian idea that motherhood erased national distinctions, that mothers from opposing sides of the conflict could find transcendent common ground based on their maternal emotions. This optimistic notion was reinforced stylistically; that is, a description of the plight of Russian mothers would inevitably be followed by a description of the similar dilemma of Chechen ones. For example, one article mentions the pilgrimages undertaken by mothers from both sides: 5,000 Russian mothers have searched for their sons in Chechnya, while 2,000 female Chechens undertook comparable journeys in search of sons detained somewhere in Russia. And the visitors, one article noted, met over 110 women from Chechnya and Ingushetia, as well as from Russia, clutching photographs of killed or missing sons and relatives. The testimonials of all of the mothers, regardless of nationality, were duly recorded.[12]

The other leitmotif of the coverage reinforced the notion that mothers could and were, indeed, morally obligated to stop the war. One woman (Eset Gorchkhanova, the leader of the women's movement from the town of Urus-Martan) called on Russian mothers to circumvent political and military authority and resolve the crisis through a simple and mutually beneficial exchange: "Dear Russian women, take your sons out of Chechnya! And we'll take ours out."[13] A member of the Russian Parliament, Gennadii Seleznev, indirectly supported this proposition by professing his belief that, where men have failed to stop the bloodshed, women are compelled to succeed.[14] And another representative of the Parliament, Mikhail Gutseriev, rallied mothers to apply their "clean hands" to the sullied endeavor of politics and secure an end to the violence, professing his faith that the "future of Russia is in women's hands."[15]

Undoubtedly, some of these rhetorical flourishes, especially on the part of the government officials, should be taken with a grain of salt. However, the goals of this June 1996 convocation of women in Ingushetia were not merely rhetorical. The participants operated under a firm and real belief that they could accomplish substantive change. Almost concurrently, a cinematic incarnation of this courageous Russian mother, intervening in violent conflicts and embodying the moral authority that men sullied by war no longer possessed, appeared in Sergei Bodrov Sr.'s 1996 film *Prisoner of the Mountains.*[16] Abdul-Murat, a Caucasian villager, captures the young and naive Russian soldier Vania Zhilin (played by Sergei Bodrov Jr.), hoping to leverage him in exchange for his own imprisoned son. When an attempted prisoner trade with the Russians fails, Abdul-Murat commands Vania to appeal to an even higher authority: his mother. After receiving Vania's letter, the mother (played by Valentina Fedotova) journeys to the heart of the conflict without hesitation, confronting both the Russian commander and Abdul-Murat with her quiet strength and steely maternal resolve. Although her efforts do not ultimately influence the sequence of events, the mother—who is not given a proper name and patronymic, thus intensifying her mythic appeal—carries significant symbolic weight as the incarnation of maternal strength and courage. This character in Bodrov's film—alongside the convocation in Ingushetia and the reverential coverage that it inspired in at least one Russian newspaper—suggested that the moral authority of the mother in Russia had, seemingly, reached a new height. Indeed, the figure of the "soldiers' mother" (and the activist group Committee of Soldiers' Mothers) emerged as one of the most politically influential and potent symbols of the antiwar movement in Russia in the 1990s.

The Committee of Soldiers' Mothers was founded in 1989. Throughout the first and second Chechen campaigns, the group staged rallies that invariably captured the attention of the Russian media, provided free consultations to parents of current or future soldiers, and worked toward achieving their main goal of converting Russia's army to an all-volunteer force. The mothers also waged a tireless battle against the dehumanizing Russian bureaucratic machine, which frequently subjected families of killed soldiers to senseless indignities, such as not having the correct papers to retrieve a son's body.[17] They assumed the role of truth-seekers, penetrating the obfuscations of the Russian military to obtain accurate statistics about dead and wounded soldiers.[18] The mothers' efforts garnered international attention, and in 1996 the group was nominated for a Nobel Peace Prize.[19]

The group utilized the exalted status of motherhood in Russian society to its tactical advantage. Whereas, during Soviet times, a woman could be considered a bad mother for wanting to keep her son away from the military service that would transform him into a "real Soviet man," the Committee of Soldiers' Mothers argued that a woman must heed a mother's biological imperative to keep her sons out of danger.[20] One sociologist speculates that the mothers are successful at gathering information inaccessible to the media or other groups precisely because they symbolize "sacred maternity."[21] The filmmaker Andrei Konchalovskii, while ruminating on the bleak reality of contemporary Russian life, cited the organization as the only proof of the existence of a Russian national consciousness: "We have no other national movements. No one is united by anything. But women are united by simple maternal emotion—they do not want to lose their children."[22] Hence, according to this argument, only motherhood (and not a sense of national or religious identity) is capable of instilling in Russians a sense of solidarity.[23] Indeed, several scholars argue that the committee, by reformulating maternal duty as civic duty, has crafted a new type of patriotism in Russia, one that centers not on military success but on the rule of law, human rights, and the strength of political institutions.[24] The committee's successful utilization of maternal mythology neutralized the tactics of their political enemies, who were understandably hesitant about attacking the embodiments of iconic Russian motherhood.[25] Their reliance upon this maternal identity may have shielded them from the direct retribution of the Russian government, since a state that professes to be democratic cannot employ overtly punitive or violent measures against mothers without facing some form of negative consequences.[26]

Media attention focused not only on the collective strength of mothers but on stories of individual maternal bravery as well. An article from 2002 exemplifies the reverential, almost hagiographical, treatment that mothers of soldiers fighting in Chechnya received throughout the press of the 1990s and early 2000s.[27] In the November 22, 2002, edition of *Parliamentary Newspaper* (*Parlamentskaia gazeta*), Natal'ia Tereb describes the "fate of a simple Siberian woman who lost her son in the war in Chechnya." At the same time, "the odyssey of her search for the remains of her son resounds as the apotheosis of a Mother's Heart."[28] The choice of the word "odyssey" points to the mythological overtones of the story, which paint the mother's journey into the heart of darkness (Chechnya) as a descent into the underworld. This opening sentence also hints at how, throughout the article, the author will portray this individual mother's story as symbolic of universal maternal devotion and sense of duty.

In 1994, the voice of Ol'ga Vladimirovna's son, crying out for her help in a dream, summons the mother to begin her quest. When she hears on the news that Russian tanks have entered the Chechen capital, Grozny, her maternal intuition tells her that her son is among them and, within two days, she arrives in the "hot zone." She recalls for the reporter that mothers had descended upon the war-torn city en masse:[29]

> There were many of us there—Ol'ga Vladimirovna recalled—losing our minds from the lack of information and because of what we'd seen . . . The burnt, disfigured bodies of young boys covered the streets of Grozny. No information, from anywhere. Just go and search. Just go and turn over corpses. And cover them up, so the dogs don't gnaw on them and the crows don't peck

> them. Those who didn't find their sons wept over the bodies of the identified. And we were so sympathetic to our "female comrades in battle"—the abandoned women. It was somehow easier for those of us who didn't find our sons—we at least still had hope.

Her description supports Konchalovskii's idea of the unity of maternal emotion, a unity in this instance forged by their collective horror as they turn over corpses in the streets of Grozny in search of their sons. Ol'ga Vladimirovna's fate is a synecdoche for the fate of all Russian mothers.

While searching for her son in Grozny a second time, she experiences firsthand the power that mothers possess to interrupt the violence of war, if only momentarily: "I was in the midst of 'enemies,' but I never felt any unkind feelings directed at me. And yet I was . . . the mother of a soldier who had burst into a Chechen house. When the 'crazy mothers' came out in their search, the fighting stopped and they let us through." The utopian notion that motherhood transcends national boundaries is validated, at least partially, by Ol'ga Vladimirovna's recollections of the respect with which the Chechen people treated them, leading her to conclude that "mothers in Chechnya are holy women."

Ol'ga Vladimirovna eventually finds the remains of her son, but she nonetheless continues her Chechen odyssey. She becomes an emissary for other Russian mothers, returning repeatedly to the underworld and negotiating with the dark spirits who populate it. At one point, she uncovers the burial place of one Russian soldier by asking a Chechen commander herself and then digging up the body. With traditional maternal self-abnegation, Ol'ga Vladimirovna denies the heroism of her feats: "Awards won't replace my son, but thank God that they remembered about us mothers. I don't consider my 'business trips' to Chechnya to be acts of bravery. I was just looking for my son." The author of the article attributes Ol'ga Vladimirovna's extraordinary courage to the strength of maternal love. The deeds recounted in the article illustrate how the powers ascribed to Russian mothers by traditional maternal mythology—the ability to neutralize discord and to mediate between disparate spheres (such as the military and civilians, or Russians and Chechens)—could be actualized in a contemporary conflict.

The Chechen conflicts of the 1990s, then, seemingly stimulated an intensification of maternal symbolism and a heightening of the rhetoric of motherhood in certain Russian media accounts. The image of the Committee of Soldiers' Mothers, valiantly facing down Russian military and political indifference and ineptitude, along with countless stories of individual heroism (such as Ol'ga Vladimirovna's), contributed to the notion that mothers had a unique role to fulfill and a moral imperative to heed in Chechnya. Mothers, united despite national and other differences, could stop the violence and save their sons.

MATERNITY AND VIOLENCE

The Chechen women who participated in the Nord-Ost Siege and committed other acts of terror were, in a sense, unwittingly responding to this call. In a perverted appropriation of a mother's moral authority, they fused the image of the noble mother, sacrificing her life on behalf of her children, with that of the criminal one, sacrificing innocent victims in pursuit of her goal. (The empathy and revulsion that they inspired in the witnesses to the Nord-Ost crisis, as discussed above, testify to this dual dynamic.)

This combination of venerable maternal authority and violence in the post-Soviet era is best encapsulated, perhaps, by a single image. A headline from the November 14, 2002, edition of the newspaper *Izvestiia* read: "Chechen woman who shot Russian soldiers may be deported from Germany." A 48-year-old Chechen woman, Asia Dombaeva, had recently made a shocking confession on live German television: during the time of the first Chechen campaign, she had killed three Russian soldiers and a Chechen policeman. Significantly, the woman surfaced to share her tale at the height of the tense Nord-Ost Siege. In a quiet voice, she recounted for the camera how, alongside her two sons (who were fighting on the side of the separatists), she calculatingly shot at Russian troops: "First I shot them in the legs, since they didn't have any body armor, and then in the head."[30] After losing both of her sons in the conflict, she was forced to flee Chechnya and settled in Germany. Dombaeva's brazen confession sparked a media sensation in her adopted country, even capturing the attention of Chancellor Gerhard Schroeder, who promised to investigate whether or not her actions warranted deportation. The image of a mother, side-by-side with her sons, relying on bullets rather than the moral superiority of a mother's supposedly "clean hands" to protect her family, succinctly captured how the symbolism of maternity now merged nobility with violence.

Violence emerged as a leitmotif not only in post-Soviet media coverage of Chechen women but also in that devoted to the cruel behavior of Russian mothers. In its focus on the increased violence and sexualization of Russian society, which it viewed as an undesirable side effect of liberalization, the press featured frequent stories of abused and neglected children, including those mistreated by mothers.[31] These press accounts were not, however, mere sensationalism; statistics about child abandonment in particular during the 1990s are sobering. During this decade, about half of the children taken under state guardianship (from 35 to 50 percent) were babies given up by their mothers and abandoned children found in public places. In Moscow, the number of children who were abandoned by their parents and accepted into children's homes increased 2.1 times during the years 1988–94. Between one and three cases of relinquishment occurred in Moscow maternity hospitals every day during 1991. In 1992, in one Moscow maternity hospital, 113 newborn babies were given up by their mothers. In 1993, the number of abandoned children in this maternity hospital rose to 156, and in 1994 to 214.[32]

The problem of child abandonment was treated in the academic as well as the popular press. Professor I. S. Stepanov, for example, writing in the January 2001 edition of *Questions of Filology* (*Voprosy filologii*), interprets abandonment as the critical issue of family dynamics in post-Soviet Russia. Referring to Ivan Turgenev's seminal 1862 novel of the same time, he deplores the current state of the "fathers and children" problem and speculates that Russia leads the world in child abandonment:

> In Moscow, indeed in all of Russia, there is an incredible number of young women, especially first-time mothers, who abandon their children, who refuse to take their newborns home from the maternity hospital. She gives birth and she abandons: "The government will take care of it!" In this area, Russia occupies one of the top places, if not the absolute first place in the world. (According to mere estimates, there are currently over one million abandoned children of all ages.) There you have the beginning of the "fathers and children" problem.

Stepanov wonders if the abandoning mother is the main type who exists in contemporary Russia, contrasting her with her antipode: the emblematic noble mother of the 1990s, the soldiers' mother.[33] He thus interprets the mother who turns away from her children as the symbol and the distillation of all that ails the contemporary Russian family.

Writing in the May 18, 1999, Moscow edition of *Workers' Tribune* (*Rabochaia tribuna*), journalist Sergei Rykov focuses not on abandoning mothers but on murdering ones. Describing his shock at reading the last month's police chronicle and finding so many accounts of infanticide, he reads off a laundry list of the most chilling offenses, hoping to scare readers into a heightened awareness of the children living around them. Rykov also rejects the often-made connection between infanticide and economic hardship: "Poverty, a sense of impending doom, and chronic hunger are more and more frequently given as the reasons for why killer-mothers [*killery-mamashi*] and killer-fathers [*killery-papashi*] murder their own little babies . . . I cannot believe this! During the blockade of Leningrad, children weren't murdered but were given the last bits. Even one's own blood."[34] Rykov's argument implies that, in post-Soviet society, the righteous bonds of maternity that spurred such selflessness during the Siege of Leningrad have worn thin. A desire to indulge in vices has replaced self-sacrifice, and parents now kill not for a "crust of bread but because of unrestrained drunkenness . . . and a parasitic way of life." He suggests that the institution of motherhood (and fatherhood) has become corroded, that the norms of the new society have weakened the previously heroic instincts of Russian parents.[35]

Several Russian commentators from the 1990s attributed grave significance to this perceived disappearance of maternal attachment, describing it in apocalyptic terms. Nina Fokina, in the March 19, 1998, edition of *Labor* (*Trud*), begins by asserting that the abandonment of a child by a mother contains no linguistic roots in the Russian language since "our ancestors could not have predicted that such a word . . . motherlessness [*bezmatershchina*] . . . would become necessary." This word is so awkward, so difficult to pronounce because it refers to a wholly unnatural and grotesque phenomenon. Fatherlessness (*bezotsovshchina*) now pales in comparison, she writes, and not because Russian fathers have en masse rediscovered their sense of paternal responsibility. Citing an increase of 43 percent in children's homes in Russia during the prior two years, Fokina suggests that, if motherly emotions begin to recede in significance within a woman's psyche, then Russian society may be on the brink of collapse: "While the maternal instinct was stronger than all other instincts, all passions and temptations . . . the world, one could say, held together. And now—it's collapsing? Judging by the speed that Russia is acquiring more orphanages, it appears that way." She also speculates that Russian mothers are devolving away from the ideal maternal qualities of tenderness and warmth: "Scholars divide women, from the point of view of motherhood, into [the categories of] 'hot,' 'warm' and 'completely cold.' There is research asserting that, until the 1960s in Russia, the first type predominated, and that in subsequent generations young mothers are more distant and cold towards their children, that they are less interested in them and in their well-being." Citing unspecified "research," Fokina contends that mothers are becoming increasingly indifferent toward their children. This assertion, if combined with the well-documented Russian demographic crisis, predicts a dark future for the country: fewer and fewer children along with increasingly miserly amounts of maternal love available from the previously nurturing and loving Russian mother.[36]

Another article that portrayed criminal motherhood as heralding the demise of the Russian nation appeared in the Moscow edition of the *Economic Newspaper* (*Ekonomicheskaia gazeta, Moskva*), on November 19, 1996. Citing the example of a mother who had recently murdered her thirteen-day-old baby because she claimed she was unable to feed him, Semen Galyshko poses the following question to his readers: "Aren't you scared to live in a country where mothers save their children from poverty by killing them?" The author argues that a nation capable of producing such mothers lacks a future, with its people doomed to gradual extinction.[37] Hence, the murdering mother foreshadows the eventual disappearance of the Russian people. Both Galyshko and Fokina assert a direct connection between the primacy of maternal emotion and the health of Russian society as a whole. This exaggerated belief in the power and significance of maternity parallels that of the psychologists and others who advocated deploying mothers to liberate the Nord-Ost hostages. Like the elderly women from the rural Starorusskii region (cited at the opening of this study) who believed that the collapse of Russian society was imminent because their local Mother of God icon had turned away from Christ, so urban Russian journalists, scholars, and other professionals attributed grave actual and symbolic significance to the maternal behavior of contemporary Russian women. Mothers can save the world, but if a mother turns away from her children, then all is lost.

"WIVES OF THE REAR"

If, in the popular press, a heated discussion about the nature and significance of Russian motherhood (and its perceived decline) unfolded during the 1990s and early 2000s, how did literature treat this subject? How have Russian writers responded to the changing dynamics of motherhood in the post-Soviet era? How is the tension between the desire to believe in a mother's supposed superhuman abilities to stop wars and stabilize an unpredictable society and the increased level of violence and abandonment that is a reality of this same post-Soviet landscape given fictional treatment? To explore these questions, I will focus first on the late-Soviet film adaptation of a Perestroika-era literary work, noting the transformation of one maternal figure from a "soldiers' mother"-esque beneficence to the cruelty and selfishness characteristic of her antipode. I will then provide close readings of two texts by Liudmila Petrushevskaia, the contemporary Russian author who has most assiduously attacked the mythology of the virtuous Russian mother.

A newspaper article written by the Russian novelist Leonid Bezhin, published in the *Independent Newspaper* (*Nezavisimaia gazeta*) in 1992, provides a useful transition from motherhood in the popular media to motherhood in literature and film.[38] In "The Power of the Mothers," Bezhin analyzes bad motherhood as both a social and a literary phenomenon, connecting historical events (World War II, in particular) with the development of a specific psychological type of masochistic mother, in literature as well as in life. Despite the essentialism of some of his conclusions, Bezhin's observations provide a useful bridge between motherhood in the popular media and motherhood in literature and film. The pattern in familial dynamics that he identifies deftly, and at times provocatively, bridges social reality and its fictional representation.

Bezhin begins by employing two nineteenth-century authors as symbols of contrasting views on Russian motherhood. A young Leo Tolstoy, filled with veneration of the maternal, submits for publication in the journal *The Contemporary* a short novel, "The Little Image of My Angel" ("Obrazok moego angela"). Nikolai Nekrasov, the editor, unable to fathom this lofty sentiment, changes the title of the work to something more terrestrial and plebian. This Nekrasov-like skepticism about motherhood, Bezhin writes, is closer to the spirit of the contemporary era than a Tolstoyan reverence toward it. Just like Nekrasov, late-twentieth-century Russian writers are anxious to pick up a pen and completely blot out the "angelic little image" of the mother.[39]

The genesis of the bad mother, Bezhin claims, is directly linked with the destruction of Russia's spiritual fathers, philosophers such as Nikolai Berdiaev, Sergei Bulgakov, and Pavel Florensky:

> These people—with their ethical way of life and insights into the spiritual depths—could have preserved in the consciousness of society the idea of sacred motherhood, of the Eternal Feminine, of the Divine Sophia. But, having been deprived of any societal influence, they were not allowed to do this, and so the idea did not last. It collapsed along with other similar ideas, and in its place emerged a kind of emptiness, a rarefaction of the spiritual space, a kind of gaping black hole from which sickly, wilted, poisonous flowers stuck out their thorns.

The decline of sacred motherhood is thus linked with the spiritual bankruptcy of the nation as a whole. The bad mother emerges, like a diseased flower, from this spiritual void.

After the Russian Revolution, the cult of motherhood was focused wholly on the mother of Lenin, Bezhin asserts. For him, the exaltation of this woman symbolizes the ruin of holy motherhood: "There you have the Bolshevik interpretation of sacred motherhood and the Eternal Feminine: a mother who raised two brothers—a tsar-murderer and, by all legal norms, a state criminal, the organizer of the violent overthrow of legitimate power." There must be something "devilish," he continues, in a woman who instilled in her sons such a destructive energy, which eventually consumed all of Russia. She became the "concrete earthly embodiment" of "revolution," which, in Russian is, significantly, a feminine noun. Sacred maternity is thus symbolically linked with the devastation and suffering of revolution. Just like the Chechen woman who shot at Russian soldiers alongside her sons and the female terrorists of Nord-Ost, then, Lenin's mother embodied the merging of maternal moral authority and violence.

The perversion of maternal symbolism was eventually followed by the emergence of a specific type of *actual* bad mother, which flourished in real life as well as in literature. Bezhin connects World War II with the breeding of this type, which he terms the "wife of the rear" (*tylovaia zhena*). It is this woman who, he believes, wields the "power of the mother over the spiritual consciousness, over the minds and souls of her unhappy, emaciated, frightened, morally crushed offspring." Left behind (in the "rear") while the men fought at the front, women acquired aggressive qualities that, according to Bezhin, are contrary to their nature. With husbands either physically or emotionally absent, the naive and trusting children of these women became the object of their mothers' masochistic tendencies: "In the consciousness of the children the sheen of sacred motherhood was preserved. This forced them to believe their mother, who instinctively bent them to her tyrannical will in the same way that the government tyrannized its subjects." Mothers, he continues, also maintained an awareness of this "sanctity of motherhood," but their love assumed a pathological form. As a result, the post–World War II Soviet family exhibited the following characteristics: "The mothers gave orders, dominated, were capricious, collapsed in hysterics, while the fathers remained silent and the sons suffered." The correspondence of Bezhin's observations to historical or sociological reality remains a highly debatable question, and one that lies beyond the scope of this study. Certain cultural works from the late-Soviet/post-Soviet period, however, reproduce the maternal psychology that Bezhin outlines to an uncanny degree. The dynamic of the controlling mother, the silent (or absent) father, and the suffering child will reoccur in the works discussed in this chapter.

THE "ANGELIC LITTLE IMAGE" FALLS FROM GRACE

Literature, Bezhin argues, attempted to penetrate this phenomenon of the bad mother, to comprehend and define it. He alludes to two contrasting types of Soviet literature dealing with motherhood, one that "sang its praises and glorified it" and another that "unmasked and mocked it." The first type, then, continued to glorify the myth of sacred motherhood even as the "wife of the rear" dismantled it, while the second exposed the stark reality of post–World War II maternity. An evocative example of this tension between "official" maternal mythology and its desacralization can be found in the 1990 film *Adam's Rib*. This film features a character that exemplifies Bezhin's "wife of the rear," and it was exactly this character that was significantly transformed from the original in the short novel by Anatolii Kurchatkin on which the film is based, *House of Women* (*Babii dom*) (published in the journal *October* in 1986). The film adaptation of Kurchatkin's story pointedly demonstrates the two strains in the representation of Russian/Soviet motherhood that Bezhin identifies: glorification on the one hand, exposure and indictment on the other. The screenplay (by Vladimir Kunin) transformed Kurchatkin's kindly, ailing grandmother from a benevolent force embodying the wisdom of the ages into a destructive and vengeful one who consumes the life force of younger generations.[40] Although screen adaptations inevitably take artistic license with the literary works on which they are based, the film preserved the essence of the other characters from Kurchatkin's novella while substantially rewriting primarily the grandmother. I will first summarize briefly the plot of *House of Women* and then discuss the reimagining of maternity found in the movie version of it, *Adam's Rib*.

The action of the novella unfolds in a cramped Moscow apartment inhabited by three generations of women: Nina Elizarovna, 50 years old; her two daughters (by two different husbands): Lida, 30 years old, and Ania, 18 years old; and her paralyzed mother. The main conflict develops around the personality clashes between Ania, a willful and somewhat wayward teenager, and her mother. Lida, the responsible older sister caught in the middle, attempts to preserve peace in the household while also navigating an affair with a married man. Nina Elizarovna and Lida dutifully empty the grandmother's bedpan and, even though Ania recoils at the distasteful task, the three younger women treat the bedridden grandmother with kindness and consideration: juggling their schedules to never leave her alone, for example.

Nina Elizarovna and her two daughters all have encounters with various men, and the entrances and exits of these men into the *House of Women* punctuate the plot of the story. First, Nina Elizarovna and Evgenii Anatol'evich, whom she meets at the museum where she works, make several ill-fated attempts at romance. The first of these is interrupted by the arrival of a handyman, who also reappears toward the end of the story, drunkenly demanding alcohol in exchange for fixing the sink currently located in the middle of the living room. Eventually Misha, Ania's boyfriend, as well as Lida's married lover and Ania's father also make appearances, but all are merely fleeting visitors. The female dominance of the household remains impenetrable.

The difficulty of navigating daily life in such a household is one of the leitmotifs of the work.[41] The sink that remains in the middle of the living room for months symbolizes this hardship, as Nina Elizarovna laments to Evgenii Anatol'evich: "It's a house of women I have here, you know; there are four of us, and all women. It's probably a trivial job, changing this sink, but if there were men's hands . . ." In fact, men are apparently more indispensable as handymen than as lovers, as Nina Elizarovna's reaction to the departure of Evgenii Anatol'evich reveals: rather than regretting the failure of their short-lived romance, she rejoices at his promise to obtain the elusive missing part for their broken sink.[42]

But, despite these daily hardships and vulnerabilities, as the violent entrance of the drunken handyman underscores, as well as the inevitable clashes between the various generations, the story paints a positive picture of female resilience and strength. After Ania experiences a brush with the law and the cruel treatment of a boyfriend, she and her mother reach a tentative truce. The wisdom and humor of the older women will help Ania forge her path in life, cushioning her from the aftermath of her inevitable mistakes. Lida's affair with the married man ends poignantly, and thus the four women now all remain without male support or companionship. But, supported by the bond between the female generations, the family can endure.

The story ends with a final dramatic and unexpected twist: the paralyzed grandmother regains the ability to walk and speak. The younger women greet this event with the expected jubilation, and it becomes clear that the grandmother embodies the maternal and elderly wisdom that supplies the family with spiritual sustenance. Fulfilling a traditionally self-sacrificial maternal role, she humbly demands no special attention to mark the occasion of her sudden resurrection, worrying only that the younger women must wake up early in the morning. She impatiently awaits the arrival of the next day so that she can begin to ease the lot of her daughter and granddaughters, thinking only of how fate has granted her an opportunity to once again serve others.[43] Although she cannot shoulder the burden of the entire household, as it becomes clear she did earlier, the grandmother will once again assume the role of the nurturing and self-abnegating maternal figure without which an all-female household cannot survive.

Kurchatkin's story, a paean to the everyday heroism and strength of Russian womanhood/motherhood, exhibits what Bezhin termed the "Tolstoyan" approach to maternity: admiring and quietly reverential. The film adaptation of *House of Women,* by contrast, adopts the "Nekrasov" stance. The "angelic little image" of the novella, the grandmother, is pulled from her lofty position as moral guardian of her family. Instead, in the film, she casts a dark shadow over the household, vengefully disrupting romantic encounters with an imperious ring of her bell. Rather than sustaining and sacrificing for the younger generations of women, the grandmother, as a lengthy monologue by Nina Elizarovna details, has selfishly interfered in her daughter's life repeatedly. The grandmother (played by Elena Bogdanova) no longer nurtures the spiritual core of the family, and the screenwriter treats her miraculous recovery at the film's end as a cataclysmic rather than a joyous event.

Adam's Rib opens with imagery that debunks the virtuous biography with which Kurchatkin had endowed the grandmother. In *House of Women,* Nina Elizarovna describes the difficulties her mother endured as the wife of a much older military husband: "Father had three kids from his previous wife, she had to raise them all, and then I came along. And moving from one garrison to the next. No university, no other private life."[44] Nina Elizarovna paints a picture of her mother as a traditionally long-suffering, self-abnegating Russian wife and mother. By the first minutes of the movie, however, an entirely different image of this character has taken shape.[45] In a grainy flashback, a young woman has a romantic encounter with a man in a sailor's uniform. This man is not her husband, the viewer quickly realizes. The flashback ends with a close-up of the paralyzed, bedridden grandmother's aged face. The memories, it becomes clear, belong to her. The photo of her husband, who holds a bell, hangs on the wall of the Moscow apartment. This opening sequence is already incompatible with the nobility that Kurchatkin had established for the grandmother. The adulterous grandmother of the movie is irreconcilable with the one from the novella, who had repeatedly flashed her "happy beatific smile."[46]

The prominence of World War II imagery in these opening frames alludes to the grandmother as possibly one of Bezhin's "wives of the rear." Her attachment to the symbols and memories of the war period betrays the centrality of World War II in the formation of her psyche. The viewer may assume that her husband died in the war, since no pictures of him from a later period hang in the apartment. According to Bezhin's schema, the maternal figure of this all-female family, which lacks a father figure and with a mother whose psychology was shaped by the war, will dominate and manipulate her children. The bell that the grandmother rings at the end of her reverie provides the first symbolic indication that the family in *Adam's Rib* fits this pattern.[47]

Having lost the power of speech, the grandmother of the film insistently rings this bell when she needs her bedpan changed or some other need met. The bell links her with her deceased husband, who also holds one in a picture that hangs next to the grandmother's own. This parallelism establishes the bell as an emblem of masculine power, and the grandmother as the one who wields this power. Her bony hands, clutching the rope and trembling with impatience as she waits for her daughter to feed her, are juxtaposed with the vitality of the younger generations. For example, in a scene where Lida (Svetlana Riabova) and Nina Elizarovna (Inna Churikova) both model a bikini Lida has bought for a proposed vacation with her married lover, the camera cuts away briefly to the grandmother preparing to ring the bell. The impulse recedes, however, and her hands limply drop from the rope. The sexual energy and vigor that mother and daughter exude overpower the decrepitude of envious old age. The defeat is temporary, however; in the scene where Nina Elizarovna entertains a visit from Evgenii Anatol'evich (Andrei Tolubeev), the grandmother and her bell exact a cruel revenge.

The screenwriter remained essentially faithful to Kurchatkin's story in his version of the first encounter between Nina Elizarovna and her suitor from the museum. In both the movie and the story, the pair is interrupted

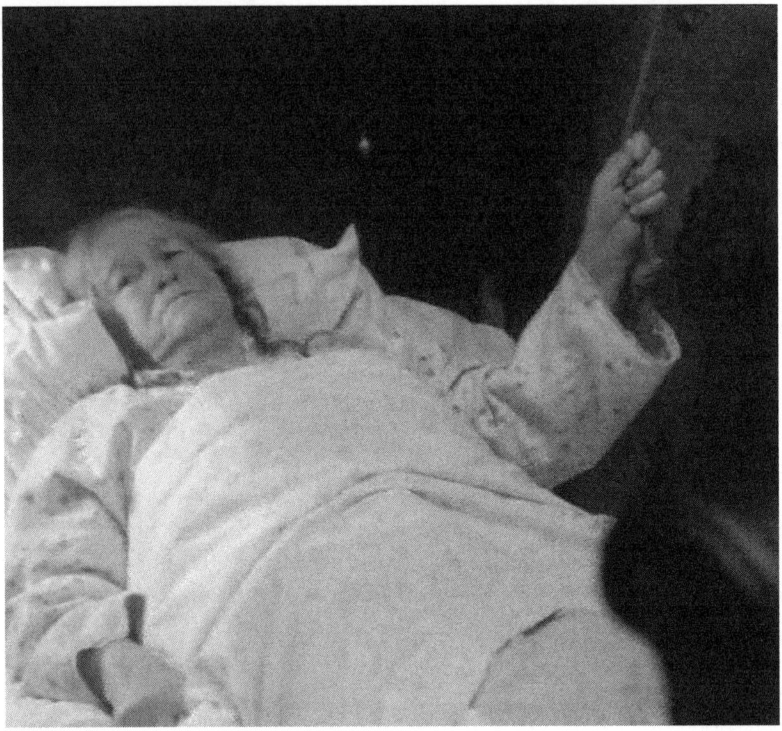

The Grandmother (Elena Bogdanova) in V. Krishtofovich's *Adam's Rib*

before they can consummate their passion. In *House of Women,* the mundane inconveniences of daily life (*byt*) in a house without men cause the disruptions. For example, the doorbell heralding the arrival of the handyman destroys one romantic mood, while the out-of-place sink ruins another. After tripping and falling over the sink, Nina Elizarovna cannot sustain the mood of romance and fantasy.[48]

In the film, however, the grandmother assumes the role that *byt* had played in the story, becoming the silent, malevolent force symbolized by the sink in *House of Women.* Nina Elizarovna leaps out of bed and answers the call of the bell, which her mother had purposefully chosen to ring at the most inopportune moment. She asks her mother in a pitifully despairing voice: "What do you need? I'm asking you, what do you need?" The grandmother's face expresses a spiteful resolve. With the atmosphere no longer conducive to seduction, Nina Elizarovna escorts her would-be suitor out and then returns to confront her mother. During her lengthy monologue, which provides significant insight into mother-daughter dynamics in the film and so

Nastia (Maria Golubkina), Nina Elizarovna (Inna Churikova), and Lida (Svetlana Riabova) in V. Krishtofovich's *Adam's Rib*

merits quoting at length, Nina Elizarovna accuses her mother of a series of manipulative, petty actions. She blames her for chasing away both of Nina Elizarovna's husbands, thus causing the family's difficult material situation as well:

> Okay, let's have it calmly now, what did you need from me? Explain to me: why did you call me? I fed you an hour ago. I changed your sheets. Your bedpan is clean. You yourself are . . . completely dry . . . What else did you need from me? . . . You lived your whole life exactly how you wanted to. And you forced me to live how you needed me to. You're the one who split me and Viktor up. You didn't want to register him in the apartment. You made him my visiting husband, do you remember? . . . Maybe I still could have made a human being out of him! But no, you didn't need a student for a son-in-law . . . And now he has everything while you and I are eating scraps . . . You ruined my whole life! Remember Sasha, Alexander Naumovich? You

> made his life a living hell, and just because he's Naumovich and his last name is Gold'berg! It was you who deprived Nastia of a father. And he loves me to this day . . . And worships Nastia . . . In half a year I'll be fifty, and for once a normal, nice man shows up . . . He wanted to take you to the sea, to seat you in the garden and let you smell the flowers, but you . . . Oh Lord, when will this end?[49]

This monologue portrays the grandmother as the true locus of power in the family, repeatedly bending her daughter to her own will. Refusing to relinquish the central role in the family to either of Nina Elizarovna's two husbands, she preserved the traditionally masculine position for herself.[50]

Certain events from Kurchatkin's text are exaggerated or altered completely for dramatic effect in *Adam's Rib.* Notably, Nastia (played by Maria Golubkina), the younger daughter (as Ania is called in the movie), becomes pregnant at age fifteen rather than merely having a brush with the law at age eighteen. Her announcement incites the movie's other climactic scene: a heated, drunken exchange between all of the characters, including Nina Elizarovna's two former husbands. The grandmother rings her bell so violently, in a vain attempt to be heard above the din of the arguing, that it breaks and hits her on the head. This leads to her "resurrection," but the screenwriter's depiction of this event differs significantly from its unequivocally positive representation in the novella.

The grandmother's miraculous recovery occurs, in fact, at the exact moment when her daughter and granddaughters had been tacitly anticipating her death. When discussing the placement of the crib for the new baby, they realize that the grandmother's bedpan will inevitably need to be carried near the infant. Old age will contaminate the air of the new generation. This prompts Nastia to remark: "But this won't go on forever, it has to end sometime." Immediately after this the three are startled by the sound of the grandmother's singing in the next room. Nina Elizarovna and her daughters greet this unexpected turn of events with horror; the camera pans across their faces, each of which expresses shock and a stony disdain. Images of the grandmother frame the movie, and the final shot lingers on her fragile figure clutching the side of the table while her daughter and granddaughters look on with dread.

In her discussion of *Adam's Rib,* Helena Goscilo has noted the symbolic connection between the grandmother and Nastia's unborn baby.[51] The grandmother's resurrection could, in fact, be interpreted as her sub- or semiconscious reaction to the loss of her role as the de facto "infant" of the family, that is, the one who requires the most attention and care. With the expected arrival of an *actual* infant, this position is threatened. But, regaining her ability to walk and speak, the grandmother can once again assume a different position of power, the masculine one that she held before her illness. She adopts an unnatural role by reclaiming her right to live, and thus taking up precious familial space that rightfully belongs to the newest, unborn generation.[52] Whereas the story celebrated the grandmother's regaining of her ability to speak—and thus to impart elderly wisdom to the younger women—the movie's closing image is of her singing an incomprehensible song in a childlike manner. While paralyzed, the grandmother remained entirely silent except for the tyrannical ringing of her bell, manipulating her daughter and granddaughters with gestures rather than words. Now, restored to some semblance of health, she will presumably employ all of her faculties for the same task. The screenwriter portrays the grandmother's recovery as devastating for Nina Elizarovna and her daughters, a fact betrayed by their stunned expressions. *Adam's Rib* ends on this somber note rather than the celebration of life and Russian womanhood that marks the finale of *House of Women.*[53] In 1986, Kurchatkin's grandmother fulfilled Ramikh's exhortations and rendered absurd the later apocalyptic forebodings of Fokina and Galyshko; by 1990, on the eve of the Soviet Union's collapse, the grandmother's cinematic incarnation no longer offered such solace or reassurance.

MATERNITY ACCORDING TO LIUDMILA PETRUSHEVSKAIA

The screen adaptation of Kurchatkin's story, then, features the transformation of a benevolent, life-affirming maternal figure into a threatening, parasitic one. As mentioned earlier, despite this, *Adam's Rib* is not completely devoid of positive maternal imagery. The grandmother exists alongside Nina Elizarovna, who bravely and selflessly navigates the complicated terrain of everyday life on the brink of the collapse of the Soviet Union. To return to Bezhin's terms, both the Tolstoy and the Nekrasov approaches to motherhood are included in one work of art.

The oeuvre of Liudmila Petrushevskaia, by contrast, presents an overwhelmingly negative and unforgiving image of the Russian mother. In her stories and plays from the post-Soviet period and earlier, Petrushevskaia catalogs the exhaustive array of indignities, manipulations, and machinations to which mothers may subject their children. Bezhin argues that her oeuvre provides an "amazing example of penetration into the pathology of Soviet motherhood."[54] To cite but a few exemplary works: "Father and Mother" ("Otets i mat'") features a hysterical, paranoid, megalomaniacal mother obsessed with her husband's supposed infidelities. In her irrational, indignant fervor, she accuses him of raping their daughters, thus finally driving him away. Her eldest daughter, Tania, the story's heroine, develops a capacity for tolerating the most wretched existence as a direct result of her mother's behavior and a desire to escape this intolerable domestic life. In "Child" ("Ditia"), a woman hides her pregnancy and later attempts to murder her newborn baby. In "Medea," a cab driver describes for a passenger how his wife murdered their daughter. Emotional and, frequently, physical violence by mothers against their children blots the landscape of everyday life in Petrushevskaia's works, assuming an almost banal predictability.[55]

In a survey of the socio-economic situation of Russian women in the aftermath of the breakup of the Soviet Union, Russian sociologist L. V. Babaeva stresses the centrality of maternal figures to the moral health of society. She argues that mothers and grandmothers are primarily responsible for the spiritual development of a child, and that only the unconditional love that they provide can ensure the transmission of morality to new generations of Russians.[56] The grandmother in Kurchatkin's *House of Women,* repository of elderly wisdom, fulfilled this obligation perfectly. Petrushevskaia's mothers and grandmothers, however, invariably fail to bequeath a positive legacy to their children. In Petrushevskaia's works, the "thin thread" of motherly love, upon which, according to Babaeva, the ethical foundation of Russian society depends, is frayed or completely severed.[57] As in Saltykov-Shchedrin's *The Golovlev Family,* the possibility of a positive maternal inheritance—either emotional or moral—appears wholly improbable.

Both Russian and Western critics frequently focus on Petrushevskaia's representation of maternity. T. Markova describes the development of what she terms "the existential drama of maternal love" in Petrushevskaia's works, where "the mother surrounds the child . . . [with] the suffocating embraces of her loving hands." Markova views Petrushevskaia's mother as inevitably abandoned by her children, the eventual victim of her own all-consuming love that cannot be reciprocated. The father in a Petrushevskaia family invariably flees from this domestic dead end. The option of escape is denied the mother, however, dooming her to play out her role in this "existential drama" that leaves her as damaged as her children. But, Markova notes, the mother in Petrushevskaia's works frequently relishes the role of victimizer as well. A surplus of supposedly benevolent maternal love deforms the adulthood of the objects of this smothering attention, rendering Petrushevskaia's mother a "mother-destroyer" who pulls maternity from its traditionally lofty heights in Russian culture.[58]

Among the foundational elements of Soviet fiction that Petrushevskaia debunks and debases in her work, Josephine Woll identifies the "sanctification of motherhood" and the notion that women derive their greatest sense of self-fulfillment from maternity as first and foremost among the targets of Petrushevskaia's satire.[59] The author's reimagining of maternity most pointedly displays her iconoclasm. Woll describes the process by which Petrushevskaia's mothers damage their children in terms similar to those later employed by Markova: "[Children in Petrushevskaia's works] genuinely benefit from maternal devotion, though they pay a price too. Carry such protective nurturing too far, however, smother children stretching toward maturity with such love, blanket grown men with its toxic honey, and what results are the emotional cripples of adulthood who populate Petrushevskaia's work." Petrushevskaia's mothers display a manic desire to be needed, projecting perpetual childhood onto adult offspring in order to ensure their own role as protector.[60] Thus, these mothers create a contradictory dynamic whereby they sacrifice, seemingly for the sake of their children, but in actuality to fulfill their own needs. The central maternal figure of *The Time: Night,* discussed below, succinctly exemplifies this contradiction.

Helena Goscilo has written extensively both about Petrushevskaia in general and on the significance of motherhood in her work in particular.[61] She argues that Petrushevskaia's original literary contribution consists "less in [the] representation of gender than in [the] refurbishment of the maternal trope—now an inimical and destructive force."[62] Goscilo views the mother/child dynamic as one of continuous repetition, where mothers and children take turns both meting out and suffering punishment. She also reads a political metaphor in the propensity of Petrushevskaia's mothers to squelch their offspring's narrative voices, whereby "the totalitarian Petrushevskaian mother mirrors the totalitarian Soviet state."[63] She extends this symbolic connection between motherhood and the state to include the film *Adam's Rib,* arguing that each can be read as a "narrative of national history." The characters in both the film and the novella are doomed to duplicate the life paths of the previous generations. Family history, like the history of Soviet Russia, is decidedly un-teleological, with the state serving not as "the optimistic nurturer, but the bad or incapacitated mother, giving birth but also blighting one's life."[64]

My discussion of the bad mother in Petrushevskaia's works draws upon these critical observations. I focus specifically, however, on her connection with the post-Soviet dynamic of maternity and violence, as identified above. A close reading of *The Time: Night* also considers the continuities between failed motherhood in Petrushevskaia's prose and the nineteenth-century works discussed in chapter 1. As it did for Arina Petrovna in *The Golovlev Family,* the manipulation of maternal self-sacrifice occupies a dominant role in the consciousness of Anna Andrianovna, the main character of *The Time: Night.* How has the legacy of sacred motherhood evolved (or remained constant) from canonical nineteenth-century prose to post-Soviet fiction? How does an awareness of maternal mythology shape the mentality of Petrushevskaia's mothers? And what effect does this awareness have on their relationship with their children?

MATERNITY AND VIOLENCE II: PETRUSHEVSKAIA'S "OUR CIRCLE"

Although "Our Circle" ("Svoi krug") was written in 1979 and first published in the late-Soviet period, in 1989, its maternal imagery resembles that which developed in the popular media of the 1990s discussed above. A mother's "clean hands" now held weapons, aiming both at Russian soldiers and at innocent hostages, but for a purportedly noble cause: the protection of her children. The mother and narrator of "Our Circle" subverts maternal moral authority even further by turning her violent impulses toward her own child. In the story's climactic moment, she delivers multiple blows to her defenseless young son in full view of the "circle" of friends to which the title alludes. The principal tension in the story develops around the interpretation of this violence: can the supposed nobility of the mother's motivation—ensuring that her son will be taken care of after her death—be reconciled with the destructive result? Do the ends justify the means? Was this an act propelled by maternal self-sacrifice or self-interest?[65]

Within the "circle," or crowd, of intellectuals to which the story's narrator belongs, children apparently constitute a crucial component of life. One member of the group is eventually alienated from the others, not least, the narrator hints, because of her inability to give birth to a living child. When a previously childless couple unexpectedly has a baby, the members of the crowd rejoice. The narrator also describes the complete devotion of a father to his exceptional daughter:

> Serge would tenderly put Sonya to bed and only afterwards set off to his other woman, and in the morning in any case Sonya woke up only just in time for school, when Serge was already on his way to work; and after work, from six until nine, Serge would be on duty again with his daughter, they'd work on her music and make up stories together.[66]

Deftly balancing his extramarital relationship with the duties of fatherhood, Serge maintains a familiar domestic routine for his daughter's benefit. This character seemingly provides a rare example of devoted and selfless fatherhood in Petrushevskaia's works. Children, then, are ostensibly necessary for entrée into the narrator's crowd, the members of which devote themselves fully to their well-being.

However, certain indicators that children are not as selflessly nurtured and cherished as it initially appears reoccur throughout the story. The narrator's first mention of her son and the reader's first introduction to him, for example, is only in flippant reference to the enviable skin of another member of the crowd.[67] And the narrator eventually exposes the relationship between

Serge and his daughter as an all-consuming, smothering, and potentially unnatural one:

> Serge, who was, on the whole, an unromantic character . . . [would] end up living with the only being he genuinely loved, with Sonya, his daughter, and his crazed love for her would lead him round every corner and down every back street and into all the dark cellars of life until he finally acknowledged it fully and abandoned all other women and lived for her sake alone, the girl whom he'd fathered from his loins. (347)

The narrator's prediction that Serge will eventually replace all other women with his daughter—along with his need to "know her fully"—hints at an inappropriate, unacknowledged sexuality in their relationship. Despite the subjectivity of the narrator's judgment of her crowd, this possibility nonetheless introduces doubt about the earlier descriptions of his seemingly selfless devotion.[68]

While valorizing the importance of children, the narrator in fact reveals their subordination to the crowd's more selfish desires. She proclaims the significance of children in the following paragraph:

> There's something absurd about not having children around, and among us it just wasn't done; the whole effect consisted in having children and messing about with puddings and mash and kindergartens, and then on Friday nights feeling human again and going on a bender full throttle, to the point where the police were sometimes even called in. (319)

Children are mere pretense and accoutrement, a justification for the weekly debauchery the crowd has engaged in for the past ten years. The narrator reveals why the absence of children precludes membership in the group: without the mundane activities of daily life *(byt)* that the raising of children dictate, the circle could not guiltlessly surrender to its established routine of drunkenness and psychosexual drama. As the historical events that unfolded during this period fail to penetrate the crowd's insularity and self-obsession, so children also remain peripheral to the group's true fixation: games of manipulation and musical beds.

The narrator's use of the word "effect" in the section quoted above is significant. To behave with an awareness of "effect" implies a potential disjuncture between a person's genuine motivations and his or her actions. Authenticity becomes impossible to identify conclusively. The narrator's statement that "there's something absurd about not having children around" (*bez detei ne priniato bylo zhit'*) reinforces the notion of a performance for the benefit of an outside observer, of an imaginary interlocutor who deems a life without children untenable. This word choice also echoes the narration of *Anna Karenina,* where Anna's consciousness of the "role of the mother living for her child" is relayed in indirect discourse, similarly introducing doubt about the sincerity of maternal emotion.[69]

The narrator's violence toward her son also betrays an acute and calculated awareness of "effect." She carefully orchestrates every detail of this dramatic interlude, designing it to elicit a specific response from its intended audience. She sends her son off on an impossible mission, knowing his failure will lead him to the hallway of the building at exactly the right moment to receive her blows (347–48). And she utilizes the group's reverence for children (in theory if not in practice) to predict their reaction to the chilling sight of her delivering a beating to her sleeping son:

> I jumped out, lifted him up and with a wild cry: "What the hell are you doing here!" and slapped him in the face, so hard that the child, not yet awake, started bleeding and choking. I started thrashing him all over, whereupon they all fell upon me, twisted me round, thrust me through the door and slammed it shut . . . My calculations had been correct. One and all of them were unable to bear the sight of a child's blood; they were quite capable of tearing each other to pieces, but children were the holy of holies for them. (345–46)

With her performance deemed a success, the narrator can ostensibly rest assured about the fate of her son after her imminent illness and death. Playing on their sympathies, she assumes they will now favor the best interests of Alesha, and that she has somehow shattered the group's solipsism: "And thus the scene of child abuse I'd staged, at such minimal cost, would provide the necessary first jolt to set in motion a new, long-lasting, romantic tradition in the life of my orphaned Alyosha, with his new, noble-spirited adoptive parents, who'd forget their own interests and instead protect his" (348). However, given the group's past history of self-involvement, this is a highly problematic assumption.

Hence, the mother's beating of her son constitutes the central interpretive question of the work. Was this violence motivated by sincere maternal concern? If so, does the end justify the means, especially given the unreliability of the members of her group as potential caretakers? The narrator's earlier statements and attitude toward her son cast some doubt on the purity of her emotions. For example, upon witnessing her husband hit Alesha after he wets the bed, she coldly leaves him to his fate: "I just smiled ironically, left the room and set off to work, leaving them to sort out the mess between them" (338). This incident provides evidence of maternal indifference to violence. So was the beating merely a sadistic display, one intended as yet another move in the endless psychological game that the narrator and her crowd have engaged in for over a decade?

On the other hand, the story's closing paragraph poignantly describes how the narrator imagines her son will visit her grave after her death:

> Alyosha, I think, will come and visit me on Easter Sundays, mentally I made that pact with him, pointing out the way there and the day; I believe he'll guess, he's a very bright boy, and there, among the painted eggs and the plastic wreaths and the disheveled, drunk and kindly crowd, he'll forgive me the fact that I didn't allow him to say goodbye, but gave him a slap in the face instead of a blessing. But it's better that way—for everyone. (348)

How, then, to reconcile this apparently genuine expression of maternal anguish with the selfishness, questionable logic, and violence that preceded it?

Critical interpretations of the mother's violence have varied. Perhaps unwittingly reproducing the mythology of the benevolent Russian mother, some have attributed nobility to the narrator's actions. M. N. Lipovetskii views the mother, and not her son, as the story's true victim, and sees her actions as springing from "a mother's pain."[70] I. Sergo analyzes the mother's violence (in both "Our Circle" and "Child") through the prism of Christian myth. She interprets the narrator's abandonment of Alesha as a symbolic offering that will "awaken compassion in the world and once again teach it to distinguish good from evil."[71] Sally Dalton-Brown also views the mother sympathetically, calling it a "harsh tale of magnificent sacrifice" and interpreting the violent act as a superficial distraction that masks the mother's true, self-abnegating nature.[72] Woll interprets the mother's actions in a more critical light, emphasizing the theatricality of the story's well-scripted climax—with the narrator playing the part of "villain" while her friends assume the role of "saviors"—and describing the scene as "a combination of farce and tragedy, worthy of a Karamazov or a Marmeladov."[73] Inna Tigountsova also wonders if, "given the *bezobrazie* [ugliness] of this circle . . . the narrator's plan is ultimately in her son's best interests, or is actually a part of a vicious vendetta."[74] And Goscilo draws a parallel between the narrator's degenerative disease, which will eventually lead to blindness, and her decision to use violence, which she deems a "failure of perception."[75] The narrator's faulty vision, both literal and figurative, thus supports a mistaken belief in her immunity to the moral repercussions of violence.

As these varying critical responses demonstrate, the tension and anxiety of interpretation caused by the narrator's violence against her son elude resolution. It remains impossible to identify authenticity in her behavior, to distinguish the genuine from that intended solely for a theatrical "effect." No clear, singular representation of maternity emerges from this work; instead,

"Our Circle" presents the mother as a destabilizing force. The story suggests, however, that the fragmentations of the maternal self in late-Soviet society now incorporate violence. The rhetoric of maternity of the post-Soviet period—as evinced by the focus on the motherhood of the female hostage-takers involved in the Moscow theater crisis, for example—also merged violence with a questionable nobility. Petrushevskaia's story is prescient in its identification and elucidation of this dynamic.

In the novella *The Time: Night* (1992), one of her best-known and most critically acclaimed works, Petrushevskaia provides an even more probing and detailed exploration of the instability of the maternal psyche. The "found manuscript" device that begins the work prefigures the complex interplay of maternal and filial voices that will characterize the novella as a whole. In a short epigraph, a (presumed) editor or publisher recounts receiving an unsolicited phone call from a woman whose mother, a poet, has died and left behind various manuscripts. Entitled "Notes from the Edge of the Table," it is these writings that, the reader assumes, comprise the text of *The Time: Night.* Thus commences the jagged, posthumous first-person narrative of Anna Andrianovna, mother of Alena—an emotionally fragile, divorced mother of three young children by various fathers, the oldest of whom she has left in Anna's care—and Andrei, a suicidal ex-convict who periodically robs her. During the course of the text, the reader learns about Alena's first sexual encounter, which leads to pregnancy and an unhappy marriage, followed by an exploitative affair with a married colleague; about Anna's delusions of literary grandeur and her desperate, cloying love for her grandson, Tima; and, most prominently, we learn in excruciating detail about the toxic, combative, and destructive nature of mother-child relations in Anna's cramped, fatherless household. If the epigraph hints at Alena's wish to preserve somehow her now-dead mother's words and thoughts, the tale that unfolds throughout the novella offers no such glimmers of optimism. As in "Our Circle," in *The Time: Night* the authenticity of the central maternal figure's motivations remains impossible to determine conclusively. The line between self-interest, self-dramatization, and self-sacrifice becomes blurred in Anna's exaggerated, acute consciousness of her own righteousness. She carefully crafts a chronicle of heroic motherhood, one that must compete with that of her wayward daughter's and emerge victorious in their war of words—a war waged not only during their heated arguments but also on the page, as Anna interjects her own caustic commentary into her daughter's diary. The self-identified nobility of her actions provides Anna with the proof of her maternal superiority, in return for which she futilely demands total obeisance from her offspring.[76] By the time Anna, abandoned by her children and grandchildren, incoherently ends her solitary narrative, the myth of the beneficent Russian mother has been thoroughly and unequivocally debased.

A MATERNAL SUPERHERO

Anna's relationship with her children is fundamentally an antagonistic and contentious one, despite her repeated proclamations of maternal devotion. For example, Anna frequently criticizes Alena's physical appearance, particularly while pregnant: "Alyona was all swollen up, so young, she looked dreadful, great hollows under her eyes, her lips bluish, her hair all lank. I've never let myself go like that, no matter what happened" (36). Whereas her daughter succumbs first to the physical burden of pregnancy and later to the emotional burden of motherhood, Anna firmly delineates her superiority in both realms. Although Alena receives the majority of Anna's critical scrutiny, this competitiveness also sometimes extends to her relations with her son, who is released from prison approximately midway through the work. For example, in the following passage, she contrasts her son's dirtiness with her own impeccable cleanliness: "[He was] all sweaty and dirty, alongside me, always spotlessly clean, twice a day in the shower for a good long session" (73). When comparing herself with her children, Anna emerges as eternally noble, wise, clean, unsullied by life. She imagines herself an oasis of wisdom and purity in which they should seek guidance and protection, much like that provided by the grandmother in Kurchatkin's *House of Women.* And not only her own children but children as a whole must be grateful for her beneficence and vigilance. Like a maternal superhero, she styles herself an intrepid savior of the small and vulnerable. "And I will have saved another child! I spend my whole life saving children!" Anna proclaims after supposedly rescuing a young girl on a tram from what she deems the inappropriate affections of her father (102). This episode becomes absurdly comic, however, when the other riders unite against Anna, much to her indignation and surprise. The incident on the tram illustrates the disjuncture between Anna's grandiose self-perception, which is built primarily on her supposed heroism on behalf of children, and reality, where her effect on these same children is decidedly more ambiguous.

To preserve these illusions of heroism, Anna employs her literary skills to rewrite the relationship with her daughter according to imaginary ideals. For example, one brief phone conversation with Alena quickly disintegrates into hysterics and name-calling and ends with Anna self-righteously hanging up the phone. Almost immediately, she mentally revises their exchange, ascribing to Alena the role of the loving, humble, daughter ("Mummy, help me, hoist just one more burden on your back"; "Mum, forgive me, I'm a fool.

I kiss you") and to herself that of the infinitely patient, comforting mother ("No, my darling, you must be strong. Look at me, I force myself to be strong, I just keep going because I'm your mother") (99–100). By privileging her own version of Alena's speech over her actual words, Anna subverts her daughter's power to craft and retell her own story, thereby attaining narrative superiority.[77] In this imaginary conversation, the maternal figure blots out all other models and human relationships in her daughter's life. Anna presents herself as the ultimate and sole example of sacrifice, constancy, and patience for her daughter to emulate.

PLANES OF BATTLE I: FOOD

One of the ways that Anna establishes her moral rectitude is through a ceremonious rejection of food. This righteousness contrasts with the selfishness of other family members, her son-in-law in particular. In the opening scene of the work, for example, she provides a detailed description of how she acts while a guest in someone's home:

> Of course I behave like the Queen of England, say no thanks to everything, won't touch a thing—not even the sugar and crackers to go with my tea. I'll only drink their tea with the bread I've brought, keep tearing off little mouthfuls to stay the pangs, it's unbearable to sit starving at someone else's table! . . . But the only thing I care about is feeding Tima, so no thanks, spread a bit more on for Tima—Tima darling would you like a bit more?[78]

This early scene establishes the symbolic value of food in constructing Anna's maternal identity. She forgoes food on behalf of her grandson, Tima, but with a consciousness of how this sacrifice appears to an outside observer.[79] Carrying with her a supply of her own bread seems like a calculated gesture, one designed to evoke sympathy for her as well as for Tima. Later in the same scene she passes up meat, again in favor of Tima, but a melodramatic, histrionic display of emotion immediately follows this supposedly self-abnegating action (8). Her tears call attention to the act of self-denial, infusing the incident with a consciously dramatic element. Like the narrator of "Our Circle," Anna exhibits an awareness of the "effect" created by her actions, particularly her exaggerated self-deprivation.

As food occupied a pivotal role in the struggles between Arina Petrovna and her son Porfiry in *The Golovlev Family,* so Anna also employs food as a weapon in the subtle manipulation of her daughter, Alena. For example, she frequently criticizes what she perceives as the gluttonous behavior of Alena's then husband, calling him a "parasite," among other insults. To stress the contrast between his selfishness and her nobility, she self-righteously offers her portion of food to her daughter (37). Alena immediately senses the manipulative subtext of this statement, as her reaction to her mother's statement—tears and a declaration of hatred—reveals.

Anna boasts of an almost superhuman ability to survive on little more than cups of tea. In illustration of this, while her son serves a prison sentence, she keeps a meager diet in supposed solidarity with him: "waiting for my one and only beloved son to come back, scrimping and saving on everything, was reduced to boiling up water in a saucepan, just plain water; bread and tea was all I had for breakfast lunch and dinner, prisoners' fare. Since that was all he had, that was all I'd have too" (39). This sparse diet contrasts with that of Alena and her husband, who entertain a series of guests with potatoes, butter, and sausage. Anna's voluntary deprivation emphasizes her virtue and, consequently, her superiority to the other members of her family. The sacrifice of food is enlisted as a tactic in the familial struggle for supremacy, and Anna always emerges victorious. Later in the work, she summarizes the centrality of food in the family's recurring battles: "Every member of our family's been a bit twisted as far as food's concerned—it's poverty that does it of course; there were always endless claims and calculations, with Mother openly accusing my husband of 'gobbling up all the children's food' and so on. But I never went in for all that" (119). Anna supposedly distinguishes herself from the primitive nature of the family dynamic, from the "masses" (i.e., the other members of the family) by not succumbing to this obsession with food, mutual recrimination, and guilt. (Her earlier comments about her son-in-law, of course, render this pronouncement highly questionable.) If the battles over food symbolize the family's animalistic nature, then Anna's ability to forgo it, in favor of Timochka or in solidarity with her imprisoned son, confirms a mother's superhuman capacity for self-abnegation. Her relationship with food thus supports Anna Andrianovna's narrative of traditional maternal self-sacrifice.

PLANES OF BATTLE II: NARRATIVE

This narrative exists in direct competition with the one her daughter attempts to craft in her diary, which Anna contradicts, debunks, and ironizes. Anna discovers Alena's diary hidden under a box on top of a bookcase while dusting, and she suffers no pangs of conscience about immediately reading it as well as passing judgment on its content (17). The first diary entry details Alena's sexual encounter with the married man who fathered her second child, as well as reminiscences of her first husband. Anna inserts her own parenthetical, sarcastic comments throughout this text, thus forcing the reader to discover Alena's most intimate thoughts only through her mother's mediation. For example, when a despairing Alena writes of her desire to throw herself under a train, à la Anna Karenina, Anna wryly comments: "A lovely man she'd found to do it for" (18). When Alena calls herself a "fool," Anna exclaims "precisely" (19). To avoid any possible ambiguity, Anna claims authorial credit by inserting her initials, A. A., after each caustic remark.

Throughout the diary, Anna also disputes her daughter's retelling of events and provides her own, alternative versions. She repeatedly paints herself in a more sympathetic light, while at the same time casting doubt on Alena's reliability as a narrator. Later in the diary, Anna proposes a counter-narrative to the one Alena unfolds. As Alena discusses the details of her affairs, her mother interjects into the text a description of Timochka's illness on the night Alena stays with her married lover. "All this is nonsense," Anna declares before enumerating the hardships she faced handling a sick child alone (21). She thus challenges not only her daughter's ability to recount events truthfully, but also her knowledge of what narratives merit development. The tawdry details of Alena's amorous affairs should remain untold, while Anna's tales of heroic grandmotherly self-sacrifice deserve textual inscription and memorializing. The diary exists, according to Anna, primarily to keep score between her and her daughter. Future readers, including her grandchildren, should refer to it as a record of her daughter's improprieties, which, in turn, underscore her own heroism: "Let them find out later who's who, let them learn sometime who their mother is and who I am!" (25).

In Alena's description of her first sexual encounter in this diary, sexual feelings combine with maternal ones: "I loved him and pitied him like my own little son." The boundary between son and lover becomes blurred, and Anna's accusatory commentary berates Alena for squandering her motherly tenderness on a grown man (23).[80] Throughout Anna's portrayal of Alena's failures as a mother, her sexual improprieties and behavior with men assume a central role. Invoking paradigmatic images of bad motherhood from Tolstoy's novel, Anna even casts herself in the role of jilted husband and Alena in that of the unfaithful wife: "It was Anna Karenina all over again, the lost mother reunited with her son—and me of course in the role of Karenin" (13). By comparing Alena with Tolstoy's heroine, she stresses the connection between the negligence of maternal duties and the privileging of romantic attachments. By drawing a parallel between herself and Karenin, Anna further establishes her own virtue and victimhood while also distancing herself from her daughter's presumed selfishness. If Anna Karenina (Alena) symbolizes the eschewing of maternal self-sacrifice, then Anna Andrianovna—raising the abandoned Tima—emerges, by contrast, as a paragon of grandmotherly modesty and heroism.[81] This literary allusion also endows their family drama with a sense of gravity and importance, elevating it from the mundane to the tragic and validating Anna's delusions of grandeur.[82]

Anna continues to emphasize Alena's perceived preference for men over Tima, accusing her, for example, of harming her unborn child by feeding her husband before herself: "The young man's hungry, I quite understand. But you need something as well if you're eating for two" (37). Alena, according to her mother, mistakenly directs her maternal impulses toward her husband rather than the child she carries (using the last three eggs in the house to make an omelet just for him, for example). This decision will lead to Alena's desiccation, to her being unable to perform her sacred maternal duty: "How are you going to feed the baby, what'll you have to feed him on, a dried-up breast? Dried up!" (38). Anna assumes the role of ultimate arbiter on appropriate maternal behavior, which, according to her, entails sacrificing—food in particular—for children rather than for husbands.

However, just as Alena combines the erotic with the maternal in her feelings toward her first lover, so Anna's grandmotherly emotions for Tima also contain sensual elements. She herself describes this love as "carnal": "I love him passionately, physically. The pleasure of holding in my hand his own tiny weightless one, of looking into those round, dark blue eyes with lashes so long . . . All parents, and grandparents especially, love their babies physically like this, make them make up for everything else in life" (58). Anna later describes similar feelings for her daughter as a child: "My beautiful daughter, how I adored her once, a baby in swaddling clothes, whose every finger washed, fondled, kissed a hundred times" (67). She admits the harmful effect that this mixture of sensuality and maternity produces: "It's a sinful love, I tell you, it makes the child callous and unbridled, as if it understands there's something unclean in it all" (58). Anna's children and grandchild, when they are young and preverbal, act as neutral vessels of sensual pleasure. Both she and her daughter conflate maternal and sensual feelings, a similarity between mother and daughter that neither woman recognizes.

Anna also attempts to define herself in opposition to her daughter by claiming superiority in her behavior with men. In her commentary to Alena's diary, she professes to never having succumbed to weakness or sexual obsession, offering the example of her own life as an instructive one for her daughter: "I'm writing this all for her sake too, so that she too should understand who's led what sort of life! Yes! I, for instance, never suffered any pain from a man, never!" (25). Biographical facts, however, discredit this claim. Anna, just like her daughter, also carried on an affair with a married man at work; also had a mother who hated her husband, just as Anna hates Alena's husband; and was also left by her husband to raise her children alone. Nonetheless, Anna remains blind to the similarities with her daughter, between her own reckless behavior with men and Alena's. Because of the verbal divide that separates them, the parallels between the "plots" in the lives of mother and daughter remain unacknowledged. Their mutual battle over words, over the power to narrate, precludes the possibility of Anna and Alena discovering the correspondences between their respective life "texts."

MOTHER VS. MOTHER

Since both she and Alena are mothers, Anna issues the final judgment on each of their maternal identities. A noble figure is established and contrasted with a selfish, weak one. It must be determined which of them successfully achieves the "effect" of motherhood, and this winner made clear and preserved for posterity. Anna's commentary on Alena's diary firmly establishes her supremacy as a mother. Once this hierarchy is documented, Anna's maternal figure subsumes her daughter completely, writing a work of prose in Alena's voice (92). The scene she imagines during this midnight burst of inspiration features, predictably, dueling maternal responses to a crisis with Tima. Alena passively stays in bed, while Anna self-righteously rejects her offers of assistance (93–94). This story erases the need for Alena's individual interpretation of her own life, since Anna—"fully self-critical, completely objective"—has successfully captured its essence (94).

Anna repeatedly points out the impossibility of true communication between mothers and children: "Ah, mothers, mothers! It's the holiest of words, but time goes by and you'll find you have nothing to say to your child, and your child has nothing to say to you. Love them and they'll tear you to pieces, don't love them and they'll leave you just the same. That's how it is" (51). After children grow out of the prelapsarian state where parents and grandparents can derive sensual pleasure from their physical closeness, a verbal barrier that cannot be transcended arises between the generations. A few pages later Anna laments that no new words or ideas can be exchanged between her and her two children, that they are trapped in a cycle of stagnation (54). Anna's feverish poetic endeavors, which her children repeatedly label "manic" (*grafomaniia*), fill this impenetrable silence. By assuming her daughter's voice in her prose and by ironizing her diary entries, Anna solves the problem of this verbal divide by eliminating the interlocutor, transforming futile dialogue into self-aggrandizing monologue.

But Anna, like the narrator of "Our Circle," also, at times, exhibits genuine poignancy in her relations with her grandson. For example, in the following passage she tenderly describes her modest efforts to feed and entertain him: "Tima came in and I smiled at him, as always ('Greet the new day with a smile'), and promised him the bread and butter from yesterday and tea with sweets . . . promised to make him a little house with windows if I could only get hold of some glue" (124). She remains fiercely loyal to him, protecting his interests and attempting to preserve his fragile mental state. She views bringing her schizophrenic mother home to live with them as a potential betrayal of Tima and her obligations toward him, fearing that the smells of old age will contaminate the child's living environment (123).[83]

This grandmotherly devotion contrasts with her lack of empathy for her daughter, whom she calls "poor miserable little female," refusing her entry into the apartment with her two other young children. And this sincerity in her love for Tima is colored by a fetishistic sensuality, and also by its all-consuming nature. When Tima defies his grandmother by opening the door for his mother and siblings, she labels him a traitor:

> A happy family! Tima had saved the day, he'd opened the door, and now he's happy and he's theirs, a member of the family! . . . So that's what all the effort was for—that's why I'd spent sleepless nights, gone hungry, nursed him, taught him—just so that Tima in one second flat would come to hate me and chuck me in . . . Oh my traitor with your silken curls, your silky little legs! (126)

She and her daughter are once again maternal adversaries, vying for the love and attention of Tima, the sole object of Anna's smothering affections. Anna interprets this reunion between mother and son as an abandonment of her, after which life loses all meaning. She bases her narrative of self almost completely on a supposed heroism on Tima's behalf. The distance between subject and object disappears, and Tima loses his discrete identity, becoming a mere stimulus for the unfolding of Anna's maternal chronicle. Alena disrupts this narrative by leaving with her children, including Tima. Anna's final descent into madness accompanies the disappearance of Alena and Tima, and perhaps erupts in anticipation of it. During the novella's final, stream-of-consciousness pages, Anna fixates on the mother's noble, solitary burden: "I'm all they've got have to rescue the lot of them, saved my son's life, yes" (142). She returns to a silent apartment, and Anna's narrative trails off with a mantra-like repetition of the names of her children and grandchildren. Whereas the early Soviet fictional mothers discussed in chapter 2 abandoned their children, *The Time: Night*'s closing image, by contrast, exposes the isolation and mental disintegration of a mother whose children and grandchildren choose instead to abandon her.

Anna Andrianovna, then, like Arina Petrovna in *The Golovlev Family*, remains acutely aware of maternal mythology, particularly the image of the mother sacrificing all on behalf of her children. Both mothers strive to achieve the "effect" of motherhood, redirecting self-sacrifice toward a selfish rather than an altruistic goal. Arina Petrovna's children, Porfiry in particular, learn to exploit their mother's delusions of maternal grandeur to satisfy their own materialistic desires. Nonetheless, the essential structure of the family, now predicated upon self-interest rather than self-sacrifice, remains intact. In *The Time: Night,* by contrast, Anna's children ridicule, try desperately to escape, and eventually abandon her, despite her proclamations of maternal beneficence. Alena, in a sense, mocks the traditional family unit by breeding indiscriminately and without a husband. And Anna's maternal identity, constructed monologically rather than dialogically, resists all manipulation.

In both *The Time: Night* and "Our Circle," the conflicting characteristics of Petrushevskaia's mothers cannot be satisfactorily reconciled. Tenderness and sincerity of emotion combine with violence—either physical or psychological—to create a destabilizing maternal presence. In both works, the boundary between self-sacrifice and self-interest in each mother's actions becomes tenuous and permeable. Both Anna Andrianovna and the narrator of "Our Circle" behave with a heightened awareness of the "effect" that sacred motherhood produces, of the nobility with which mythologized maternity endows them. This awareness renders problematic the distinguishing of pretense from authenticity in their maternal actions.[84]

Petrushevskaia's mothers fail to harmonize the potentially chaotic forces—such as vanity, greed, selfishness, megalomania—that threaten familial stability, rejecting the mediating function that characterizes the iconic Russian mother. This failure, in turn, challenges the notion that motherhood can somehow ameliorate the consequences of the rapid social change that occurred in Russia during the 1990s. Anna Andrianovna and the narrator of "Our Circle," with their stark isolation from any kind of female network, could not be any further from the collective maternal strength harnessed by the Committee of Soldiers' Mothers. Bezhin argues that the spiritual power of the mother, previously so prominent and well developed in Russian culture, is disappearing. The literature and film discussed in this chapter support Bezhin's dire prognostications, as well as those of the other Russian observers who lamented the extinction of the mythologized, self-sacrificial Russian mother. The works of Petrushevskaia—and, to a lesser extent, the film *Adam's Rib*—question the notion of maternity as a redemptive force capable of counteracting the social, political, or economic instability of the post-Soviet period. Instead, these mothers, these "women with a thirst for destruction," to borrow Petrushevskaia's evocative phrase, bequeath to the next generation a questionable psychological, moral, and spiritual legacy.[85]

Conclusion

"THE SPECTER OF ANNA KARENINA always hover[s] over Russian mothers," the literary scholar G. S. Smith has observed.[1] In *The Italian* (*Ital'ianets,* dir. A. Kravchuk), a Russian film released in 2005, the ghost not only of Anna Karenina but also of the other nineteenth-century mother discussed in this study, Arina Petrovna Golovleva, haunts the bleak and frigid provincial landscape. The film takes place in a post-Soviet orphanage, inhabited by the sons and daughters of those numerous Russian mothers who turned away from their children in the years after the collapse of the Soviet Union. When the women of the Starorusskii district observed their local Mother of God spurning Christ, deeming this a signal of the decline of motherhood and Russian society's consequent impending doom, it may have been the mothers of precisely such orphans who provoked their ominous predictions. During the course of the film, however, one of the abandoning mothers decides to turn back *toward* her son and retrieve him from the orphanage. The mother's pleading eyes and hollow face underscore her desperation. The realization that, without her son, she remained utterly alone had inspired her quest for reunion with him. Like Anna Karenina in her last hours, the mother appears overwhelmed by isolation and despair, alienated from all affective ties and links to the outside world. The mother's final action confirms an even more explicit link with the fate of Tolstoy's heroine: after discovering that her son had already been adopted and that she could never see him again, she jumps under a train. The mother's punishment for renouncing maternity, then, is a descent into impenetrable isolation and eventual suicide.

The spirit of Arina Petrovna pervades the film in a less direct but nonetheless palpable way. As the Golovlev matriarch infused familial dynamics with the spirit of capitalism, so the abandoned children of *The Italian* find themselves subject to pricing, buying, and selling. Shepherded by an opportunistic and overbearing woman called "Madame," wealthy western European couples visit the orphanage and select a child to take home with them, in exchange for enough euros to afford "Madame" a fancy car and the orphanage's director a regular supply of alcohol. Like Saltykov-Shchedrin's novel, which took place during a period of economic transformation in nineteenth-century Russia, so *The Italian* reflects the destabilizing effects of post-Soviet Russia's rapid and erratic embrace of capitalism after 1991. The film's young hero, however, six-year-old Vania Solntsev, refuses to surrender himself to the demands of the marketplace, rebuffing an adoption attempt by Italians and instead undertaking an epic journey to locate his biological mother. The steely shrewdness and coldheartedness of "Madame" as she attempts first to coerce and later to capture the innocent Vania testify to the corrosive effects of money on the Russian character. As the sympathetic night watchman of Vania's first orphanage remarks, "When children are exchanged for dollars, it's a sign that the country is dying." Vania's unshakeable faith in his mother is counterpoised to the cynicism and indifference that he encounters along his journey. His mother's name, Vera (which means "faith" in Russian), accentuates the symbolism of Vania's quest. The film ends with a close-up of Vania's joyous face as he basks in the light emitted by his mother, who remains unseen and thus more capable of embodying the abstract maternal qualities of tenderness, mercy, and boundless love. *The Italian* presents the iconic Russian mother, and the unflagging devotion that she inspires even in a child from whom she has turned away, as an antidote to the deleterious effects of capitalism on post-Soviet life.[2]

I have chosen to conclude with this film because it synthesizes several of the motifs of bad motherhood touched upon in earlier chapters of this study. In addition to the intersections with *Anna Karenina* and *The Golovlev Family* already mentioned, *The Italian* also contains variations on the image of the abandoning mother that figured so prominently in the popular fiction of the 1920s. In both the film and the works discussed in chapter 2, a mother's decision to abandon her child contains profound significance not only for her personal fate, but for that of the (Soviet or post-Soviet) nation as a whole. In the fiction of the 1920s that I have analyzed, the needs of the nation supersede those of the child, thus rendering abandonment a positive or, at the very least, a wholly justifiable choice. Abandonment without such a noble cause deems the mother incompetent and in desperate need of the intervention of the Soviet state. In *The Italian*, on the other hand, it is a mother's reunion with her abandoned son that holds the promise of positive consequences for post-Soviet society. The disembodied mother of Vania Solntsev offers hope for the rebirth of severed familial ties, and this hope, in turn, provides reassurance that Russian society can also recapture the positive values endangered by the dislocations of both the Soviet and post-Soviet period. The contrasting images of abandoning mothers developed in the film also link it with both the panic about and the valorization of Russian motherhood that characterized the 1990s, as detailed in chapter 3. The suicidal mother—and the countless other mothers whom she represents and whose relinquished children languish in orphanages—confirms the ominous prognostications of those observers of Russian society who feared the extinction of the iconic Russian mother. At the same time, Vera Solntseva's reunion with her son figuratively and literally highlights the power of motherhood to initiate both personal and societal transformation. The reclamation of a bad mother prefigures redemption on a much wider scale.

The ambivalent image of maternity that emerges from this film encapsulates the multifaceted and elusive significance of the central figure of this study. Does the bad mother reaffirm the enduring centrality of the mother archetype in Russian culture? Or, rather, does it reveal the fallibility of a figure rooted in pre-Christian and Christian belief patterns that no longer exert the same sustaining power that they once did? The answer, perhaps unsurprisingly, to both of these questions is "yes." On the one hand, the bad mother upholds the importance of the maternal archetype by revealing the often dire individual and societal consequences of its subversion. Seemingly, important paradigm shifts cannot occur in Russian society without the symbolic figure of the mother transforming into contested territory, with all warring factions declaring victory on the field of maternity as a prelude to a wider triumph. On the other hand, attacks on sacred maternity, such as those waged by Saltykov-Shchedrin or Petrushevskaia, ultimately besmirch and mock the notion of motherhood as a force that binds Russian society together. Such selfish and devious mothers highlight the folly of appealing to the supposedly beneficent and tender Russian mother for comfort or reassurance during times of chaos and tumult. The fact that, during the 1990s, both of these tendencies can be observed simultaneously testifies to the intense dislocation that Russia experienced during that decade.

In his essay "The Mythologization of Reality," the Polish-Jewish artist and writer Bruno Schulz observes: "There is not even one of our ideas that is not derived from mythology, a mythology that has been transformed, mutilated, remolded."[3] The various permutations of the bad mother during periods of pronounced societal shift identified in this study—from the mother who gradually subsumes her maternal identity, to the mother who lightheartedly abandons her child to communal care, to the Chechen mother shooting at Russian soldiers alongside her sons—all contribute to the "transformation, mutilation, and remolding" of the mythology of the noble, self-sacrificing, unity-inspiring and conflict-mediating Russian mother. The figure of the bad mother in the periods I have focused upon has intersected with social and cultural upheaval and, hopefully, illuminated our understanding of these disruptions. Russia's uniqueness lies, perhaps, in the frequency with which the negative maternal image emerges at the intersection of multiple spheres, such as the religious, political, and economic, as well as in how often the "mutilated" myth of Russian motherhood has been enlisted in the battles over Russia's familial and national destiny. At the end of *The Italian,* the abstract maternal figure Vera Solntseva emits a warm light that fulfills the promise embodied by both her first ("faith") and her last names (*solntse* = "sun"). The transformation of an abandoning mother into an iconic one presages a light-filled future not only for her son but also for the other orphans toward whom Russia's mothers may once again turn. The bad mothers at the center of this study produce no such light; instead, their absence or, even worse, their destructive presence casts a dark shadow over their children and, frequently, over their own lives as well. The interpretation of this shadow has varied significantly according to the exigencies of Russian, Soviet, and post-Soviet history. Despite the contingent and historically variable emanations of the bad mother, and the contrasting interpretations of the shadow she casts, this "mutilated" myth has emerged as a central and recurring motif in Russian culture of roughly the previous 150 years.

Notes

INTRODUCTION

1. T. Shchepanskaia, "Materinskoe prokliatie," in *Muzhiki i baby: Muzhskoe i zhenskoe v russkoi traditsionnoi kul'ture* (St. Petersburg: Iskusstvo-SPB, 2005), 337. For more on the well-established tradition of tracking Russia's historical development through changes in Marian icons, see Vera Shevzov, *Russian Orthodoxy on the Eve of Revolution* (New York: Oxford University Press, 2004), 244.

2. Theodor H. Gaster, "Myth and Story," in *Sacred Narrative: Readings in the Theory of Myth,* ed. Alan Dundes (Berkeley: University of California Press, 1984), 112–13.

3. Nikolai Berdiaev, *The Russian Idea,* trans. R. M. French (Hudson, N.Y.: Lindisfarne, 1992), 24.

4. E. Ann Kaplan, *Motherhood and Representation: The Mother in Popular Culture and Melodrama* (London: Routledge, 1992), 17.

5. Helena Goscilo, "The Gendered Trinity of Russian Cultural Rhetoric," in *Soviet Hieroglyphics,* ed. Nancy Condee (Bloomington: Indiana University Press, 1995), 75.

6. Joanna Hubbs, *Mother Russia: The Feminine Myth in Russian Culture* (Bloomington: Indiana University Press, 1988); Catriona Kelly, "Educating Tat'yana: Manners, Motherhood and Moral Education (*Vospitanie*), 1760–1840," in *Gender in Russian History and Culture,* ed. Linda Edmondson, 1–28 (Hampshire, Eng.: Palgrave, 2001); and Catriona Kelly, *Refining Russia: Advice Literature, Polite Culture, and Gender from Catherine to Yeltsin* (Oxford: Oxford University Press, 2001); Andrew Wachtel, *The Battle for Childhood: Creation of a Russian Myth* (Palo Alto, Calif.: Stanford University Press, 1990). For a comprehensive history of Russian childhood, see Catriona Kelly, *Children's World: Growing Up in Russia, 1890–1991* (New Haven, Conn.: Yale University Press, 2007). Barker employs a psychoanalytic approach and focuses primarily on mother-son relations, as developed in Russian folklore and in the works of such nineteenth-century male authors as Pushkin and Dostoevsky: Adele Marie Barker, *The Mother Syndrome in the Russian Folk Imagination* (Columbus,

Ohio: Slavica, 1986). For a historical account of interrelations between mothers and daughters in nineteenth-century Russia, see Barbara Alpern Engel, *Mothers and Daughters: Women of the Intelligentsia in Nineteenth-Century Russia* (Evanston, Ill.: Northwestern University Press, 2000). For a discussion of literature's treatment of the same relationship, see Joe Andrew, "Mothers and Daughters in Russian Literature of the First Half of the Nineteenth Century," *Slavonic and East European Review* 73 (1995): 37–60.

7. Ann Taylor Allen, *Feminism and Motherhood in Western Europe, 1890–1970* (New York: Palgrave Macmillan, 2005), 1.

8. Anne Cova, "Où en est l'histoire de la maternité?" *CLIO: Histoire, femmes et sociétés* 21 (2005): 189–211, http://clio.revues.org/index1465.html. See also Seth Koven and Sonya Michel, eds., *Mothers of a New World: Maternalist Politics and the Origins of Welfare States* (New York: Routledge, 1993). For the reception of maternalist ideology in Russia, see Marlyn L. Miller, "Russian Motherhood Discourse in *Zhenskii vestnik,* 1904–14," (master's thesis, Brandeis University, 2002).

9. Allen, *Feminism and Motherhood,* 2.

10. Qtd. in Allen, *Feminism and Motherhood,* 228. For more on the relationship between motherhood and Western feminism, see Adrienne Rich's pathbreaking *Of Woman Born: Motherhood as Experience and Institution* (New York: Norton, 1995).

11. For more on the concept of the individual in Russian history, see Oleg Kharkhordin, *The Collective and the Individual in Russia: A Study of Practices* (Berkeley: University of California Press, 1999). On the complicated relationship between Russian women and feminism, see Nancy Ries, "The Burden of Mythic Identity: Russian Women at Odds with Themselves," in *Feminist Nightmares,* ed. Susan Ostrov Weisser and Jennifer Fleischner, 242–68 (New York: NYU Press, 1994).

12. Elisabeth Badinter, *Mother Love, Myth and Reality: Motherhood in Modern History* (New York: Macmillan, 1981), 4.

13. O.V. Riabov, *Russkaia filosofiia zhenstvennosti* (Ivanovo: Isdatel'skii tsentr 'Iunona', 1999), 300. In another work, Riabov argues that the "matrifocality" of Russian culture is part of what has rendered it the "Other" in the eyes of Western observers. See his *"Rossiia-matushka": Natsionalizm, gender, i voina v Rossii XX veka* (Stuttgart: Ibidem-Verlag, 2007).

14. Barbara Heldt, "Motherhood in a Cold Climate: The Poetry and Career of Maria Shkapskaya," in *Sexuality and the Body in Russian Culture,* ed. Jane T. Costlow, Stephanie Sandler, and Judith Vowles (Palo Alto, Calif.: Stanford University Press, 1993), 237; Riabov, *Russkaia filosofiia,* 46.

15. Vera Ramikh, *Materinstvo i kul'tura (Filosofsko-kul'turologicheskii analiz)* (Rostov-na-Donu: Izdatel'skii tsentr DGTU, 1997), 15; Riabov, *Russkaia filosofiia,* 46.

16. Ramikh, *Materinstvo i kul'tura,* 4.

17. Riabov, *Russkaia filosofiia,* 46.

18. Hubbs, *Mother Russia,* xv–xvi, 21, 20. The philosopher Vasily Rozanov illustrated how imagery of Moist Mother Earth penetrated into twentieth-century maternal symbolism when he defined a woman's primary task as "to rework our civilization, to bring it closer to her kind, to moisten its dry features with the dampness of motherhood." See V. V. Rozanov, *Religiia: Filosofiia: Kul'tura* (Moscow: "Respublika," 1992), 189. Qtd. in Ramikh, *Materinstvo i kul'tura,* 17.

19. Barker, *The Mother Syndrome,* 48; Riabov, *Russkaia filosofiia,* 36–37.

20. T. Shchepanskaia, "Mat'-zemlia," in *Muzhiki i baby,* 344; Hubbs, *Mother Russia,* 23, 98, 99. For an interesting discussion of how the Ukrainian pagan goddess known as "Berehynia" continues to merge with the Christian Virgin Mary in defining women's identity in post-communist Ukraine, see Marian J. Rubchak, "Christian Virgin or Pagan Goddess: Feminism versus the Eternally Feminine in Ukraine," in *Women in Russia and Ukraine,* ed. Rosalind Marsh (Cambridge: Cambridge University Press, 1996), 315–30. For a description of how specific veneration of Moist Mother Earth continues to be practiced in traditional Russian culture, see Shchepanskaia, "Mat'-zemlia."

21. Nikolai Berdiaev, *The Russian Idea,* trans. R. M. French (Hudson, N.Y.: Lindisfarne, 1992), 24.

22. Riabov, *Russkaia filosofiia,* 29, 39–40.

23. Elena Hellberg-Hirn, *Soil and Soul: The Symbolic World of Russianness* (Aldershot, Eng.: Ashgate, 1998), 117. Hellberg-Hirn also notes that "the proverb emphasizes peasant identity as a familial attachment in terms of a mother-child relationship."

24. Shevzov, *Russian Orthodoxy,* 221.

25. G. P. Fedotov, *The Russian Religious Mind* (New York: Harper, 1960), 361.

26. Shevzov, *Russian Orthodoxy,* 214.

27. Leonid Ouspensky and Vladimir Lossky, *The Meaning of Icons,* trans. G. E. H. Palmer and E. Kadloubovsky (Crestwood, N.Y.: St. Vladimir's Seminary, 1982), 92; Joan Delaney Grossman, "Feminine Images in Old Russian Literature and Art," *California Slavic Studies* 11 (1980): 36.

28. Ouspensky and Lossky, *The Meaning of Icons,* 93.

29. Shevzov, *Russian Orthodoxy,* 220.

30. Grossman, "Feminine Images," 37.

31. Serge A. Zenkovsky, *Medieval Russia's Epics, Chronicles and Tales* (New York: E. P. Dutton, 1974), 153–60. Ivan Karamazov references this story in the preface to his "The Grand Inquisitor" tale in F. Dostoevsky's *The Brothers Karamazov.* Interestingly, by the time of the *Domostroi* (the sixteenth-century Russian treatise on household management that clearly delineated the role of women), the mother's warm and tender image, so prominent in medieval icons, had assumed a much more practical guise. In this text, as Dorothy Atkinson ob-

serves, "the mother's essential relationship with her children . . . is not emotional or spiritual but material; her function is to provide the comforts of a well-run home and to accumulate a dowry for her daughters." See Atkinson, "Society and the Sexes in the Russian Past," in *Women in Russia,* ed. Dorothy Atkinson, Alexander Dallin, and Gail Warshofsky Lapidus (Palo Alto, Calif.: Stanford University Press, 1977), 15.

32. Grossman, "Feminine Images," 69.

33. Natalia Pushkareva, *Women in Russian History,* trans. and ed. Eve Levin (New York: M. E. Sharpe, 1997), 41; Natalia Pushkareva, *Chastnaia zhizn' russkoi zhenshchiny: Nevesta, zhena, liubovnitsa* (Moscow: Ladomir, 1997), 68, 71. Pushkareva also points out that, in medieval Rus', the tradition of giving children "matronymics" instead of patronymics remained until the fourteenth century, a sign of respect for mothers that has no analogue in western Europe (*Chastnaia zhizn',* 70). For more on the potential causes of the particular reverence shown toward mothers in Russian families, see James Billington, *The Icon and the Axe* (New York: Alfred A. Knopf, 1966), 19–20.

34. Hubbs, *Mother Russia,* 100. See also Daniel Rancour-LaFerriere, *The Joy of All Who Sorrow: Icons of the Mother of God in Russia* (Moscow: Ladomir, 2005), chapter 13, "More a Mother Than a Virgin."

35. Fedotov, *The Russian Religious Mind,* 360.

36. Judith Deutsch Kornblatt, *Divine Sophia: The Wisdom Writings of Vladimir Solovlyov* (Ithaca, N.Y.: Cornell University Press, 2009), 52.

37. Barker, *The Mother Syndrome,* 48.

38. I. A. Il'in, "O russkoi kul'ture," in *Sobranie sochinenii,* vol. 6, book 2 (Moscow: Russkaia kniga, 1996), 549. Qtd. in Riabov, *Russkaia filosofiia,* 228.

39. Medieval Russian iconography presents her as "the source of all power, unit[ing] heaven and earth" (Hubbs, *Mother Russia,* 104).

40. S. Bulgakov, *Kupina neopalimaia: Opyt dogmaticheskogo istolknovaniia nekotorykh chert v pravoslavnom pochitanii Bogomateri* (Vilnius, 1991), 206, 205. Qtd. in Riabov, *Russkaia filosofiia,* 134.

41. Riabov, *Russkaia filosofiia,* 27.

42. Barbara Engel, *Women in Russia, 1700–2000* (Cambridge: Cambridge University Press, 2004), 6; Gary Marker, *Imperial Saint: The Cult of St. Catherine and the Dawn of Female Rule in Russia* (DeKalb, Ill.: Northern Illinois University Press, 2007), 14.

43. On how this belief continues to manifest itself in contemporary instances of domestic violence, see Rebecca Kay, *Russian Women and Their Organizations: Gender, Discrimination and Grassroots Women's Organizations* (New York: St. Martin's, 2000), 96.

44. T. Shchepanskaia, "Mat'," in *Muzhiki i baby,* 342–43; Pushkareva, *Chastnaia,* 87; S. B. Adon'ieva, "O ritual'noi funktsii zhenshchiny v russkoi traditsii," *Zhivaia starina* 1 (1998): 27; Shevzov, *Russian Orthodoxy,* 222.

45. *The Domostroi: Rules for Russian Households in the Time of Ivan the Terrible,* ed. and trans. Carolyn Johnston Pouncy (Ithaca, N.Y.: Cornell University Press, 1994), 100.

46. L. V. Poliakov, "Women's Emancipation and the Theology of Sex in Nineteenth-Century Russia," *Philosophy East and West* 42 (1992): 299.

47. Andrzej Walicki, *A History of Russian Thought* (Palo Alto, Calif.: Stanford University Press, 1979), 99.

48. A. S. Khomiakov, *O starom i novom* (Moscow, 1988), 286. Qtd. in Poliakov, "Women's Emancipation," 299.

49. Laura J. Olson, "Russianness, Femininity and Romantic Aesthetics in *War and Peace,*" *Russian Review* 56 (1997): 516.

50. Ibid., 528.

51. Shari L. Thurer, *The Myths of Motherhood* (Boston: Houghton Mifflin, 1994), 141; Badinter, *Mother Love,* 169; Kaplan, *Motherhood and Representation,* 76.

52. Badinter, *Mother Love,* 117, 130. See also Yvonne Knibiehler and Catherine Fouquet, *L'histoire des mères du moyen-âge à nos jours* (Paris: Editions Montalba, 1980), chapter 6, "La découverte de l'amour maternel."

53. Barbara Alpern Engel, "Mothers and Daughters: Family Patterns and the Female Intelligentsia," in *The Family in Imperial Russia,* ed. David Ransel (Urbana, Ill.: University of Illinois Press, 1978), 51; Pushkareva, *Chastnaia,* 191. Based on her analysis of thick journals and children's magazines of the 1840s, Diana Greene concludes that, by this decade, "the Russian periodic press was energetically promulgating [the] domestic ideology" that originated in western Europe. She speculates that this ideology entered Russia through one of two channels: either upper-class girls' boarding schools (*instituty*) or translations of conduct books from the original English, French, or German that were reviewed in the Russian press. See Greene, "Mid-Nineteenth-Century Domestic Ideology in Russia," in *Women and Russian Culture: Projections and Self-Perceptions,* ed. Rosalind Marsh (New York: Berghahn Books, 1998), 79. Engel also argues that these Western ideas were reaching a section of the population beyond the elite of the two major cities, "due to increased educational opportunities and the proliferation of journals" (Engel, "Mothers and Daughters: Family Patterns," 53). For an overview of the reception of Rousseau and various advice manuals designed for mothers that arrived in Russia from France in the late eighteenth and nineteenth centuries, see Kelly, *Refining Russia,* chapter 1.

54. Barbara Alpern Engel, *Breaking the Ties That Bound: The Politics of Marital Strife in Late Imperial Russia* (Ithaca, N.Y.: Cornell University Press, 2011), 166.

55. "Although [this] 'new domesticity' was primarily a middle-class phenomenon," as Michelle Marrese explains, "the emphasis on motherhood as the vital center of female experience was adopted by the [Russian] aristocracy as well."

See Marrese, *A Woman's Kingdom: Noblewomen and the Control of Property in Russia, 1700–1861* (Ithaca, N.Y.: Cornell University Press, 2002), 172. On the emergence of the mother as conservator of morality in American society, see Ruth H. Bloch, "American Feminine Ideals in Transition: The Rise of the Moral Mother, 1785–1815," *Feminist Studies* 4 (1978): 100–126.

56. Marrese, *A Woman's Kingdom,* 198.

57. Nikolai Solov'ev, *Zhenshchina i deti* (Moscow, 1869), 47, 44.

58. Richard Wortman, "The Russian Empress as Mother," in *The Family in Imperial Russia,* ed. David Ransel (Urbana, Ill.: University of Illinois Press, 1978), 61, 63.

59. Bram Dijkstra, *Idols of Perversity: Fantasies of Feminine Evil in Fin-de-Siècle Culture* (New York: Oxford University Press, 1986), 9.

60. Riabov, *Russkaia filosofiia,* 81.

61. A. Kriuchnikovaia, "Zadacha russkoi materi," *Sem'ia i shkola* 2 (1874): 26, 29, 28. *Sem'ia i shkola* (*Family and School*) was one of the first pedagogical journals published in imperial Russia.

62. Natalia Chernyaeva, "Childcare Manuals and Construction of Motherhood in Russia, 1890–1990" (Ph.D. diss., University of Iowa, 2009), 66.

63. Riabov, *Russkaia filosofiia,* 133.

64. Nikolai Berdiaev, *O naznachenii cheloveka* (Moscow, 1993), 207. Qtd. in Riabov, *Russkaia filosofiia,* 133.

65. Vasily Rozanov, "Opavshie list'ia: Korob vtoroi," in *Sobranie sochinenii v dvukh tomakh,* vol. 2 (Moscow, 1990), 285. Qtd. in Riabov, *Russkaia filosofiia,* 134.

66. Silver Age philosopher and writer Vladimir Solovev's concept of Sophia (the Eternal Feminine, or Divine Wisdom) also stressed her mediatory function. As Judith Deutsch Kornblatt explains, Sophia "is not merely a person but a relationship, the principle or energy or potential that can conjoin. She does not exist in either a sacred or a natural world, but mediates dynamically between the two" (Kornblatt, *Divine Sophia,* 93). Kornblatt identifies the pagan Moist Mother Earth as well as the Orthodox veneration of the Mother of God as important components in the evolution of Solovev's concept of Sophia. See ibid., 51–60. However, Solovev's Sophia ultimately took on multiple guises and drew on numerous predecessors, not only the maternal ones, as Kornblatt clarifies: "[Sophia] is never solely female, just as she is never solely divine or solely earthly, solely abstract or solely material, solely ideal or solely debased. Instead, her truest manifestation is at once incarnated and transfigured into a new whole, both male and female" (ibid., 82).

67. William G. Wagner, "Orthodox Domesticity: Creating a Social Role for Women," in *Sacred Stories: Religion and Spirituality in Modern Russia,* ed. Mark D. Steinberg and Heather J. Coleman (Bloomington: Indiana University Press, 2007), 130.

68. *Mat' i ditia: Pribavlenie k Khoziaike* 53 (St. Petersburg, 1902): 3. Qtd. in Chernyaeva, "Childcare Manuals," 62.

69. Katerina Clark, *The Soviet Novel* (Bloomington: Indiana University Press, 2000), 53.

70. Maxim Gorky, *Mother,* trans. Margaret Wettlin, in *Collected Works in Ten Volumes,* vol. III (Moscow: Progress, 1978), 88, 130, 221–22.

71. Ibid., 176, 346.

72. Vera S. Dunham, *In Stalin's Time: Middleclass Values in Soviet Fiction* (Duke, N.C.: Duke University Press, 1990), 14.

73. A. S. Makarenko, *The Collective Family: A Handbook for Russian Parents,* trans. Robert Daglish (Garden City, N.Y.: Anchor Books, 1967), 38. Qtd. in Greta Bucher, "Stalinist Families: Motherhood, Fatherhood, and Building the New Soviet Person," in *The Making of Russian History,* ed. John W. Steinberg and Rex A. Wade (Bloomington, Ind.: Slavica, 2009), 135. Makarenko's texts retained their prominence and were widely reprinted throughout the Soviet era. *A Book for Parents,* for example, went through thirteen editions between 1953 and 1987. See Kelly, *Children's World,* 125 n. 137.

74. Wendy Z. Goldman, *Women, the State and Revolution: Soviet Family Policy and Social Life, 1917–1936* (Cambridge: Cambridge University Press, 1993), 336, 338.

75. Dunham, *In Stalin's Time,* 34, 35.

76. Beth Holmgren, "Writing the Female Body Politic (1945–1985)," in *A History of Women's Writing in Russia,* ed. Adele Marie Barker and Jehanne M. Gheith (Cambridge: Cambridge University Press, 2002), 231; Lynne Attwood, "Rationality versus Romanticism: Representations of Women in the Stalinist Press," in *Gender in Russian History and Culture,* ed. Linda Edmondson (Hampshire, Eng.: Palgrave, 2001), 170–71. Holmgren argues that this emergence of the home and romantic love as themes in postwar fiction "saw the feminization of Soviet literature, in contrast and reaction to the 1920s' myth of a new, masculinized society," precisely the myth that produced the abandoning mother as a positive role model. As "the steelbodied male worker and soldier 'softened' and aged into the family man . . . the do-all wife and mother stepped into a lead role" (Holmgren, "Writing the Female Body Politic," 229).

77. Bucher, "Stalinist Families," 141.

78. Dunham, *In Stalin's Time,* 14, 35, 214; Mary Buckley, *Women and Ideology in the Soviet Union* (Ann Arbor: University of Michigan Press, 1989), 131–33.

79. Elisabeth Waters, "The Modernisation of Russian Motherhood, 1917–37," *Soviet Studies* 44 (1992): 131. The physical and psychic toil of this double burden was first explored in Soviet fiction by Natalia Baranskaia in her 1969 novella, "A Week Like Any Other." Anna Rotkirch employs the term "the contract of the wage working mother" to refer to "the type of gender relations that the Soviet state offered and forced women into from the early 1930s." This contract maintained that "all women were supposed to do wage work and have children, while the socialist state was supposed to provide improved versions of traditional

domestic work by establishing state canteens and nurseries. Any abolition of the family or housework was no longer on the agenda . . . as it had been briefly in the 1920s." See Rotkirch, "'Coming to Stand on Firm Ground': The Making of a Soviet Working Mother," in *On Living Through Soviet Russia,* ed. Daniel Bertaux, Paul Thompson and Anna Rotkirch (New Brunswick, N.J.: Transaction, 2005), 158–59. On representations of motherhood in Soviet film of the 1930s, see Alison Rowley, "Where Are All the Mother-Heroines? Images of Maternity in Soviet Films of the 1930s," *Canadian Journal of History* 44 (2009): 25–38. On motherhood in Soviet cinema during the Khrushchev era, see John Haynes, "Reconstruction or Reproduction? Mothers and the Great Soviet Family in Cinema After Stalin," in *Women in the Khrushchev Era,* ed. Melanie Ilič, Susan E. Reid and Lynne Attwood, 114–30 (Hampshire, Eng.: Palgrave, 2004).

80. Linda Edmondson, "Putting Mother Russia in a European Context," in *Art, Nation and Gender: Ethnic Landscapes, Myths and Mother-Figures,* ed. Tricia Cusack and Síghle Breathnach-Lynch (Hampshire, Eng.: Ashgate, 2003), 53. For a discussion of how World War II–era films also utilized the symbolism of the *Rodina-mat'* poster, see Elena Baraban, "The Return of Mother Russia: Representations of Women in Soviet Wartime Cinema," *Aspasia* 4 (2010): 121–38.

81. Victoria E. Bonnell, *Iconography of Power: Soviet Political Posters Under Lenin and Stalin* (Berkeley: University of California Press, 1997), 261; Irina Sandomirskaia, *Kniga o rodine: Opyt analiza diskursivnikh praktik* (Vienna: Wiener Slawistischer Almanach, 2001), 84–85. For more on female imagery in World War II posters, see also Jeffrey Brooks, *Thank You, Comrade Stalin! Soviet Public Culture from Revolution to Cold War* (Princeton, N.J.: Princeton University Press, 2000), 178–79; and Susan Corbesero, "Femininity (Con)scripted: Female Images in Soviet Wartime Poster Propaganda, 1941–45," *Aspasia* 4 (2010): 103–20.

82. Lisa A. Kirschenbaum, "'Our City, Our Hearths, Our Families': Local Loyalties and Private Life in Soviet World War II Propaganda," *Slavic Review* 59 (2000): 838. Kirschenbaum convincingly argues that it was not until World War II that official policies making "motherhood the essence of Soviet womanhood" and imagery and rhetoric began to converge (840).

83. Susan E. Reid, "The Khrushchev Kitchen: Domesticating the Scientific-Technological Revolution," *Journal of Contemporary History* 40 (2005): 292. On a much more pragmatic level, the catastrophic population losses suffered by the Soviet Union during World War II—and the accompanying severely imbalanced ratio of males to females—prompted the government to legitimize single motherhood, encouraging women to have children irrespective of the presence or absence of a husband. The Family Law of 1944 created a separate, legal category of fatherless children for the first time in Soviet history. See Mie Nakachi, "Population, Politics and Reproduction: Late Stalinism and Its Legacy," in *Late Stalin-*

ist Russia, ed. Juliane Fürst (New York: Routledge, 2006), 23–45; and Greta Bucher, *Women, The Bureaucracy and Daily Life in Postwar Moscow, 1945–1953* (Boulder, Colo.: East European Monographs, 2006), 42–44.

84. G. N. Kaminskii, "Rech' narkoma zdravookhraneniia na vtoroi sessii Vserossiiskogo TsIK XVI soiuza," *Voprosy materinstva i mladenchestva* 3 (1936): 1–4. Qtd. in Olga Issoupova, "From Duty to Pleasure? Motherhood in Soviet and Post-Soviet Russia," in *Gender, State and Society in Post-Soviet Russia,* ed. Sarah Ashwin (London: Routledge, 2000), 33.

85. Attwood, "Rationality versus Romanticism," 172.

86. Engel, *Women in Russia,* 253–55. Although official rhetoric enticed women with the prospect of choice, "policy," as Engel explains, "pointed in a different direction. Virtually every policy initiative aimed to encourage women to bear and raise children, rather than to help them advance on the job or combat discrimination at the workplace" (ibid., 255–56).

87. Issoupova, "From Duty?" 31.

88. Sarah Ashwin, "Introduction," in *Gender, State and Society in Post-Soviet Russia,* 10–11. For a detailed discussion of the reasons for the collapse of plans to implement communal child-rearing, see Goldman, *Women, the State and Revolution,* chapter 2.

89. Waters, "The Modernisation," 124.

90. Qtd. in Riabov, *Matushka-Rus'* (Moscow: Nauchnyi-isdatel'skii tsentr Ladomir, 2001), 105 n. 6. Riabov argues that the Communist Party's personification as a mother began with Gorky's novel. See Riabov, *"Rossiia-matushka,"* 216. See also Hubbs, *Mother Russia,* 234.

91. Sandomirskaia, *Kniga o rodine,* 85.

92. Jennifer Marie Utrata, "Counting on Motherhood, Not Men: Single Motherhood and Social Change in the New Russia" (Ph.D. diss., University of California–Berkeley, 2008), 21, 71.

93. Issoupova, "From Duty?" 39, 46.

94. Utrata, "Counting on Motherhood," 93.

95. Allen, *Feminism and Motherhood,* 184–85. The reasons that a woman chooses to have children are, of course, multifaceted and difficult to quantify. Utrata demonstrates how, during the Soviet period, women perceived the bond between mothers and children as stronger than that between husbands and wives, and how children were seen as a more reliable source of rewarding love than husbands (Utrata, "Counting on Motherhood," 66).

96. Michele Rivkin-Fish, "From Demographic Crisis to Dying Nation. The Politics of Language and Reproduction in Russia," in *Gender and National Identity in Twentieth-Century Russian Culture,* ed. Helena Goscilo and Andrea Lanoux (DeKalb: Northern Illinois University Press, 2006), 161, 168.

97. Ramikh, *Materinstvo i kul'tura,* 60, 124.

98. Ibid., 124.

CHAPTER ONE

1. Fedor Dostoevsky, *A Writer's Diary,* trans. Kenneth Lantz (Evanston, Ill.: Northwestern University Press, 1993), 383–84.

2. Carolyn Johnston Pouncy, "Introduction" in *The Domostroi,* ed. and trans. Carolyn Johnston Pouncy (Ithaca, N.Y.: Cornell University Press, 1994), 50.

3. Laura Engelstein, *The Keys to Happiness: Sex and the Search for Modernity in Fin-de-Siècle Russia* (Ithaca, N.Y.: Cornell University Press, 1992), 32.

4. Jessica Tovrov, *The Russian Noble Family: Structure and Change* (New York: Garland, 1987), 45. Although I focus here on family relations among the gentry and nobility, a similar dynamic dominated in peasant households. Changes in peasant families began to be observed in the post-Emancipation period, contemporaneously with those taking place in gentry households as well, as discussed below. As Boris Mironov explains, "Although the patriarch continued to occupy a central position in the family, the unlimited and arbitrary scope of his power gradually declined as it fell more and more under the purview of custom and law. In the last third of the nineteenth century, the weakening of the family's old patriarchal system accelerated." See Boris Mironov, *The Social History of Imperial Russia, 1700–1917,* vol. 1, trans. Ben Eklof (Boulder, Colo.: Westview, 1999), 150.

5. Qtd. in William Wagner, *Marriage, Property and Law in Late Imperial Russia* (New York: Oxford University Press, 1994), 73. Russian fathers of the nineteenth century did not, of course, always live up to this ideal. As Andrew Wachtel summarizes, "Most fathers in the gentry tradition fall into two basic categories: the 'stern but fair' man who works hard to manage his estate, or the extravagant father who is unable to deal with the realities of life, is self-indulgent, and has a passion for cards and/or a certain eccentric bent." See Andrew Wachtel, *The Battle for Childhood: Creation of a Russian Myth* (Palo Alto, Calif.: Stanford University Press, 1990), 99. The father and husband of the Golovlev family, mentioned later in this chapter, provides but one example of an irrelevant and weak paternal figure in nineteenth-century Russian literature.

6. Wagner, *Marriage,* 62.

7. Interestingly, in 1876, Dostoevsky and Saltykov-Shchedrin met and discussed the "family question," as I. B. Pavlova describes. In the December 1876 edition of *A Writer's Diary,* Dostoevsky sums up their conversation on the topic as follows: "'We don't have families at all anymore,' one of our most talented writers recently observed, contradicting me." This comment by Saltykov-Shchedrin apparently haunted Dostoevsky, for he mentioned it several more times, including during his discussion of the family as portrayed by Tolstoy, in the July/August 1877 *Diary.* In his notebooks from 1876–77, he refers to Saltykov-Shchedrin's comment at least two more times. See I. B. Pavlova, *Tema sem'i i roda u Saltykova-Shchedrina v literaturnom kontekste epokhi* (Moscow: IMLI

RAN, "Nasledie," 1999), 148–49. For a comparative analysis of the family theme as developed by the two authors, see ibid., chapter 3.

8. Kaplan, *Motherhood and Representation,* 76.

9. Toni Bowers, *The Politics of Motherhood: British Writing and Culture, 1680–1760* (Cambridge: Cambridge University Press, 1996), 96.

10. Tovrov, *Russian Noble Family,* 161.

11. Harriet Murav, *Russia's Legal Fictions* (Ann Arbor: University of Michigan Press, 1998), 138.

12. Priscilla Roosevelt, *Life on the Russian Country Estate* (New Haven, Conn.: Yale University Press, 1995), 182.

13. Tovrov, *Russian Noble Family,* 162.

14. Kelly, "Educating Tat'yana," 15. As Kelly observes, the two conflicting models of moral education in existence in the late-eighteenth and early-nineteenth century in Russia revolved around the role of the mother: the first advocated "'*education maternelle,*' or indoctrination by the mother," while the second, "'conjugal education,' [supported] the view that women should marry as tabulae rasae upon which husbands wrote what they wanted" (Kelly, "Educating Tat'yana," 3).

15. Qtd. in Tovrov, *Russian Noble Family,* 163.

16. Eduard Pomperi, *Zhenshchina po otnosheniiu k muzhchin v ispolnenii ee materinskikh, sestrinskikh i supruzheskikh obiazannostei* (Moscow, 1866), 30.

17. Ibid., 58.

18. Qtd. in Tovrov, *Russian Noble Family,* 275. For a more detailed account of the plentiful images of maternal self-sacrifice in turn-of-the-century Russian moralistic literature, see ibid., 276.

19. S. N., "Despotizm materinskoi liubvi," *Zhurnal dlia vospitaniia* 3 (1859): 136.

20. Ibid., 205.

21. Konstantin Grum, *Rukovodstvo k vospitaniiu I* (St. Petersburg, 1843–45), 57. Qtd. in Tovrov, "Mother-Child Relationships Among the Russian Nobility," in *The Family in Imperial Russia,* ed. David Ransel (Urbana: University of Illinois Press, 1978), 225.

22. Tovrov, "Mother-Child Relationships," 25.

23. Rebecca Jo Plant, *Mom: The Transformation of Motherhood in Modern America* (Chicago: University of Chicago Press, 2010), 120–21.

24. Wachtel, *The Battle for Childhood,* 49.

25. L. N. Tolstoi, "Detstvo," in *Polnoe sobranie sochinenii,* vol. 1 (Moscow: 'Nauka', 2000), 77, 79.

26. Mary W. Cavender, *Nests of the Gentry: Family, Estate and Local Loyalties in Provincial Russia* (Newark: University of Delaware Press, 2007), 46.

27. Tovrov, *Russian Noble Family,* 290.

28. Wachtel, *Battle for Childhood,* 99. Scholars disagree about the extent to

which the reality of women's family lives reproduced the mythological ideals that these autobiographical and literary traditions had created. Many have argued that the self-sacrificial model did not translate into a high level of involvement by noble women in the daily lives of their children. For example, Barbara Engel notes that, "although less formidable [than fathers], mothers often proved nearly as remote. Whatever the depth of maternal feeling, no one expected a noblewoman of means to nurture or socialize her small children. One of the prerogatives of wealth was freedom from the daily responsibilities of childcare. The more conscientious mother might assume a supervisory role, but most seemed satisfied to inspect their children in the morning and evening, and to receive reports from nurse, governess, or tutor" (Engel, "Mothers and Daughters: Family Patterns," 47). Tovrov also contends that "the self-sacrifice that characterized the ideal mother should not be confused with a nurturing attitude or emotional generosity, which did not become part of the maternal ideal until later" (Tovrov, *Russian Noble Family,* 277). Natal'ia Pushkareva, however, in her comprehensive study of the private lives of Russian women, adds nuance to the debate. On the basis of memoir literature, she convincingly divides Russian gentry women into two "psychological types." The first were those women raised primarily in the countryside, whose behavior was closer to folk ideals and for whom motherhood, and everything associated with it, comprised the entirety of their private lives. The second type of woman lived in a large city and occupied herself almost exclusively with the intrigues of society life rather than with the daily rigors of motherhood (Pushkareva, *Chastnaia,* 207). After the Emancipation, women representing both of these types were undoubtedly deprived of some of the freedom to choose their degree of involvement in the raising of children, a fact attested to by the increase in child-rearing literature and manuals on housekeeping published in the 1860s (Marrese, *A Woman's Kingdom,* 201; Engel, "Mothers and Daughters: Family Patterns," 59).

29. Wagner, *Marriage,* 101.

30. William Wagner, "The Trojan Mare: Women's Rights and Civil Rights in Late Imperial Russia," in *Civil Rights in Imperial Russia,* ed. Olga Crisp and Linda Edmondson (Oxford: Clarendon, 1989), 74; Wagner, *Marriage,* 206.

31. Engel, *Breaking the Ties That Bound,* 3–4; Wagner, "Trojan Mare," 78.

32. Gregory L. Freeze, "Bringing Order to the Russian Family: Marriage and Divorce in Imperial Russia, 1760–1860," *Journal of Modern History* 62 (1990): 710.

33. Richard Stites, "M. L. Mikhailov and the Emergence of the Woman Question in Russia," *Canadian Slavic Studies* 3 (1969): 192. According to Stites, "the emergence of the woman question took place in the half-decade following the Crimean War and its clearest statement was made at the end of the decade by M. L. Mikhailov, a minor poet and revolutionary figure of the 1860s" (178–79).

34. Ibid., 192.

35. Jane T. Costlow, "The Pastoral Source: Representations of the Maternal Breast in Nineteenth-Century Russia," in *Sexuality and the Body in Russian Culture,* ed. Jane T. Costlow, Stephanie Sandler, and Judith Vowles (Palo Alto, Calif.: Stanford University Press, 1993), 224.

36. Barbara Heldt Monter, "Rassvet and the Woman Question," *Slavic Review* 36 (1977): 77.

37. Stites, "Mikhailov," 198.

38. Ironically, self-sacrifice also became a salient part of the image cultivated by the Russian female radicals of the 1870s and 1880s, those who had escaped the tyranny of domestic bonds. As Barbara Engel writes, "radical women's selflessness and readiness for self-sacrifice greatly endeared them to their comrades, who regarded them as moral exemplars and inspirations" (Engel, *Women in Russia,* 84).

39. Engel, "Mothers and Daughters: Family Patterns," 51–52. A literary representation of such a retrograde mother can be found, for example, in Chernyshevsky's extremely influential novel *What Is to Be Done?* (1863), in which the heroine, Vera Pavlovna, escapes her mother's tyranny through a fictional marriage and eventually becomes one of the exemplary "new people" introduced in the text.

40. Kelly, *Refining Russia,* 128. In her autobiography, Natalia Grot (1825–1899), who was born into an old gentry family and later became the wife of a distinguished scholar, articulated this stance when she wrote that Russian society needs "educated women far less than intelligent mothers, housewives, and workers in various fields who will enlighten and purify all the dark and dirty corners in our society with their own example and good works." See *Russia Through Women's Eyes,* ed. Toby W. Clyman and Judith Vowles (New Haven, Conn.: Yale University Press, 1996), 240.

41. Costlow, "The Pastoral Source," 224.

42. Marrese, *A Woman's Kingdom,* 7.

43. As I. P. Foote observes, "Porfiry's character and the manner of his end have been the dominant themes of critical discussion of the novel" (Foote, "Introduction: Saltykov and 'The Golovlyovs,'" in *Saltykov-Shchedrin's "The Golovlyovs": A Critical Companion,* ed. I. P. Foote [Evanston, Ill.: Northwestern University Press, 1997], 20). See, for example, William Mills Todd III, "The Anti-Hero with a Thousand Faces: Saltykov-Shchedrin's Porfiry Golovlev," *Studies in the Literary Imagination* 9 (1976): 87–105. Western criticism on Saltykov-Shchedrin and the novel is much less voluminous than the Soviet contribution. For the only comprehensive study of his life and works in a Western language, see Kyra Sanine, *Saltykov-Chtchédrine, Sa vie et ses oeuvres* (Paris: Institut d'Études Slaves, 1955).

44. See, for example, Pavlova, *Tema sem'i i roda,* 9–10; and Sanine,

Saltykov-Chtchédrine, 213. For a biographical account of Olga Mikhailovna's life, see Sergei Makashin, *Saltykov-Shchedrin, Biografiia* (Moscow: Khudozhestvennaia literatura, 1951), 30–39. For the lengthy list of fictional characters supposedly inspired by her, including Arina Petrovna, see Makashin, *Biografiia,* 31.

45. Marrese, *A Woman's Kingdom,* 1, 117; Wachtel, *The Battle for Childhood,* 98. For a comparative study (France, England, and Russia) of how differing female property rights have affected how women writers have represented the institution of marriage, see Sally Livingston, "Owning Property, Being Property: Medieval and Modern Women Shape the Narratives of Marriage" (Ph.D. diss., Harvard University, 2008).

46. Emil Draitser, *Techniques of Satire: The Case of Saltykov-Shchedrin* (Berlin: Walter de Gruyter, 1994), 15.

47. Karl Marx and Frederick Engels, "The Communist Manifesto," in *The Woman Question: Selections from the Writings of Karl Marx, Frederick Engels, V. I. Lenin, Joseph Stalin* (New York: International Publishers, 1972), 34; Susan McReynolds, "'You Can Buy the Whole World': The Problem of Redemption in *The Brothers Karamazov,*" *Slavic and East European Journal* 52 (2008): 98.

48. A. S. Bushmin, *Evoliutsiia satiry Saltykova-Shchedrina* (Leningrad: 'Nauka,' 1984), 89.

49. Qtd. in Pavlova, *Tema sem'i i roda,* 66.

50. Alfred J. Rieber, *Merchants and Entrepreneurs in Imperial Russia* (Chapel Hill: University of North Carolina Press, 1982), 82; Hans Rogger, *Russia in the Age of Modernisation and Revolution 1881–1917* (Essex, Eng.: Longman Group, 1983), 3; Thomas C. Owen, *Capitalism and Politics in Russia* (Cambridge: Cambridge University Press, 1981), 53.

51. Rieber, *Merchants and Entrepreneurs,* 149. The merchant was almost universally disdained by Russian writers of the nineteenth century. As Beth Holmgren has pointed out, the merchant's "image in [Russian] literature . . . was marginalized and frequently ambiguous" (Beth Holmgren, *Rewriting Capitalism: Literature and the Market in Late Tsarist Russia and the Kingdom of Poland* [Pittsburgh: University of Pittsburgh Press, 1998], 18). Valentine Tschebotarioff Bill argues that the economic transformation summarized above failed to interest the major Russian writers of the period. Exhibiting the "hostility toward a pecuniary society prevalent among Russia's literary circles . . . Pushkin, Dostoevsky, and Tolstoy condemned, each in his own way, the world of acquisition and retention and set the mood of hostility toward a monetary culture which permeates Russia's intellectual and literary world throughout all of the nineteenth century" (Bill, "The Dead Souls of Russia's Merchant World," *Russian Review* 15 [1956]: 247). For an insightful discussion of the image of the merchant in nineteenth-century Russian literature, see Holmgren, *Rewriting Capitalism,* chapter 2.

52. Roberta Thompson Manning, *The Crisis of the Old Order in Russia* (Princeton, N.J.: Princeton University Press, 1982), 5.

53. Ibid., 6, 21. In keeping with the general trend outlined by Bill, Saltykov-Shchedrin exhibited a distinctly skeptical attitude toward the emergence of capitalism in Russia. By the late 1860s, as his biographer S. Makashin has observed, the writer was increasingly focusing his satirical lens on the proponents and profiteers of this new system. In works such as *Gentlemen from Tashkent* (1869) and *Diary of a Provincial in St. Petersburg* (1872), Saltykov-Shchedrin wondered whether the rising bourgeoisie were reformers who would recklessly "destroy the old temple" without bothering to build a new one. See *Gospoda Tashkentsy,* in *Sobranie sochinenii,* vol. 10 (Moscow: Khudozhestvennaia literatura, 1970), 267. Andrei Anikin argues that Saltykov possessed a "populist understanding of capitalism and of its particular development in Russia: this analysis denied the progressive nature of capitalist development and expressed revulsion at capitalism's negative effects both on the city and the countryside" (Anikin, "Money and the Russian Classics," trans. Thomas Epstein, *Diogenes* 162 [1993]: 107). For a more detailed discussion of the writer's attitude toward capitalism, see S. Makashin, *Saltykov-Shchedrin: Seredina puti, 1860e–1870e gody* (Moscow: Khudozhestvennaia literatura, 1984), 447–51; and Bushmin, *Evoliutsiia satiry,* 84–89.

54. This and all subsequent citations of the novel are from *The Golovlyov Family,* trans. Ronald Wilks (London: Penguin Books, 1988), and are noted in the text. I have occasionally modified the translation.

55. Arina Petrovna does, of course, succeed unequivocally in improving the family's material situation while also providing some of the novel's few examples of positive character traits, such as industry and dedication to the pursuit of a goal. "Of all the characters in the novel," Eva V. Wampuszyc writes, "Arina Petrovna most fully functions in both the pre- and post-emancipation periods . . . With her sight set on future progeny . . . and in the name of the family, she builds the Golovlyov fortune from a small, insignificant estate to one of the largest in the province . . . She exemplifies pre-reform industry and possesses the talent of a 'statesman' and 'business woman' to acquire, build, negotiate, and develop the Golovlyov estate" (Wampuszyc, "The Narrative of Noble Decline and the Discourse of Money in Late 19th C. Russia and the Kingdom of Poland: M. E. Saltykov-Shchedrin and B. Prus." [Ph.D. diss., University of Michigan, 2004], 67).

56. For some of the recurrences of this phrase, see pages 16, 17, and 22.

57. As Wampuszyc observes, "Arina Petrovna 'chucks a cut' to three of four children, all of whom lack a sense of future, both financial and personal, and have proven irresponsible with money. By doing this, she makes a choice to prematurely sever ties with her children and abandon her maternal responsibilities. She exchanges family relations for economic security. Her greatest transgression, thus, is viewing material acquisition as convertible into familial relations" (Wampuszyc, "Narrative of Noble Decline," 69–70).

58. Ibid., 60.

59. It is in reality a "maternal" rather than "parental" blessing, since Arina Petrovna runs the estate without the assistance or participation of her husband, who remains peripheral and irrelevant.

60. These sentences recur on pages 57 and 81.

61. Tovrov, *Russian Noble Family,* 276.

62. In discussing Saltykov-Shchedrin's memoir, *Old Times of Poshekhona* (*Poshekhonskaia Starina*), Tovrov observes: "In his memoir Saltykov-Shchedrin showed the force of this ideal [of sacrifice for the family] in describing how it could be used, if not oppressively, then at least to justify oppression. His mother was a cruel tyrant, but rationalized her every vicious act by saying that it was for the good of the family. Even those children who suffered the most from her despotism agreed that she made momentous personal sacrifices for the sake of her family and praised her for it" (Tovrov, *Russian Noble Family,* 96).

63. Alexander Gerschenkron, "Time Horizon in Russian Literature," *Slavic Review* 34 (1975): 692, 705.

64. Todd, "Anti-Hero," 97; Draitser, *Techniques of Satire,* 16.

65. Todd, "Anti-Hero," 94.

66. Darra Goldstein, "Domestic Porkbarrelling in Nineteenth-Century Russia, or Who Holds the Keys to the Larder?" in *Russia, Women, Culture,* ed. Helena Goscilo and Beth Holmgren (Bloomington: Indiana University Press, 1996), 140.

67. As Karl D. Kramer observes, "A striking collection of metaphors centers on the business of feeding. In these situations nature is turned upside down so that the mother figuratively devours her own children." See Kramer, "Satiric Form in Saltykov's *Gospoda Golovlevy,*" in *Saltykov-Shchedrin's "The Golovlyovs": A Critical Companion,* ed. I. P. Foote (Evanston, Ill.: Northwestern University Press, 1997), 125.

68. Goldstein points out that "the more obsessed Arina Petrovna and Judas become with food, the more they run off at the mouth; here food as a manipulative device is connected with that other source of oral gratification, talking" (Goldstein, "Domestic Porkbarreling," 143).

69. Ibid., 142.

70. Gerschenkron, "Time Horizon," 704. This combination of frugal management leading to starvation and disaster was developed earlier in the century by Nikolai Gogol, in his description of Pliushkin in *Dead Souls.* Given that Pliushkin is a kind of feminized figure (Chichikov mistakes him for a woman), he may be viewed as a precursor "bad" mother. I am grateful to Andrew Wachtel for this observation.

71. As Foote observes, "It is she [Annin'ka] who in the final scene discerns the truth of his repentance and, by her compassionate embrace, symbolically returns him to the human fold" (Foote, "Introduction," 15).

72. Pavlova, *Tema sem'i i roda,* 62.

73. M. E. Saltykov-Shchedrin, "Sovremennye prizraki," in *Sobranie sochinenii,* vol. 6 (Moscow: Khudozhestvennaia literatura, 1968), 389, 393.

74. This theme of a mother exploiting maternal mythology to cement her power within a family is a recurring one in the works of the contemporary Russian author Liudmila Petrushevskaia, who will be discussed in chapter 3.

75. The corrosive effect of money on the female soul in particular seems to have been a recurrent theme in Saltykov-Shchedrin's works (Pavlova, *Tema sem'i i roda,* 39). His few writings on the Women's Question indicate that he viewed it as part of the larger issue of societal reform that should not be treated separately (ibid., 76).

76. Anikin, "Money and the Russian Classics," 109.

77. Saltykov-Shchedrin, "Sovremennye prizraki," 394.

78. The publication histories of the two works overlap somewhat: *The Golovlev Family* was serialized in *Notes of the Fatherland* between 1875 and 1880, while *Anna Karenina* appeared in the *Russian Messenger* between 1874 and 1877.

79. Edwina Cruise, for example, observes that the "opposed and competing attractions of lover versus son, and of the rich erotic potential of her body's yearnings versus a mother's sacrifices of self for children and family are mutually exclusive. Therein lies her tragedy." See Edwina Cruise, "Women, Sexuality and the Family in Tolstoy," in *The Cambridge Companion to Tolstoy,* ed. Donna Tussing Orwin (Cambridge: Cambridge University Press, 2002), 203. Wachtel similarly observes that Anna "truly becomes a tragic heroine" at the moment when she fully grasps the mutual exclusivity of her love for Vronsky and for her son. See Wachtel, "Death and Resurrection in *Anna Karenina,*" in *In the Shade of the Giant: Essays on Tolstoy,* ed. Hugh McLean (Berkeley: University of California Press, 1989), 107. Gary Saul Morson argues that Anna had an opportunity to resolve this conflict in part 4 of the novel, when Karenin offers her a divorce and accompanying custody of both Serezha and her child with Vronsky, Annie, who would legally have been considered his child. For an explanation of Anna's refusal, see Morson, *Anna Karenina in Our Time* (New Haven, Conn.: Yale University Press, 2007), 113–17. Regardless of whether or not Anna herself shoulders the blame for not resolving the conflict, this tension between Serezha and Vronsky waxes and wanes until Anna's suicide.

80. Costlow, "The Pastoral Source," 230.

81. Leo Tolstoy, *Anna Karenina,* trans. Constance Garnett, ed. Leonard J. Kent and Nina Berberova (New York: Modern Library, 2000), 6. All subsequent citations are from this edition and are noted in the text. I have occasionally modified the translation.

82. Amy Mandelker, *Framing Anna Karenina* (Columbus, Ohio: Ohio State University Press, 1993), 51.

83. Engel, *Breaking the Ties That Bound,* 1.

84. Qtd. in Gregory L. Freeze, "Profane Narratives About a Holy Sacrament: Marriage and Divorce in Late Imperial Russia," in *Sacred Stories: Religion and Spirituality in Modern Russia,* ed. Mark D. Steinberg and Heather J. Coleman (Bloomington: Indiana University Press, 2007), 146.

85. Gregory L. Freeze, "Krylov vs. Krylova: 'Sexual Incapacity' and Divorce in Tsarist Russia," in *The Human Tradition in Modern Russia,* ed. William B. Husband (Wilmington, Del.: Scholarly Resources, 2000), 8–9.

86. Engel, *Breaking the Ties That Bound,* 16–17.

87. Amy Mandelker defines this volatility in the following manner: "Tolstoy's depiction of an adulterous heroine who is both passionately maternal (at least in the first half of the novel) and sexual thus represents the threatening combination of maternity and sexuality that the Western Judeo-Christian ethic has sought to fragment. Within this ideology, a good woman is a good mother—that is, endowed with a proper maternal instinct that supersedes and eclipses all other drives." See Mandelker, *Framing Anna Karenina,* 51. Olga Karpushina even argues that Anna's physical beauty presages her later devolution as a mother. Because, in Tolstoy's moral universe, a woman's body should be "functional rather than beautiful . . . There is something questionable about Anna's beauty, as well as about her only child, as if her beauty betrays her status as a bad mother and foreshadows her later neglect of her daughter." See Olga Karpushina, "The Idea of the Family in Tolstoy's *Anna Karenina:* The Moral Hierarchy of Families," *Studies in Slavic Cultures II:* "Anna Karenina on Page and Screen" (January 2001): 80.

88. Edward Wasiolek, *Tolstoy's Major Fiction* (Chicago: University of Chicago Press, 1978), 133.

89. The issue also lays bare and perhaps hastens the estrangement of Dolly and Anna. As Donna Orwin has observed, "Birth control is the issue that reveals the newly formed rift between the two friends. Anna has rejected the natural consequence of sexual relations and family life, namely, pregnancy, because it would interfere with the pleasures of the individual on which her relationship with Vronsky is based. Dolly, who has herself dreamed of freedom from motherhood . . . on her ride to Vronsky's estate . . . is shocked into reaffirmation of her role as keeper of the hearth by the appearance of a truly 'liberated' woman in the person of Anna." See Donna Orwin, *Tolstoy's Art and Thought, 1847–1880* (Princeton, N.J.: Princeton University Press, 1993), 181–82. Thus, Anna's stance on birth control underscores how consequential her decisions about maternity are for the pivotal relationships in her life.

90. Caryl Emerson, "Prosaics in *Anna Karenina:* Pro and Con," *Tolstoy Studies Journal* 8 (1995–96): 164.

91. The union of Kitty and Levin, presumably, represents the transcendence of this division.

92. This singularity is also reinforced later in the novel, during the scene

between Dolly and the peasant women. As Costlow observes, this scene reveals how motherhood unites women despite external differences: "The description of Dolly's work as mother ends with her conversing with peasant women: their maternal experiences erase class boundaries; they share a common language" (Costlow, "The Pastoral Source," 229).

93. Morson also contends that Dolly is the true hero of the novel, since she "best exemplifies its governing values." See Morson, "Prosaics and *Anna Karenina*," *Tolstoy Studies Journal* 1 (1988): 4; and his *Anna Karenina in Our Time*, 38–48.

94. Engel, *Breaking the Ties That Bound*, 248.

95. Mandelker argues that Anna's combining of maternity with sexuality is what "most distinguishes Anna's narrative from that associated with the continental tradition of adulteresses . . . Anna is thus unique in literature in that she combines the maternal aspect of the Victorian fallen woman with the passionate sensuality of the French mistress" (Mandelker, *Framing Anna Karenina*, 61). This unique linkage constitutes one aspect, according to Mandelker, of Tolstoy's polemic with the Victorian novel in *Anna Karenina*.

96. As Wasiolek observes, "By her elaborate drama she protects herself against conscious acknowledgement of the true cause of her shame, but cannot annihilate the shame. The shame and guilt remain even though Anna attempts to relieve them by retreating to the habitual pattern of the guiltless mother" (Wasiolek, *Tolstoy's Major Fiction*, 137).

97. This is seen, to name but one example, in Kitty's misguided attempt to pattern her life according to the template of Varen'ka's.

98. The modified Garnett translation imprecisely renders *derzhava* as "support," and I have altered the translation accordingly.

99. Engel, *Breaking the Ties That Bound*, 243–44.

100. "Intensely as Anna had longed to see her son, and much as she had been thinking of it and preparing herself for it, she had not in the least expected that seeing him would affect her so deeply" (611).

101. See Morson, "Prosaics and *Anna Karenina*," 6. Justin Weir argues that, in the novel, "memory functions as one of the cornerstones of personal identity, uniting the often-interrupted flow of consciousness." See Justin Weir, "Anna Incommunicada: Language and Consciousness in *Anna Karenina*," *Tolstoy Studies Journal* 8 (1995–96): 101.

102. Mandelker maintains that Anna's attitude toward her daughter "does not necessarily imply an absence of maternal feeling. Just as an infertile woman who desperately longs for children of her own may find the presence of other people's children intolerable, so Ani is a continual, painful reminder to Anna that she has lost Serezha" (*Framing Anna Karenina*, 191 n. 73). This observation does not account, however, for Anna's enlistment of her daughter as a source of power in the battle with Vronsky, as discussed above.

103. Priscilla Meyer astutely observes that the disintegration of Anna's maternal identity also leads to her separation from God and religion. "That the maternal instinct can be driven out by sexual passion is the most reprehensible aspect of her conduct," she writes, "and is the proof of the sacrilegious nature of adultery for Tolstoy . . . the shame of it makes religious solace impossible." See Priscilla Meyer, *How the Russians Read the French: Lermontov, Dostoevsky, Tolstoy* (Madison: University of Wisconsin Press, 2008), 172.

104. Vladimir Alexandrov, *Limits to Interpretation* (Madison: University of Wisconsin Press, 2004), 261. Svetlana Grenier contends that Anna had been isolated from the "indispensable feminine-familial network of human relations" from the beginning of the novel, as a result of her residing in the "masculine and anti-familial city of Petersburg." See Svetlana Grenier, "A Tale of Two Cities: Tolstoy's Gendered Moral Geography in *Anna Karenina*," in *Mapping the Feminine: Russian Women and Cultural Difference*, ed. Hilde Hoogenboom, Catherine Theimer Nepomnyashchy, and Irina Reyfman (Bloomington: Indiana University Press, 2008), 108. For an insightful discussion of the importance of the "bond of women's friendship" in *Anna Karenina* and in Tolstoy's works as a whole, see Anne Eakin Moss, "Tolstoy's Politics of Love: 'That Passionate and Tender Friendship That Exists Only Among Women,'" *Slavic and East European Journal* 53 (2009): 566–86.

105. Qtd. in Pavlova, *Tema sem'i i roda,* 93, 96.

106. Freeze, "Trojan Mare," 79–80.

107. Freeze, "Profane Narratives," 168.

108. Engelstein, *The Keys to Happiness,* 225, 247–48, 353.

CHAPTER TWO

1. Il'ia Rents, "Ekskursiia v 'sviatye mesta'," *Zhenskii zhurnal* 6 (1926): 9. Vorsheva's husband is also mentally handicapped, and she assumes that her son has inherited this trait from his father.

2. Ibid., 9–10.

3. "Pis'mo Raisy Vorshevoi," *Zhenskii zhurnal* 3 (1927): 13.

4. Rents, "Ekskursiia," 10.

5. "Otkliki chitatel'nits," *Zhenskii zhurnal* 2 (1927): 12.

6. Another of the key issues Vorsheva touches upon in her text, eugenics, received fictional treatment in Sergei Tret'iakov's censored 1926 play, *I Want a Child!* For an insightful discussion of eugenics in 1920s Soviet society and in the play itself, see Christina Kiaer, "Delivered from Capitalism: Nostalgia, Alienation, and the Future of Reproduction in Tretiakov's *I Want a Child!*" in *Everyday Life in Early Soviet Russia,* ed. Christina Kiaer and Eric Naiman (Bloomington: Indiana University Press, 2006), 183–216.

7. Wendy Z. Goldman, *Women, the State and Revolution: Soviet Family*

Policy and Social Life, 1917–1936 (Cambridge: Cambridge University Press, 1993), 1, 51. For the theoretical underpinnings of Marxist ideas about the Women's Question, see Mary Buckley, *Women and Ideology in the Soviet Union* (New York: Harvester Wheatsheaf, 1989), chapter 1. For a discussion of the roots of anti-family sentiment in the Russian philosophical tradition, see Eric Naiman, *Sex in Public* (Princeton, N.J.: Princeton University Press, 1997), chapter 1.

8. Zlata Lilina, the wife of G. Zinoviev, qtd. in Lynne Attwood, *Creating the New Soviet Woman: Women's Magazines as Engineers of Female Identity, 1922–53* (London: Macmillan, 1999), 7.

9. Lisa A. Kirschenbaum, *Small Comrades: Revolutionizing Childhood in Soviet Russia, 1917–1932* (New York: RoutledgeFalmer, 2001), 51, 58.

10. Qtd. in Orlando Figes, *A People's Tragedy: The Russian Revolution 1891–1924* (New York: Penguin, 1998), 734.

11. David E. Powell, *Antireligious Propaganda in the Soviet Union: A Study of Mass Persuasion* (Cambridge, Mass.: MIT Press, 1975), 37. The paintings of K. S. Petrov-Vodkin (1878–1939) represent a notable exception to the Bolshevik imperative to purge Russian culture of religiosity, including the Mother of God. In works such as *1918 in Petrograd* (commonly referred to as *The Petrograd Madonna;* 1920) and *Motherhood* (1925), Petrov-Vodkin set icon-inspired images of mothers against contemporary, Soviet backgrounds, infusing quotidian scenes with sacred imagery. His headscarf-donning madonnas represent the successful merging of the new Soviet woman with the archetypal mother of medieval icon painting and transcendent maternal imagery. For a more detailed examination of the maternal theme in Petrov-Vodkin's works, see Vasilii Uspenskii, *K. S. Petrov-Vodkin: Materinstvo* (St. Petersburg: Arka, 2010).

12. Goldman, *Women,* 1.

13. Ibid., 8.

14. N. K. Krupskaia, *Zhenshchina-Rabotnitsa,* 2nd ed. (Moscow-Leningrad, 1926), 34.

15. Goldman, *Women,* 62. Goldman notes that the daunting social problems faced by the new government—namely, the overwhelming numbers of homeless children—cast serious doubt on the viability of this utopian vision from the very beginning: "Despite their hopeful schemes and honorable intentions, the delegates still had to face the forbidding problems of the present. Outside the doors of the Congress, thousands of children were starving in institutions that lacked even the most basic provisions" (ibid., 63).

16. Alexandra Kollontai, "Tezisy o kommunisticheskoi morali v oblasti brachnykh otnoshenii," *Kommunistka* 12–13 (1921): 30.

17. Alexandra Kollontai, "Communism and the Family," in *Selected Writings* (New York: W. W. Norton, 1977), 134, 257–58. Qtd. in Goldman, *Women,* 10.

18. A. G. Goikhbarg, *Brachnoe, semeinoe, i opekunskoe pravo Sovetskoi respubliki* (Moscow, 1920), 5. Qtd. in Goldman, *Women,* 9.

19. Elizabeth A. Wood, *The Baba and the Comrade: Gender and Politics in Revolutionary Russia* (Bloomington: Indiana University Press, 1997), 29, 79.

20. Goldman, *Women,* 9.

21. Elizabeth Waters, "The Modernisation of Russian Motherhood, 1917–1937," *Soviet Studies* 4 (1992): 128; Goldman, *Women,* 9; Tricia Starks, *The Body Soviet: Propaganda, Hygiene, and the Revolutionary State* (Madison: University of Wisconsin Press, 2008), 158. Naiman describes the emergence of similar ideas about the egotism and baseness of motherhood in early-twentieth-century Russian thought. See Naiman, *Sex in Public,* 39–45.

22. Issoupova, "From Duty?" 35. On the Soviet government's (mainly unsuccessful) attempts to transform the practices of rural mothers in the 1920s, see David L. Ransel, *Village Mothers* (Bloomington: Indiana University Press, 2000), chapter 2.

23. Starks, *The Body Soviet,* 136, 145, 146. The Soviet campaign to convince mothers to turn away from their traditional female networks and toward the expertise of medical science had a precedent in the West. Historians have identified the turn of the twentieth century as the period when the ideology of "scientific motherhood" first achieved prominence in Europe and the United States. "Scientific motherhood" imparted the message to women that they could not successfully raise a healthy child without the intercession of scientific and medical experts, and that motherhood resembled a profession requiring the proper training and education. See Rima Apple, *Perfect Motherhood: Science and Childrearing in America* (Rutgers, N.J.: Rutgers University Press, 2006).

24. Frances Bernstein, *The Dictatorship of Sex: Lifestyle Advice for the Soviet Masses* (DeKalb: Northern Illinois University Press, 2007), 122–28.

25. Barbara Evans Clements, "The Birth of the New Soviet Woman," in *Bolshevik Culture: Experiment and Order in the Russian Revolution,* ed. Abbott Gleason, Peter Kenez, and Richard Stites (Bloomington: Indiana University Press, 1985), 221. The Bolsheviks also held a similar view of peasants, as Wood observes: "Both peasants and women were contrasted with the conscious, active, dedicated skillful male worker comrade" (Wood, *Baba,* 117).

26. Wood, *Baba,* 1, 3.

27. Attwood, *Creating,* 11, 26; Nancy Glick Vavra, "Rabotnitsa, Constructing a Bolshevik Ideal: Women and the New Soviet State" (Ph.D. diss., University of Colorado, 2002), 3.

28. Attwood, *Creating,* 12, 168.

29. "Mat'," *Rabotnitsa* 12 (1923): 14. The author of the story is listed only as "Rit." The children's father, the reader learns, was hanged for his revolutionary activities before the birth of the youngest son.

30. Ibid., 15. Aunt Varia apparently had at least one real-life counterpart in Mariia Baryshnikova, a revolutionary who, after the death of her husband during the Civil War, left her only child with another family and volunteered for

the Polish front as a nurse. See Elizabeth Jones Hemenway, "Mothers of Communists: Women Revolutionaries and the Construction of a Soviet Identity," in *Gender and National Identity in Twentieth-Century Russian Culture,* ed. Helena Goscilo and Andrea Lanoux (DeKalb: Northern Illinois University Press, 2006), 84–85.

31. D. Chetverikov, "Semeinye dela," *Rabotnitsa i krest'ianka* 20 (1926): 11. All subsequent citations are noted in the text.

32. The narrator does, however, introduce the possibility that these disapproving reactions are merely a figment of Anna Vlas'evna's imagination, that she projects her own fears on to the workers.

33. All citations are from P. Kudriashev, "Mat' i syn," *Rabotnitsa* 2 (1925): 17.

34. Surveys of other Soviet journals from the period have produced similar conclusions about the positive portrayal of abandoning mothers. Clements observes that, in articles published in another women's magazine, *Female Communist* (*Kommunistka*), during the same period: "The writers . . . speak approvingly of the new women's decisions to leave their children. They are praised for their autonomy" (Clements, "The Birth," 227). In her survey of the journal *Issues of Motherhood and Infancy* (*Voprosy materinstva i mladenchestva*), Olga Issoupova similarly notes that, during this decade, a "line of propaganda was the idea that mothers had to be freed from the burden of their children, something which, it seems, a number of women achieved through abandonment." See Issoupova, "From Duty?" 38. Elena Bonner describes her real-life experiences growing up as the daughter of one such "abandoning mother" in her memoir, *Mothers and Daughters,* trans. Antonina W. Bouis (New York: Alfred A. Knopf, 1992). Her mother, Ruth, a dedicated and influential Communist Party member, left Bonner and her brother almost exclusively in the care of nannies while she unapologetically pursued her professional activism. Bonner poignantly describes her mother's transformation into a loving mother and grandmother in the last years of her life: "Could I have ever imagined that my mother, a Party worker, antibourgeois and maximalist, who never allowed herself to use a tender word to Egorka or me . . . could turn into a 'crazy' grandmother and great-grandmother, for whom her grandchildren and great-grandchildren would be the chief 'light in the window,' the justification for all the losses of her entire life?" (Bonner, *Mothers,* 89–90). For a discussion of Bonner's work, see Helena Goscilo, "The Italics Are Hers: Matrophobia and the Family Romance in Elena Bonner's *Mothers and Daughters,*" in *The Russian Memoir,* ed. Beth Holmgren (Evanston, Ill.: Northwestern University Press, 2003), 53–69.

35. The agitational trial, a mock trial that attempted to re-create the environment of a Soviet courtroom as accurately and in as much detail as possible, was an especially popular form of propaganda throughout the 1920s in the Soviet Union. Productions of these dramatized trials would typically travel to venues such as factories and workers' clubs. See Elizabeth A. Wood, *Performing Justice:*

Agitation Trials in Early Soviet Russia (Ithaca, N.Y.: Cornell University Press, 2005); and Julie A. Cassiday, *The Enemy on Trial* (DeKalb: Northern Illinois University Press, 2000).

36. Tricia Starks, "A Fertile Mother Russia: Pronatalist Propaganda in Revolutionary Russia," *Journal of Family History* 28 (2003): 413.

37. Waters, "The Modernisation," 126. See also Starks, *The Body Soviet,* chapter 5; and Frances Bernstein, "Envisioning Health in Revolutionary Russia: The Politics of Gender in Sexual-Enlightenment Posters of the 1920s," *Russian Review* 57 (1998): 211–15.

38. Wood, *Performing Justice,* 147.

39. Ibid., 273 n. 76. Other contributions to the "trial of the mother" genre include *Sud nad mater'iu po obvineniiu v nevezhestvennom ukhode za det'mi i neprivitii ospy, povlekshem za soboi smert' rebenka* (*Trial of a Mother Accused of the Ignorant Care of Her Children and Not Inoculating Them Against Smallpox, Leading to the Death of a Child*) (Omsk, 1925 or 1926) and *Sud nad mater'iu vinovnoi v rasprostranenii skarlatiny* (*Trial of a Mother Guilty of Spreading Scarlet Fever*) (Moscow, 1925), both by Dr. B. Sigal. For a detailed list of both published and unpublished agitational trials, see Wood, *Performing Justice,* 221–30.

40. Cassiday, *The Enemy,* 59.

41. Wood, *Performing Justice,* 6; Cassiday, *The Enemy,* 64.

42. Cassiday, *The Enemy,* 65.

43. Wood, *Performing Justice,* 129, 130. For more on the role of gender in these trials, see *Performing Justice,* chapter 7, "The Trial of the New Woman."

44. B. S. Ginzburg, *Sud nad mater'iu, podkinuvshei svoego rebenka* (Moscow: Otdel okhrany materinstva i mladenchestva narkomzdrava, 1924), 3. All further citations are to this edition and are noted in the text. The author of the preface is V. Lebedeva, head of the Department for the Protection of Motherhood and Infancy, which published the text of the play.

45. Ransel, *Village Mothers,* 79.

46. Cassiday observes that a working-class background frequently provided the only acceptable defense in the agitational trials: "Any member of the proletariat or peasantry could be rehabilitated and reintegrated into the new society regardless of the severity of his crime. Conversely, any member of the leftover social classes . . . was beyond redemption even if his crime was trivial" (*The Enemy,* 78).

47. A. G., "'Sud nad mater'iu, podkinuvshei svoego rebenka,'" *Rabotnitsa* 13–14 (1924): 44.

48. Starks, "A Fertile Mother Russia," 421.

49. Clark, *The Soviet Novel,* 69. For a discussion of how the image of the female heroine, Dasha Chumalova, influenced later female characters in socialist realist works, see Xenia Gasiorowska, "Daša Čumalova and Her Successors,"

Slavic and East European Journal 1 (1957): 260–71. For a survey of the varied responses of the reading public to the novel, see Naiman, *Sex in Public,* 89–90, 95–96. The novel was apparently a favorite of Stalin, and so its circulation reached into the millions (Edward J. Brown, *Russian Literature Since the Revolution* [Cambridge, Mass.: Harvard University Press, 1963], 131).

50. Fedor Gladkov, *Cement,* trans. A. S. Arthur and C. Ashleigh (Evanston, Ill.: Northwestern University Press, 1994), 2. All subsequent citations are to this edition and are noted in the text.

51. Eliot Borenstein, *Men Without Women* (Durham, N.C.: Duke University Press, 2000), 16.

52. Catriona Kelly writes that the Bolsheviks connected children (like women) with the "physical sphere," allowing them entrance "to the Bolshevik heaven only if they were purified and inculcated in reasonable modes of thought and in ascetic, self-denying modes of behavior. The drive to propagandize hygiene in children . . . was also a form of externally imposed discipline, a means of control over a population whose lack of ability to regulate its own physical needs was sensed as potentially troublesome." The image of children intermingling with goats succinctly captures why the Bolsheviks felt the need to implement a regime that instilled physical discipline in its youngest citizens. See Catriona Kelly, "Shaping the 'Future Race': Regulating the Daily Life of Children in Early Soviet Russia," in *Everyday Life in Early Soviet Russia,* ed. Christina Kiaer and Eric Naiman (Bloomington: Indiana University Press, 2006), 258.

53. Thea Margaret Durfee, "*Cement* and *How the Steel Was Tempered:* Variations on the New Soviet Woman," in *A Plot of Her Own: The Female Protagonist in Russian Literature,* ed. Sona Stephan Hoisington (Evanston, Ill.: Northwestern University Press, 1995), 91.

54. In his review of the novel, the avant-garde writer and literary critic Osip Brik argues that these two plot lines, "which have absolutely nothing to do with each other," are part of what render *Cement* a "bad" work of literature. See O. M. Brik, "Pochemu ponravilsia 'Tsement,'" *Na literaturnom postu* 1 (1926): 30.

55. Durfee, "*Cement,*" 95.

56. N. K. Krupskaia, "Kollektivnaia mat'," *O nashikh detiakh* 3 (1930): 1. Natalia Chernyaeva argues that the concept of "collective motherhood" emerged as an attempt to escape from a particular "ideological cul-de-sac" faced by Bolshevik theorists working at the Department for the Protection of Motherhood and Infancy in the 1920s: how to admit the existence of a biological bond between mother and child while simultaneously advocating for women's full-time participation in the labor force, which potentially threatened that bond. The solution lay in an attempt to "redraw the very definition of motherhood," with the delegates of the First All-Russian Congress of the Department for the Protection of Motherhood and Infancy being greeted with the following banner: "Be a mother not only to your own child, but to all children of the working class and the peas-

antry." See Natalia Chernyaeva, "Childcare Manuals and Construction of Motherhood in Russia, 1890–1990" (Ph.D. diss., University of Iowa, 2009), 95.

57. Durfee, "*Cement,*" 92. For Clark's original definition of these two terms, see *The Soviet Novel,* 19–24.

58. The Greens were peasant armies that fought for both the Whites and the Reds during the Russian Civil War.

59. Eric Laursen has challenged Clark's "spontaneity-consciousness paradigm" as applied to *Cement.* Relying on the concept of "instinct" to replace "spontaneity," he identifies the following pattern for successful revolutionary development in the novel: "Having undergone a near-death experience, successful characters are reborn in revolution and guided by revolutionary instinct and class instinct to fight for the bright future." Dasha's progression, accompanied by the weakening of her maternal attachment to Nurka, adheres to this pattern. See Eric Laursen, "'A New Enigmatic Language': The Spontaneity-Consciousness Paradigm and the Case of Gladkov's *Cement,*" *Slavic Review* 65 (2006): 69. For another, broader critical discussion of "spontaneity-consciousness," which Laursen draws upon, see Anna Krylova, "Beyond the Spontaneity-Consciousness Paradigm: 'Class Instinct' as a Promising Category of Historical Analysis," *Slavic Review* 62 (2003): 1–23.

60. The other aspect of Dasha's "sacrifice" involves her sexual identity. After her rape and the subsequent abandonment of her domestic life, she begins to sleep with other men, in service of the revolution: "Thus it was, for the first time, of her own free will, without being untrue to Gleb in her own soul, Dasha had relations with other men; and when she recalled it she had no regret. It was as if this had become part of her perilous work under the eyes of the counter-espionage. Some dull-eyed soldier would come to her and would not go away into the mountains . . . It is true there were moments when she also lost her head, but this was her sacrifice" (169–70). The "birth" of Dasha's "strength" stimulates not only a recession of her maternal instincts but also the awakening (or liberating) of her sexual ones. This direct link is illustrated in chapter 13, "Burning Days," when Dasha is captured, whipped, and nearly executed by a band of Cossacks. After her escape, she spends the night with Badin, whose unwanted advances she had until then repeatedly spurned: "And in the guest room of the Executive Committee, Dasha (how it came about she never knew) spent the night with him in one bed, and for the first time during the past years his stormy blood brought to her in the night hours the unforgettable passion of a woman" (134). Emboldened by her bravery while a captive of the Cossacks, Dasha exhibits strength that matches that of the rough, animal-like Badin. They can unite as equals. This contrasts Dasha with the weak and fragile Polia, whom Badin victimizes later in the novel.

61. Laursen argues that Dasha's transformation requires conquering not only maternal attachment to Nurka but also the defeat of her own childlike state.

Dasha "struggles against her desire for the child, both her 'inner child' and her daughter Nurka. Both would prevent her from assuming her role as leader in the new society. Her struggle ends only with Nurka's death, which is symbolic of the death of her own child-self, and which allows her transformation into conscious 'adult'" (Laursen, "A New Enigmatic," 77–78).

62. Vera S. Dunham, *In Stalin's Time: Middleclass Values in Soviet Fiction* (Duke, N.C.: Duke University Press, 1990), 65.

63. In Gladkov's subsequent revisions of the original 1925 text of the novel, the internal struggle within Dasha becomes much less pronounced. In the 1947 revision, for example, as Robert L. Busch notes: "Dasha's image is greatly enhanced both professionally and domestically . . . The children's home she set up is improved. This indicates greater success on her part, while keeping her daughter there ceases to be considered a sacrifice of the child's well-being for Dasha's freedom to engage in social work." See Robert L. Busch, "Gladkov's *Cement:* The Making of a Soviet Classic," *Slavic and East European Journal* 22 (1978): 354. Focusing on the gender aspects of Gladkov's many revisions, Pavla Veselá observes that "while earlier versions of Gladkov's novel discussed the results of uprooted traditional, patriarchal gender relations, later editions muted these conflicts, questioned the past order less, and focused instead on issues connected with motherhood." She also adds that Dasha becomes a "more responsible mother" in these later versions, a change "enabled by a more favorable portrayal of the communal children's home." See Pavla Veselá, "The Hardening of *Cement:* Russian Women and Modernization," *NWSA Journal* 15 (2003): 105, 116.

64. Naiman presents the character of Polia as an illustration of Gothic thematics during the New Economic Policy. See Naiman, *Sex in Public,* 173–79.

65. Laursen points out that Gleb's attraction for Polia stems from his failure to "force Dasha back into the childlike role of prerevolutionary wife," a role Polia appears well-suited to assume (Laursen, "*Cement,*" 78).

66. Jones Hemenway describes how communist memorial literature of the 1920s details a comparable transfer of maternal emotions from "biological children to fellow revolutionaries and the Russian masses" in the narratives of real-life female Bolsheviks of the period. See Jones Hemenway, "Mothers of Communists," 85.

67. Durfee, "*Cement,*" 100.

68. As Sharon Kowalsky has detailed, infanticide revealed fissures in the Soviet project for the transformation of society. Criminologists in the 1920s endowed this act with significant symbolism, and it "embodied the gulf between urban and rural, modern and backward, proletariat and peasant, and male and female." See Sharon Kowalsky, *Deviant Women: Female Crime and Criminology in Revolutionary Russia, 1880–1930* (DeKalb: Northern Illinois University Press, 2009), 181.

69. Evgeny Dobrenko, *The Making of the State Reader* (Palo Alto, Calif.: Stanford University Press, 1997), 63–64.

70. Naiman, *Sex in Public,* 90–91.

71. Issoupova, "From Duty?" 38. Soviet viewers would encounter a cinematic representation of a mother abandoning her child for the sake of the revolutionary struggle only in the final years of the Soviet state, when Aleksander Askoldov's film *The Commissar,* which was produced in 1967, was finally released in 1988. The film's central character, Klavdiia Vavilova, the commissar of a Bolshevik regiment during the time of the Civil War, finds herself unexpectedly pregnant and thus unable to continue her military activities. Billeted with a poor Jewish family, Vavilova experiences a resurgence of maternal emotions under the influence of the mother of the household, the aptly named Maria. When faced with the decision to join her regiment in the ongoing struggle or stay with her son, however, Vavilova, eventually chooses the former, leaving her child in Maria's care. Askoldov does not present Vavilova as an unequivocally positive figure, as the propaganda of the 1920s discussed above had done. Rather, as Elena Stishova has argued, this film was perhaps "the first which questioned that most sacred of things: the ethics of the revolution," explaining its lengthy banning from public viewing. See Elena Stishova, "The Mythologization of Soviet Woman: *The Commissar* and Other Cases," in *Red Women on the Silver Screen,* ed. Lynne Attwood (London: Pandora, 1993), 181.

72. Melanie Ilič, "Introduction," in *Women in the Khrushchev Era,* ed. Melanie Ilič, Susan E. Reid, and Lynne Attwood (Hampshire, Eng.: Palgrave, 2004), 10. The societal pressure to exude a "natural" feminine beauty also led Soviet women to assume an additional burden that Yulia Gradskova has termed the "beauty shift." This frequently involved exerting significant effort in order to obtain the scarce consumer goods necessary to conform to the beauty ideal. See Yulia Gradskova, *Soviet People with Female Bodies: Performing Beauty and Maternity in Soviet Russia in the Mid 1930s–1960s* (Stockholm: Stockholm University, 2007), 221.

73. Attwood, *Creating,* 116; Choi Chatterjee, "Soviet Heroines and the Language of Modernity, 1930–39," in *Women in the Stalin Era,* ed. Melanie Ilič (Hampshire, Eng.: Palgrave, 2001), 62–63; Sheila Fitzpatrick, *Everyday Stalinism* (New York: Oxford University Press, 1999), 142–43.

74. Fitzpatrick, *Everyday Stalinism,* 143.

75. These relatively mild punishments failed to deter women from seeking abortions, however, and offenders did eventually face imprisonment. As Attwood details, by 1941, the women's magazine *Female Worker* "adopted a sterner tone . . . reminding readers that 'abortion performed outside of medical facilities is a crime,' and insisting that citizens should take it on themselves to report any cases they heard of to the authorities." See Attwood, *Creating,* 124.

76. Chatterjee, "Soviet Heroines," 61.

77. David Hoffmann, *Stalinist Values: The Cultural Norms of Soviet Modernity 1917–1941* (Ithaca, N.Y.: Cornell University Press, 2003), 112.

78. Hans Guenther, "'Broad Is My Motherland': The Mother Archetype and Space in the Soviet Mass Song," in *The Landscape of Stalinism: The Art and Ideology of Soviet Space,* ed. Evgeny Dobrenko and Eric Naiman (Seattle: University of Washington Press, 2003), 80.

79. Baraban, "Return of Mother Russia," 122.

80. See the section titled "The Motherland Calls!" of the introduction to this study for more on the significance of this poster.

81. Keith A. Livers, *Constructing the Stalinist Body* (Lanham, Md.: Lexington Books, 2004), 14.

82. This absence of contemporary detail distinguishes Deineka's painting from the earlier, maternity-themed works of Petrov-Vodkin.

83. I. Sofenov, "Problema sinteza v metro," *Iskusstvo* 2 (1938): 40. Qtd. in Hans Guenther, "Archetipy sovetskoi kul'tury," in *Sotsrealisticheskii kanon,* ed. Hans Guenther and Evgeny Dobrenko (St. Petersburg: Gumanitarnoe agenstvo "Akademicheskii proekt," 2000), 778.

84. The Five-Year Plan marked a departure from earlier Soviet economic policy that had allowed limited elements of capitalism in an attempt to reinvigorate an economy devastated after years of war. The Five-Year Plan prioritized rapid industrialization and mandated the collectivization of agriculture.

85. Clark, *The Soviet Novel,* 134–35.

86. Guenther, "'Broad Is My Motherland,'" 92.

87. Eric Naiman, "Historectimies: On the Metaphysics of Reproduction in a Utopian Age," in *Sexuality and the Body in Russian Culture,* ed. Jane T. Costlow, Stephanie Sandler, and Judith Vowles (Palo Alto, Calif.: Stanford University Press, 1993), 276.

88. See Sarah Ashwin and Tatyana Lytkina, "Men in Crisis in Russia: The Role of Domestic Marginalization," *Gender and Society* 18 (2004): 189–206.

89. Beth Holmgren, *Women's Works in Stalin's Time: On Lidiia Chukovskaia and Nadezhda Mandelstam* (Bloomington: Indiana University Press, 1993), 55.

90. See Buckley, *Women and Ideology,* chapter 3: "The Stalin Years: The Woman Question Is Solved."

91. Lidia Chukovskaia, "Sof'ia Petrovna" in *Izbrannoe* (Moscow: Gorizont, 1997), 43. All subsequent citations are to this edition and are noted in the text. The translations are mine.

92. The prose foreword was added in 1957, and the epigraph derives from a poem Akhmatova wrote in 1961. Like *Sof'ia Petrovna,* Akhmatova's work did not see publication in Russia until the Perestroika period (1987). Chukovskaia, a confidante of the poet, kept a journal of her encounters with Akhmatova, which

was published in two volumes as *Notes on Anna Akhmatova,* covering the years 1938–41 and 1952–62. For more on the *Notes* and the relationship between the two women, see Holmgren, *Women's Works,* chapter 4.

93. Anna Akhmatova, *Selected Poems,* trans. Richard McKane (Newcastle-upon-Tyne, Eng.: Bloodaxe Books, 1989), 281, 282. All subsequent citations are to this translation and are noted in the text.

94. This connection would be emphasized in official Soviet World War II–era films, such as Mark Donskoi's *The Rainbow* (1944), which utilized the "Virgin Mary as the archetype of saintly maternity." See Baraban, "Return of Mother Russia," 132.

95. For a discussion of how this demythologizing took place in Soviet film of the period, see Haynes, "Reconstruction or Reproduction?" 114–30.

96. Amy E. Randall, "'Abortion Will Deprive You of Happiness!': Soviet Reproductive Politics in the Post-Stalin Era," *Journal of Women's History* 23 (2011): 18. See also Deborah A. Field, *Private Life and Communist Morality in Khrushchev's Russia* (New York: Peter Lang, 2007), chapter 4.

97. Buckley, *Women and Ideology,* 171, 174.

98. Lynne Attwood, "Conclusion," in *Red Women on the Silver Screen,* ed. Lynne Attwood (London: Pandora, 1993), 127. See ibid. for examples of films from the 1970s that explore this tension.

99. I. Grekova, "Vdovii parokhod, " in *Vdovii parokhod: Izbrannoe* (Moscow: "Tekst," 1998), 193–328.

100. *Malen'kaia Vera,* dir. V. Pichul, perf. N. Negoda, A. Sokolov, and Y. Nazarov, Gorky Film Studios, 1988.

CHAPTER THREE

1. A newspaper account from September 2003 lists four suicide bombings carried out by the "black widows" prior to the Nord-Ost Siege, with the first dating from June 2000. See Svetlana Shubaeva, "Ukus chernoi vdovy," *Nasha obshcheregional'naia gazeta,* September 11, 2003. Nord-Ost was the first act of terror carried out by the women in Moscow. Subsequently, they would also be responsible for the death of 15 people at a rock concert in Moscow in July 2003; for bringing down two Russian airplanes in August 2004, killing 89 people; and for two subway bombings in Moscow in March 2010, which killed 40 people. See Rosemarie Skaine, *Female Suicide Bombers* (Jefferson, N.C.: McFarland, 2006), 100–108. Two women were also apparently involved in the taking of hundreds of hostages at an elementary school in the North Ossetian town of Beslan. The incident left approximately 300 hostages dead. Some sources claim that the women disagreed with the rebel leader over the killing of innocent children. See Anne Nivat, "The Black Widows: Chechen Women Join the Fight for Independence—and Allah," *Studies in Conflict and Terrorism* 28 (2005): 415. The three

days that the standoff at Nord-Ost lasted provided unique insight into the characters of the women, insight obviously not attainable from the other terrorist acts. For an analysis of media representations of the female Chechens, see P. V. Romanov, V. V. Shcheblanova, and E. R. Iarskaia-Smirnova, "Politicheskii diskurs: Zhenshchiny-terroristki v interpretativnikh modeliakh rossiiskikh SMI (Diskurs-analiz gazetnikh publikatsii)," *Politicheskie issledovaniia,* December 31, 2003, 144–54.

2. See *Kommersant,* November 4, 2002, section "gvozd' programmy."

3. Anna Politkovskaia, "Nord-Ost: 6-i riad, 30-e mesto," *Novaia gazeta,* November 14, 2002.

4. Aleksandra Samarina, "Nikto ne khotel umirat'," *Vremia-MN,* November 2, 2002.

5. See Shubaeva, "Ukus chernoi vdovy."

6. Viktoriia Molodtsova, "U terrorizma zhenskoe litso," *Uchitel'skaia gazeta,* November 13, 2002.

7. "Zhenshchin-kamikadze v Chechne gotoviat araby," *Komsomol'skaia pravda,* October 25, 2002.

8. A. S. Gieroglifov, "Obshchestvennoe priznanie zhenshchiny," *Otechestvennye zapiski* 8 (1863): 518. Qtd. in A. V. Popova, "Zhenskii vopros v russkikh zhurnalakh 60-x godov XIX veka," in *Vzaimodeistvie tvorcheskikh individual'nostei russkikh pisatelei,* ed. V. N. Aniushkina (Moscow: Moscow Pedagogical Institute, 1994), 520.

9. V. A. Ramikh, *Materinstvo kak sotsiokul'turnyi fenomen* (Rostov-na-Donu: Izdatel'skii tsentr DGTU, 1995), 127.

10. Ibid., 32, 117. Former Soviet premier Mikhail Gorbachev made similar arguments a decade earlier in his book on Perestroika, where he lamented that the Soviet Union's success in ensuring female equality had, paradoxically, led to the "loosening of familial ties" and thus to a host of societal ills. The solution to this situation was to "return women to their authentic, female mission": motherhood and domesticity. See M. S. Gorbachev, *Perestroika i novoe myshlenie* (Moscow: Izdatel'stvo politicheskoi literatury, 1987), 117.

11. Ramikh, *Materinstvo kak sotsiokul'turnyi fenomen,* 124.

12. *Moskvichka* 17 (1996): 6–7.

13. Ibid., 8. Qtd. in Issoupova, "From Duty?" 44–45.

14. *Moskvichka* 17 (1996): 7.

15. Mikhail Gutseriev, member of the Duma, qtd. in *Moskvichka* 17 (July 1996): 9. Qtd. in Issoupova, "From Duty?" 44.

16. *Kavkazskii plennik,* dir. S. Bodrov-starshii, perf. S. Bodrov-mladshii, O. Menshikov, and D. Sikharulidze, "Karavan," 1996.

17. See Tatiana Kuznetsova, "Mat' soldata," *Argumenty i fakty,* September 5, 2001, Moscow edition. For a more detailed analysis of the functioning and significance of the group, see Amy Caiazza, *Mothers and Soldiers: Gender, Citi-*

zenship and Civil Society in Contemporary Russia (New York: Routledge, 2002), chapter 7; Valerie Sperling, "The Last Refuge of a Scoundrel: Patriotism, Militarism and the Russian National Idea," *Nations and Nationalism* 9 (2003): 235–53; Serguei Oushakine, *The Patriotism of Despair* (Ithaca, N.Y.: Cornell University Press, 2009), chapter 4; Maya Eichler, "Russia's Post-Communist Transformation: A Gendered Analysis of the Chechen Wars," *International Feminist Journal of Politics* 8 (2006): 486–511; Brenda Vallance, *The Rule of Law and Russian Military Reform: The Role of Soldiers' Mothers in Russian Society* (Pittsburgh: Center for Russian and East European Studies, 2000); and Kathryn Pinnick, "When the Fighting Is Over: The Soldiers' Mothers and the Afghan Madonnas," in *Post-Soviet Women: From the Baltic to Central Asia,* ed. Mary Buckley (Cambridge: Cambridge University Press, 1997), 143–56.

18. See, for example, "Materi idut v ataku," *Za rubezhom,* March 2, 2000, Moscow edition.

19. Caiazza, *Mothers and Soldiers,* 130. The Committee of Soldiers' Mothers has an analogue in the Argentinean activist group, the Mothers of the Plaza de Mayo. These mothers also harnessed the power of collective maternal strength to try and uncover the fates of their children (and the tens of thousands of other children) who had been "disappeared" during the so-called "Dirty War" waged by Argentina's military dictatorship in the mid-1970s and early 1980s. They take their name from a square in Buenos Aires that became the site of weekly protests beginning in 1977. See Marguerite Guzman Bouvard, *Revolutionizing Motherhood: The Mothers of the Plaza de Mayo* (Wilmington, Del.: Scholarly Resources, 1994).

20. Eichler, "Russia's Post-Communist Transformation," 451; Caiazza, *Mothers and Soldiers,* 125.

21. See "Materi idut v ataku."

22. Marina Murzina, "Andrei Konchalovskii: 'My vse v avtomobile bez tormozov,'" *Argumenty i fakty,* February 16, 2000.

23. At least one Russian observer has speculated, however, that the heightened public and media attention that the Committee of Soldiers' Mothers received during the first Chechen campaign subsided during the second one, in the late 1990s. Journalist Elena Grueva claims that the support of most of Russian society for this new campaign rendered them less receptive to the "crying of new mothers for new victims." See "Zhertvy," *Itogi,* December 14, 1999.

24. Caiazza, *Mothers and Soldiers,* 126; Sperling, "The Last Refuge of a Scoundrel," 248.

25. Caiazza, *Mothers and Soldiers,* 126, 158.

26. Sperling, "The Last Refuge of a Scoundrel," 244.

27. The *Moskvichka* coverage of the 1996 convocation of women in Ingushetia, to cite but one example, included a pathos-inspiring account of an Ingush woman significantly headlined "Mother Maria." This "multi-child mother"

lost both her husband and one of her sons in the war and was herself wounded. The president of the Ingush republic asked to be accepted as her adopted son. The story is a paean to a mother's moral fortitude and capacity for suffering. See *Moskvichka* 9.

28. Natal'ia Tereb, "Sestra nasha zhizn'," *Parlamentskaia gazeta,* November 22, 2002. All subsequent citations of the interview are to this article.

29. A group of mothers was able to secure the release of some 100 Russian soldiers in January 1995, and a mother's march from Moscow to Grozny took place in March 1995. See Sperling, "The Last Refuge of a Scoundrel," 243.

30. Konstantin Getmanskii and Boris Lysenko, "Rasstreliavshuiu rossiiskikh soldat chechenku mogut deportirovat' iz Germanii," *Izvestiia,* November 14, 2002.

31. Issoupova, "From Duty?" 45. For examples of headlines, see ibid., 52 n. 21. On the proliferation of violence in Russian popular culture during the 1990s, see Eliot Borenstein, *Overkill: Sex and Violence in Russian Popular Culture* (Ithaca, N.Y.: Cornell University Press, 2008).

32. Ol'ga Issoupova, "Problematic Motherhood: Child Abandonment, Abortion, Adoption and Single Motherhood in Russia in the 1990s," *Slavonica* 6 (2000): 69.

33. I. S. Stepanov, "Deti—nashe budushchee (K kontseptu 'Otsy i deti')," *Voprosy filologii* 1 (2001): 5.

34. Ramikh makes a similar point, claiming that child abandonment cannot be explained by poverty or difficult living conditions alone. She also cites the adoption of orphaned children during and after the war as evidence. See Ramikh, *Materinstvo i kul'tura,* 120.

35. Sergei Rykov, "Mama, otnimaiushchaia zhizn'," *Rabochaia tribuna,* Moscow edition, May 18, 1999.

36. Nina Fokina, "Materinskii zov," *Trud,* March 19, 1998. The Russian Federation experienced negative population growth for the first time in 1992. As Michele Rivkin-Fish observes, "the Russian media seized on this demographic event as an ominous sign of physical loss and linked it conceptually with a range of other signs of Russia's diminishing vitality." See Rivkin-Fish, "From Demographic Crisis to Dying Nation: The Politics of Language and Reproduction in Russia," in *Gender and National Identity in Twentieth-Century Russian Culture,* ed. Helena Goscilo and Andrea Lanoux (DeKalb: Northern Illinois University Press, 2006), 153.

37. Semen Galyshko, "Kogda stranoi praviat vory i p'ianitsy—akademiki streliaiutsia, a materi ubivaiut svoikh detei," *Ekonomicheskaia gazeta,* November 19, 1996, Moscow edition.

38. Bezhin was born in Moscow in 1949. He began publishing works of prose in 1979 and is also a well-known scholar and translator of Asian languages and cultures. His major works include *Metro Stop Turgenev* (*Metro "Turgenev-*

skaia"; 1979) and *The Humanitarian Boom* (*Gumanitarnyi bum;* 1985). Bezhin received the M. Sholokhov prize in 1990. See the entry on Bezhin in Sergei I. Chuprinin, ed., *Novaia Rossiia: Mir literatury: Entsiklopedicheskii slovar'-spravochnik v dvukh tomakh,* vol. 1 (Moscow: Ripol klassik, 2002).

39. All citations are from Leonid Bezhin, "Vlast' materei," *Nezavisimaia gazeta,* December 23, 1992.

40. Kunin also wrote the screenplay for *Intergirl* (*Interdevochka;* 1989), a film examining the life of a Russian hard-currency prostitute during the late-Perestroika era.

41. On the evolution of the quotidian as a theme in Russian women's writing from the 1960s to the post-Soviet period, see Benjamin M. Sutcliffe, *The Prose of Life: Russian Women Writers from Khrushchev to Putin* (Madison: University of Wisconsin Press, 2009).

42. Anatolii Kurchatkin, "Babii dom," *Oktiabr'* 6 (1986): 11, 39. For a brief overview of female characters in Kurchatkin's works, see Arch Tait, "Russian Women in Anatoly Kurchatkin," in *Women and Russian Culture,* ed. Rosalind Marsh (New York: Berghahn Books, 1998), 275–80.

43. Kurchatkin, "Babii dom," 52, 53, 54.

44. Ibid., 12.

45. Vladimir Kunin's screenplay (*kinopovest'*) provides a much more detailed alternative biography for the grandmother. As Rimgaila Salys observes: "The Kunin *kinopovest'* buttresses, confirms, and makes explicit what Krishtofovich's film quietly suggests regarding the grandmother's Stalinist past and its villain-victim paradigm . . . The grandmother's persona is developed more extensively in the *kinopovest',* which is constructed as an alternation of successive flashbacks with the present, and her life experience is set against that of the other family women." See Rimgaila Salys, "Three-Rib Circus: Women and Historical Discourse in *Rebro Adama,*" *Russian Review* 60 (2001): 628. For Kunin's text, see *Rebro Adama: Povesti* (St. Petersburg: Novyi Gelikon, 1994).

46. Kurchatkin, "Babii dom," 52.

47. Salys has suggested that the film "maps the sociohistorical landscape of the country through its representation of women." She interprets each generation of women in the film as symbolic of one of the periods of Soviet history—"Stalinist, Thaw, Stagnation, and Glasnost"—with the grandmother representing "the party elite of the first Stalinist generation, which was able, for a time, to live as it liked, while exerting its will on others and often at their expense." See Salys, "Three-Rib Circus," 621.

48. Kurchatkin, "Babii dom," 39.

49. *Rebro Adama,* dir. V. Krishtofovich, perf. I. Churikova, E. Bogdanova, S. Riabova, and M. Golubkina, Mosfil'm, 1990.

50. Viktor Vital'evich (Rostislav Yankovskii), father of Lida, confirms Nina Elizarovna's version of events later in the movie, pointing accusingly at the grand-

mother while saying: "If it hadn't been for her (*indicating the grandmother*), Nastia could have been my daughter."

51. Helena Goscilo, "The Gendered Trinity of Russian Cultural Rhetoric," in *Soviet Hieroglyphics,* ed. Nancy Condee (Bloomington: Indiana University Press, 1995), 75.

52. In this the grandmother evokes comparisons with the Baba Yaga figure of folklore. As Andreas Johns explains, Baba Yaga's literal consumption of her offspring "is unnatural not only because it is cannibalistic, but also because she attempts to prevent the normal succession or cycle of the generations. Her wish to devour children can be seen as incestuous desire, as jealousy, as the selfish wish to keep the younger generation from growing up and taking her place, or as the wish to usurp that place herself." See Andreas Johns, *Baba Yaga: The Ambiguous Mother and Witch of the Russian Folktale* (New York: Peter Lang, 2004), 106.

53. To the best of my knowledge, no Soviet critic explored the connection between the novella and the film. Most Soviet commentators, as Salys has noted, failed to acknowledge the ambiguity of the film's ending in their "rush toward humanistic affirmation" (Salys, "Three-Rib Circus," 626). Boris Berman, for example, proclaims that the film "reveals a truth that makes one want to live," while Eduard Grafov, unwittingly reading the novella into the film, writes of the "grandeur of the grandmother's . . . primeval . . . love for her 'girls.'" See Boris Berman, "A zhit', okazyvaetsia, eshche mozhno," *Ekran i stsena,* December 6, 1990; and Eduard Grafov, "Teni zabytykh zhenshchin," *Sovetskaia kul'tura,* February 23, 1991.

54. Bezhin, "Vlast'," 8.

55. Liudmila Petrushevskaia, "Otets i mat'," in *Sobranie sochinenii,* vol. 1 (Moscow: TKO AST, 1996), 31–35; ibid., "Ditia," 41–44; Liudmila Petrushevskaia, "Medea," in *Sobranie sochinenii,* vol. 2 (Moscow: TKO AST, 1996), 41–48.

56. L. V. Babaeva, *Zhenshchiny v Rossii v usloviakh sotsial'nogo pereloma: Rabota, politika, povsednevnaia zhizn'* (Moscow: Rossiiskii obshchestvennyi nauchnyi fond, 1996), 155.

57. Ibid., 156.

58. T. Markova, "Vzgliad iz zazerkal'ia: Zhenshchiny i muzhchiny v proze Liudmily Petrushevskoi," in *Tolerantnost' v kontekste mnogokladnosti rossiiskoi kul'tury,* ed. O. L. Deviatova, A. V. Medvedev, and S. L. Kropotov (Ekaterinburg: Izdatel'stvo Ural'skogo Universiteta, 2001), 142, 143.

59. Josephine Woll, "The Minotaur in the Maze: Remarks on Lyudmila Petrushevskaya," *World Literature Today* 67 (Winter 1993): 127. For an excellent discussion of Petrushevskaia's works in the context of post-Soviet "alternative prose," see Carol Adlam, *Women in Russian Literature After Glasnost: Female Alternatives* (London: Legenda, 2005), chapter 5.

60. Woll, "The Minotaur," 127, 128.

61. In particular, see Helena Goscilo, "Mother as Mothra: Totalizing Narrative and Nurture in Petrushevskaia," in *A Plot of Her Own: The Female Protagonist in Russian Literature,* ed. Sona Stephan Hoisington (Evanston, Ill.: Northwestern University Press, 1995), 102–13.

62. Goscilo, "Gendered Trinity," 77.

63. Goscilo, "Mother as Mothra," 105.

64. Goscilo, "Gendered Trinity," 77.

65. The ending of Lidia Chukovskaia's *Sof'ia Petrovna,* discussed in chapter 2, evokes a similar anxiety of interpretation.

66. Liudmila Petrushevskaia, "Our Circle," trans. Sally Laird, in *Immortal Love* (London: Virago, 1995), 335. All subsequent citations of the story are from this edition and are noted in the text. This image strikes an uncanny parallel with that of Anna Karenina similarly putting her son to bed before setting off for a ball, as mentioned in chapter 1.

67. The reference to Alesha is parenthetical to a lengthy and rapturous description of the radiance of Lenka's skin: "Lenka indeed had unusually delicate natural skin; her white flesh and red blood made a quite fantastic combination at any hour of the day, no matter whether at sunet or dawn; and her lips were truly as red as blood. All children of course have skin like this—take my Alyosha, for example" (317).

68. On the "failure of [Petrushevskaia's] narrative persona to provide a focal point of moral authority," see Monika Katz, "The Other Woman: Character Portrayal and the Narrative Voice in the Short Stories of Liudmila Petrushevskaia," in *Women and Russian Culture,* ed. Rosalind Marsh (New York: Berghahn Books, 1998), 194.

69. Leo Tolstoy, *Anna Karenina,* trans. Constance Garnett, ed. Leonard J. Kent and Nina Berberova (New York: Modern Library, 2000), 331.

70. M. N. Lipovetskii, *"Svobody chernaia rabota": Stat'i o literature* (Sverdlovsk: Sredne-Ural'skoe knizhnoe izdatel'stvo, 1991), 153.

71. I. Sergo, "Siuzhet antichnogo i khristianskogo v zhenskom prochtenii ('Teshcha Edipa' i 'Ditia' Liudmily Petrushevskoi)," in *Tolerantnost' v kontekste mnogokladnosti russkoi kul'tury,* ed. O. L. Deviatova, A. V. Medvedev, and S. L. Kropotov (Ekaterinburg: Izdatel'stvo Ural'skogo Universiteta, 2001), 171.

72. Sally Dalton-Brown, *Voices from the Void: The Genres of Liudmila Petrushevskaia* (New York: Berghahn Books, 2000), 36, 37. Katz also minimizes the narrator's guilt, arguing that she "is not an intrinsically evil character" but is instead simply the product of a corrupt and selfish environment "in which each individual egotistically seeks his own gain" (Katz, "The Other Woman," 191).

73. Woll, "The Minotaur," 125.

74. Inna Tigountsova, *The Ugly in Russian Literature* (Saarbruecken, Ger.: Lambert Academic, 2010), 163. Like Woll, Tigountsova also foregrounds a Dostoevskian link in Petrushevskaia's prose, and her use of the term *bezobrazie* re-

lates specifically to Dostoevsky's poetics of the ugly. See Tigountsova, *The Ugly*, chapter 5, for a fuller development of this connection.

75. Goscilo, "Mother as Mothra," 106–7.

76. Ibid., 108; Woll, "The Minotaur," 127.

77. As Goscilo notes, "Anna Andrianovna['s] 'telling power' . . . assumes the tyrannical form of censorship over all narrative within the story" (Goscilo, "Mother as Mothra," 112).

78. Liudmila Petrushevskaia, *The Time: Night,* trans. Sally Laird (Evanston, Ill.: Northwestern University Press, 1994), 2–3. All subsequent citations are from this edition and are noted in the text.

79. Anna Andrianovna's posturing and frequently ridiculous affectations, her delusions of grandeur contrasted with the banal background of her surroundings, provide *The Time: Night* with its overall tone of black humor. For example, some drug addicts con Anna into buying horse tranquilizers for them, skillfully manipulating her vanity to reach their goal. Anna's description of their supposed chivalry, this lofty imagery juxtaposed with their obviously mercenary goals, is absurdly comic. This effect is heightened by Anna's confession that she faithfully waits for her "Friend," as she calls him, to show up at her apartment and return to her the money that he owes for the drugs (15–16).

80. Ramikh argues that a woman's relations even with her husband become maternal: "A woman [also] displays her motherly feelings . . . to the man who must become the father of her child. He is already her child in a certain sense." See Ramikh, *Materinstvo i kul'tura,* 119.

81. In her dissertation on single motherhood in Russia, Jennifer Utrata describes the social pressure that grandmothers experience to become precisely the kind of self-sacrificing figure that Anna imagines herself to be. See Jennifer Utrata, "Counting on Motherhood, Not Men: Single Motherhood and Social Change in the New Russia" (Ph.D. diss., University of California–Berkeley, 2008), 234.

82. Anna similarly accomplishes this elevation of family drama to the level of tragedy through literary allusion with her citation of Anna Akhmatova's poem "Requiem": "my son in prison, pray for me, pray for me (as *she* wrote, our great genius)" (81). This reference implicitly equates the fate of Anna's son, who is sent to prison after a fight, with that of Akhmatova's son, an innocent man imprisoned for political reasons during the Stalin era. It also connects Anna's troubles with her children to a noble, poetic tradition of maternal suffering. See T. Prokhorova, "Rasshirenie vozmozhnostei kak avtorskaia strategiia: Liudmila Petrushevskaia," *Voprosy literatury* 3 (2009), http://magazines.russ.ru/voplit/2009/3/pro7-pr.html.

83. This is reminiscent of the discussion about not putting a crib near the path of the grandmother's bedpan in *Adam's Rib.*

84. Tigountsova identifies both works as "dystopias with Dostoevskian characters and locus. The house/home is a place of dystopia for both Dostoevsky and

Petrushevskaia; its oppressive nature is represented in the narrowing of space and the tyranny taking place within that home" (Tigountsova, *The Ugly,* 163).

85. *The Time: Night,* 62.

CONCLUSION

1. G. S. Smith, "Mothers and Sons in Russian Literature," *Journal of European Studies* 34 (2004): 299.

2. *Ital'ianets,* dir. A. Kravchuk, perf. K. Spiridonov, M. Kuznetsova, and N. Reutov, Lenfilm Studio and Tulos Cinema, 2005.

3. Bruno Schulz, "The Mythologization of Reality," trans. John M. Bates, http://www.babelmatrix.org/works/pl/Schulz,_Bruno/Mityzacja_rzeczywisto%C5%9Bci/en/1455-The_Mythologization_of_Reality.

Bibliography

Adlam, Carol. *Women in Russian Literature After Glasnost: Female Alternatives.* London: Legenda, 2005.

Adon'ieva, S. B. "O ritual'noi funktsii zhenshchiny v russkoi traditsii." *Zhivaia starina* 1 (1998): 26–28.

Akhmatova, Anna. *Selected Poems.* Translated by Richard McKane. Newcastle-upon-Tyne, Eng.: Bloodaxe Books, 1989.

Alexandrov, Vladimir. *Limits to Interpretation.* Madison: University of Wisconsin Press, 2004.

Allen, Ann Taylor. *Feminism and Motherhood in Western Europe, 1890–1970.* New York: Palgrave Macmillan, 2005.

Andrew, Joe. "Mothers and Daughters in Russian Literature of the First Half of the Nineteenth Century." *Slavonic and East European Review* 73, no. 1 (1995): 37–60.

Anikin, Andrei V. "Money and the Russian Classics." Translated by Thomas Epstein. *Diogenes* 162 (1993): 99–109.

Apple, Rima. *Perfect Motherhood: Science and Childrearing in America.* Rutgers, N.J.: Rutgers University Press, 2006.

Ashwin, Sarah. "Introduction." In *Gender, State and Society in Post-Soviet Russia,* edited by Sarah Ashwin, 1–29. London: Routledge, 2000.

Ashwin, Sarah, and Tatyana Lytkina. "Men in Crisis in Russia: The Role of Domestic Marginalization." *Gender and Society* 18, no. 2 (2004): 189–206.

Atkinson, Dorothy. "Society and the Sexes in the Russian Past." In *Women in Russia,* edited by Dorothy Atkinson, Alexander Dallin, and Gail Warshofsky Lapidus, 3–28. Palo Alto, Calif.: Stanford University Press, 1977.

Attwood, Lynne. "Conclusion." In *Red Women on the Silver Screen,* edited by Lynne Attwood, 124–30. London: Pandora, 1993.

———. *Creating the New Soviet Woman: Women's Magazines as Engineers of Female Identity, 1922–53.* London: Macmillan, 1999.

———. "Rationality versus Romanticism: Representations of Women in the Stalinist Press." In *Gender in Russian History and Culture,* edited by Linda Edmondson, 158–76. Hampshire, Eng.: Palgrave, 2001.

Babaeva, L. V. *Zhenshchiny v Rossii v usloviakh sotsial'nogo pereloma: Rabota, politika, povsednevnaia zhizn'.* Moscow: Rossiiskii obshchestvennyi nauchnyi fond, 1996.

Badinter, Elisabeth. *Mother Love, Myth and Reality: Motherhood in Modern History.* New York: Macmillan, 1981.

Baraban, Elena. "The Return of Mother Russia: Representations of Women in Soviet Wartime Cinema." *Aspasia* 4 (2010): 121–38.

Baranskaia, Natalia. *Nedelia kak nedelia: povest'.* Paris: Institut d'Études Slaves, 1988.

Barker, Adele Marie. *The Mother Syndrome in the Russian Folk Imagination.* Columbus, Ohio: Slavica, 1986.

Berdiaev, Nikolai. *O naznachenii cheloveka.* Moscow, 1993.

———. *The Russian Idea.* Translated by R. M. French. Hudson, N.Y.: Lindisfarne, 1992.

Berman, Boris. "A zhit', okazyvaetsia, eshche mozhno." *Ekran i stsena,* December 6, 1990.

Bernstein, Frances. *The Dictatorship of Sex: Lifestyle Advice for the Soviet Masses.* DeKalb: Northern Illinois University Press, 2007.

———. "Envisioning Health in Revolutionary Russia: The Politics of Gender in Sexual-Enlightenment Posters of the 1920s." *Russian Review* 57, no. 2 (1998): 191–217.

Bezhin, Leonid. "Vlast' materei." *Nezavisimaia gazeta,* December 23, 1992.

Bill, Valentine Tschebotarioff. "The Dead Souls of Russia's Merchant World." *Russian Review* 15, no. 4 (1956): 245–58.

Billington, James. *The Icon and the Axe.* New York: Alfred A. Knopf, 1966.

Bloch, Ruth H. "American Feminine Ideals in Transition: The Rise of the Moral Mother, 1785–1815." *Feminist Studies* 4, no. 2 (1978): 100–126.

Bonnell, Victoria E. *Iconography of Power: Soviet Political Posters Under Lenin and Stalin.* Berkeley: University of California Press, 1997.

Bonner, Elena. *Mothers and Daughters.* Translated by Antonina W. Bouis. New York: Alfred A. Knopf, 1992.

Borenstein, Eliot. *Men Without Women: Masculinity and Revolution in Russian Fiction, 1917–1929.* Durham, N.C.: Duke University Press, 2000.

———. *Overkill: Sex and Violence in Russian Popular Culture.* Ithaca, N.Y.: Cornell University Press, 2008.

Bouvard, Marguerite Guzman. *Revolutionizing Motherhood: The Mothers of the Plaza de Mayo.* Wilmington, Del.: Scholarly Resources, 1994.

Bowers, Toni. *The Politics of Motherhood: British Writing and Culture, 1680–1760.* Cambridge: Cambridge University Press, 1996.

Brik, O. M. "Pochemu ponravilsia 'Tsement.'" *Na literaturnom postu* 1 (1926): 30–32.

Brooks, Jeffrey. *Thank You, Comrade Stalin! Soviet Public Culture from Revolution to Cold War.* Princeton, N.J.: Princeton University Press, 2000.

Brown, Edward J. *Russian Literature Since the Revolution.* Cambridge, Mass.: Harvard University Press, 1963.

Bucher, Greta. "Stalinist Families: Motherhood, Fatherhood, and Building the New Soviet Person." In *The Making of Russian History,* edited by John W. Steinberg and Rex A. Wade, 129–52. Bloomington, Ind.: Slavica, 2009.

———. *Women, the Bureaucracy and Daily Life in Postwar Moscow, 1945–1953.* Boulder, Colo.: East European Monographs, 2006.

Buckley, Mary. *Women and Ideology in the Soviet Union.* Ann Arbor: University of Michigan Press, 1989.

Bulgakov, S. *Kupina neopalimaia: Opyt dogmaticheskogo istolknovaniia nekotorykh chert v pravoslavnom pochitanii Bogomateri.* Vilnius, 1991.

Busch, Robert L. "Gladkov's *Cement:* The Making of a Soviet Classic." *Slavic and East European Journal* 22, no. 3 (1978): 348–61.

Bushmin, A. S. *Evoliutsiia satiry Saltykova-Shchedrina.* Leningrad: 'Nauka,' 1984.

Caiazza, Amy. *Mothers and Soldiers: Gender, Citizenship and Civil Society in Contemporary Russia.* New York: Routledge, 2002.

Cassiday, Julie A. *The Enemy on Trial.* DeKalb: Northern Illinois University Press, 2000.

Cavender, Mary W. *Nests of the Gentry: Family, Estate and Local Loyalties in Provincial Russia.* Newark: University of Delaware Press, 2007.

Chatterjee, Choi. "Soviet Heroines and the Language of Modernity, 1930–39." In *Women in the Stalin Era,* edited by Melanie Ilič, 49–68. Hampshire, Eng.: Palgrave, 2001.

Chernyaeva, Natalia. "Childcare Manuals and Construction of Motherhood in Russia, 1890–1990." Ph.D. diss., University of Iowa, 2009.

Chernyshevsky, N. G. *Chto Delat'?: Iz Rasskazov o Novykh Liudiakh.* Leningrad: Khudozhestvennaia literatura, 1967.

Chetverikov, D. "Semeinye dela." *Rabotnitsa i krest'ianka* 20 (1926): 11–15.

Chukovskaia, Lidia. "Sof'ia Petrovna." In *Izbrannoe,* 5–80. Moscow: Gorizont, 1997.

Chuprinin, Sergei I., ed. *Novaia Rossiia: Mir literatury: Entsiklopedicheskii slovar'-spravochnik v dvukh tomakh.* Vol. 1. Moscow: Ripol klassik, 2002.

Clark, Katerina. *The Soviet Novel.* Bloomington: Indiana University Press, 2000.

Clements, Barbara Evans. "The Birth of the New Soviet Woman." In *Bolshevik Culture: Experiment and Order in the Russian Revolution,* edited by Abbott Gleason, Peter Kenez, and Richard Stites, 220–37. Bloomington: Indiana University Press, 1985.

Corbesero, Susan. "Femininity (Con)scripted: Female Images in Soviet Wartime Poster Propaganda, 1941–45." *Aspasia* 4, no. 1 (2010): 103–20.

Costlow, Jane T. "The Pastoral Source: Representations of the Maternal Breast in Nineteenth-Century Russia." In *Sexuality and the Body in Russian Culture,* edited by Jane T. Costlow, Stephanie Sandler, and Judith Vowles, 223–36. Palo Alto, Calif.: Stanford University Press, 1993.

Cova, Anne. "Où en est l'histoire de la maternité?" *CLIO: Histoire, femmes et sociétés* 21 (2005), http://clio.revues.org/index1465.html.

Cruise, Edwina. "Women, Sexuality and the Family in Tolstoy." In *The Cambridge Companion to Tolstoy,* edited by Donna Tussing Orwin, 191–205. Cambridge: Cambridge University Press, 2002.

Dalton-Brown, Sally. *Voices from the Void: The Genres of Liudmila Petrushevskaia.* New York: Berghahn Books, 2000.

Dijkstra, Bram. *Idols of Perversity: Fantasies of Feminine Evil in Fin-de-Siècle Culture.* New York: Oxford University Press, 1986.

Dobrenko, Evgeny. *The Making of the State Reader.* Palo Alto, Calif.: Stanford University Press, 1997.

The Domostroi: Rules for Russian Households in the Time of Ivan the Terrible, edited and translated by Carolyn Johnston Pouncy. Ithaca, N.Y.: Cornell University Press, 1994.

Dostoevsky, Fedor. *A Writer's Diary.* Translated by Kenneth Lantz. Evanston, Ill.: Northwestern University Press, 1993.

Draitser, Emil. *Techniques of Satire: The Case of Saltykov-Shchedrin.* Berlin: Walter de Gruyter, 1994.

Dugin, A. *Metafizika blagoi vesti.* Moscow, 1996.

Duma o Kavkaze s nadezhdoi i veroi. Special issue of *Moskvichka* no. 17 (1996): 6–12.

Dunham, Vera S. *In Stalin's Time: Middleclass Values in Soviet Fiction.* Duke, N.C.: Duke University Press, 1990.

Durfee, Thea Margaret. "*Cement* and *How the Steel Was Tempered:* Variations on the New Soviet Woman." In *A Plot of Her Own: The Female Protagonist in Russian Literature,* edited by Sona Stephan Hoisington, 89–101. Evanston, Ill.: Northwestern University Press, 1995.

Edmondson, Linda. "Putting Mother Russia in a European Context." In *Art, Nation and Gender: Ethnic Landscapes, Myths and Mother-Figures,* edited by Tricia Cusack and Síghle Breathnach-Lynch, 53–64. Hampshire, Eng.: Ashgate, 2003.

Eichler, Maya. "Russia's Post-Communist Transformation: A Gendered Analysis of the Chechen Wars." *International Feminist Journal of Politics* 8, no. 4 (2006): 486–511.

Emerson, Caryl. "Prosaics in *Anna Karenina:* Pro and Con." *Tolstoy Studies Journal* 8 (1995–96): 150–76.

Engel, Barbara Alpern. *Breaking the Ties That Bound: The Politics of Marital Strife in Late Imperial Russia.* Ithaca, N.Y.: Cornell University Press, 2011.

———. "Mothers and Daughters: Family Patterns and the Female Intelligentsia." In *The Family in Imperial Russia,* edited by David Ransel, 44–59. Urbana: University of Illinois Press, 1978.

———. *Mothers and Daughters: Women of the Intelligentsia in Nineteenth-Century Russia.* Evanston, Ill.: Northwestern University Press, 2000.

———. *Women in Russia, 1700–2000.* Cambridge: Cambridge University Press, 2004.

Engelstein, Laura. *The Keys to Happiness: Sex and the Search for Modernity in Fin-de-Siècle Russia.* Ithaca, N.Y.: Cornell University Press, 1992.

Fedotov, G. P. *The Russian Religious Mind.* New York: Harper, 1960.

Field, Deborah A. *Private Life and Communist Morality in Khrushchev's Russia.* New York: Peter Lang, 2007.

Figes, Orlando. *A People's Tragedy: The Russian Revolution 1891–1924.* New York: Penguin, 1998.

Fitzpatrick, Sheila. *Everyday Stalinism.* New York: Oxford University Press, 1999.

Fokina, Nina. "Materinskii zov." *Trud,* March 19, 1998.

Foote, I. P. "Introduction: Saltykov and 'The Golovlyovs.'" In *Saltykov-Shchedrin's "The Golovlyovs": A Critical Companion,* edited by I. P. Foote, 3–44. Evanston, Ill.: Northwestern University Press, 1997.

Freeze, Gregory L. "Bringing Order to the Russian Family: Marriage and Divorce in Imperial Russia, 1760–1860." *Journal of Modern History* 62, no. 4 (1990): 709–46.

———. "Krylov vs. Krylova: 'Sexual Incapacity' and Divorce in Tsarist Russia." In *The Human Tradition in Modern Russia,* edited by William B. Husband, 5–17. Wilmington, Del.: Scholarly Resources, 2000.

———. "Profane Narratives About a Holy Sacrament: Marriage and Divorce in Late Imperial Russia." In *Sacred Stories: Religion and Spirituality in Modern Russia,* edited by Mark D. Steinberg and Heather J. Coleman, 146–78. Bloomington: Indiana University Press, 2007.

G., A. "'Sud nad mater'iu, podkinuvshei svoego rebenka.'" *Rabotnitsa* 13–14 (1924): 44.

Galyshko, Semen. "Kogda stranoi praviat vory i p'ianitsy—akademiki streliaiutsia, a materi ubivaiut svoikh detei." *Ekonomicheskaia gazeta,* November 19, 1996, Moscow edition.

Gasiorowska, Xenia. "Daša Čumalova and Her Successors." *Slavic and East European Journal* 1, no. 4 (1957): 260–71.

Gaster, Theodor H. "Myth and Story." In *Sacred Narrative: Readings in the Theory of Myth,* edited by Alan Dundes, 110–36. Berkeley: University of California Press, 1984.

Gerschenkron, Alexander. "Time Horizon in Russian Literature." *Slavic Review* 34, no. 4 (1975): 75–91.

Getmanskii, Konstantin, and Boris Lysenko. "Rasstreliavshuiu rossiiskikh soldat chechenku mogut deportirovat' iz Germanii." *Izvestiia,* November 14, 2002.

Gieroglifov, A. S. "Obshchestvennoe priznanie zhenshchiny." *Otechestvennye zapiski* 8 (1863): 518–34.

Ginzburg, B. S. *Sud nad mater'iu, podkinuvshei svoego rebenka.* Moscow: Otdel okhrany materinstva i mladenchestva narkomzdrava, 1924.

Gladkov, Fedor. *Cement.* Translated by A. S. Arthur and C. Ashleigh. Evanston, Ill.: Northwestern University Press, 1994.

Goikhbarg, A. G. *Brachnoe, semeinoe, i opekunskoe pravo Sovetskoi respubliki.* Moscow, 1920.

Goldman, Wendy Z. *Women, the State and Revolution: Soviet Family Policy and Social Life, 1917–1936.* Cambridge: Cambridge University Press, 1993.

Goldstein, Darra. "Domestic Porkbarrelling in Nineteenth-Century Russia, or Who Holds the Keys to the Larder?" In *Russia, Women, Culture,* edited by Helena Goscilo and Beth Holmgren, 125–51. Bloomington: Indiana University Press, 1996.

Gorbachev, M. S. *Perestroika i novoe myshlenie.* Moscow: Izdatel'stvo politicheskoi literatury, 1987.

Gorky, Maxim. *Mother.* Translated by Margaret Wettlin. In *Collected Works in Ten Volumes,* vol. 3. Moscow: Progress, 1978.

Goscilo, Helena. "The Gendered Trinity of Russian Cultural Rhetoric." In *Soviet Hieroglyphics,* edited by Nancy Condee, 68–92. Bloomington: Indiana University Press, 1995.

———. "The Italics Are Hers: Matrophobia and the Family Romance in Elena Bonner's *Mothers and Daughters.*" In *The Russian Memoir,* edited by Beth Holmgren, 53–69. Evanston, Ill.: Northwestern University Press, 2003.

———. "Mother as Mothra: Totalizing Narrative and Nurture in Petrushevskaia." In *A Plot of Her Own: The Female Protagonist in Russian Literature,* edited by Sona Stephan Hoisington, 102–13. Evanston, Ill.: Northwestern University Press, 1995.

Gradskova, Yulia. *Soviet People with Female Bodies: Performing Beauty and Maternity in Soviet Russia in the Mid 1930s–1960s.* Stockholm: Stockholm University, 2007.

Grafov, Eduard. "Teni zabytykh zhenshchin." *Sovetskaia kul'tura,* February 23, 1991.

Greene, Diana. "Mid-Nineteenth-Century Domestic Ideology in Russia." In *Women and Russian Culture: Projections and Self-Perceptions,* edited by Rosalind Marsh, 78–97. New York: Berghahn Books, 1998.

Grekova, I. "Vdovii parokhod." In *Vdovii parokhod: Izbrannoe,* 193–328. Moscow: "Tekst," 1998.

Grenier, Svetlana. "A Tale of Two Cities: Tolstoy's Gendered Moral Geography in *Anna Karenina.*" In *Mapping the Feminine: Russian Women and Cultural Dif-*

ference, edited by Hilde Hoogenboom, Catherine Theimer Nepomnyashchy, and Irina Reyfman, 93–111. Bloomington: Indiana University Press, 2008.

Grossman, Joan Delaney. "Feminine Images in Old Russian Literature and Art." *California Slavic Studies* 11 (1980): 33–70.

Grot, Natalia. "From a Family Chronicle: Reminiscences for Children and Grandchildren." Translated by Lesli LaRocco. In *Russia Through Women's Eyes,* edited by Toby W. Clyman and Judith Vowles, 220–41. New Haven, Conn.: Yale University Press, 1996.

Grueva, Elena. "Rodina i mat'." *Itogi,* December 14, 1999.

Grum, Konstantin. *Rukovodstvo k vospitaniiu I.* St. Petersburg, 1843–45.

Guenther, Hans. "Archetipy sovetskoi kul'tury." In *Sotsrealisticheskii kanon,* edited by Hans Guenther and Evgeny Dobrenko, 743–84. St. Petersburg: Gumanitarnoe agenstvo "Akademicheskii proekt," 2000.

———. "'Broad Is My Motherland': The Mother Archetype and Space in the Soviet Mass Song." In *The Landscape of Stalinism: The Art and Ideology of Soviet Space,* edited by Evgeny Dobrenko and Eric Naiman, 77–95. Seattle: University of Washington Press, 2003.

"Gvozd' programmy." *Kommersant,* November 4, 2002, http://www.kommersant.ru/doc.html?path=/daily/2002/201m/25432274.htm.

Haynes, John. "Reconstruction or Reproduction? Mothers and the Great Soviet Family in Cinema After Stalin." In *Women in the Khrushchev Era,* edited by Melanie Ilič, Susan E. Reid, and Lynne Attwood, 114–30. Hampshire, Eng.: Palgrave, 2004.

Heldt, Barbara. "Motherhood in a Cold Climate: The Poetry and Career of Maria Shkapskaya." In *Sexuality and the Body in Russian Culture,* edited by Jane T. Costlow, Stephanie Sandler, and Judith Vowles, 237–54. Palo Alto, Calif.: Stanford University Press, 1993.

———. "Rassvet and the Woman Question." *Slavic Review* 36, no. 1 (1977): 76–85.

Hellberg-Hirn, Elena. *Soil and Soul: The Symbolic World of Russianness.* Aldershot, Eng.: Ashgate, 1998.

Hemenway, Elizabeth Jones. "Mothers of Communists: Women Revolutionaries and the Construction of a Soviet Identity." In *Gender and National Identity in Twentieth-Century Russian Culture,* edited by Helena Goscilo and Andrea Lanoux, 75–92. DeKalb: Northern Illinois University Press, 2006.

Hoffmann, David. *Stalinist Values: The Cultural Norms of Soviet Modernity 1917–1941.* Ithaca, N.Y.: Cornell University Press, 2003.

Holmgren, Beth. *Rewriting Capitalism: Literature and the Market in Late Tsarist Russia and the Kingdom of Poland.* Pittsburgh: University of Pittsburgh Press, 1998.

———. *Women's Works in Stalin's Time: On Lidiia Chukovskaia and Nadezhda Mandelstam.* Bloomington: Indiana University Press, 1993.

———. "Writing the Female Body Politic (1945–1985)." In *A History of Women's Writing in Russia,* edited by Adele Marie Barker and Jehanne M. Gheith, 225–42. Cambridge: Cambridge University Press, 2002.

Hubbs, Joanna. *Mother Russia: The Feminine Myth in Russian Culture.* Bloomington: Indiana University Press, 1988.

Ilič, Melanie. "Introduction." In *Women in the Khrushchev Era,* edited by Melanie Ilič, Susan E. Reid, and Lynne Attwood, 5–28. Hampshire, Eng.: Palgrave, 2004.

Issoupova, Olga. "From Duty to Pleasure? Motherhood in Soviet and Post-Soviet Russia." In *Gender, State and Society in Post-Soviet Russia,* edited by Sarah Ashwin, 30–54. London: Routledge, 2000.

———. "Problematic Motherhood: Child Abandonment, Abortion, Adoption and Single Motherhood in Russia in the 1990s." *Slavonica* 6, no. 2 (2000): 68–87.

Ital'ianets. Dir. A. Kravchuk. Perf. K. Spiridonov, M. Kuznetsova, and N. Reutov. Lenfilm Studio and Tulos Cinema, 2005.

Johns, Andreas. *Baba Yaga: The Ambiguous Mother and Witch of the Russian Folktale.* New York: Peter Lang, 2004.

Kaminskii, G. N. "'Rech' narkoma zdravookhraneniia na vtoroi sessii Vserossiiskogo TsIK XVI soiuza." *Voprosy materinstva i mladenchestva* 3 (1936): 1–4.

Kaplan, E. Ann. *Motherhood and Representation: The Mother in Popular Culture and Melodrama.* London: Routledge, 1992.

Karpushina, Olga. "The Idea of the Family in Tolstoy's *Anna Karenina:* The Moral Hierarchy of Families." *Studies in Slavic Cultures II:* "Anna Karenina on Page and Screen" (2001): 63–92.

Katz, Monika. "The Other Woman: Character Portrayal and the Narrative Voice in the Short Stories of Liudmila Petrushevskaia." In *Women and Russian Culture,* edited by Rosalind Marsh, 188–97. New York: Berghahn Books, 1998.

Kavkazskii plennik. Dir. S. Bodrov-starshii. Perf. S. Bodrov-mladshii, O. Menshikov, and D. Sikharulidze. "Karavan," 1996.

Kay, Rebecca. *Russian Women and Their Organizations: Gender, Discrimination and Grassroots Women's Organizations, 1991–96.* New York: St. Martin's, 2000.

Kelly, Catriona. *Children's World: Growing Up in Russia, 1890–1991.* New Haven, Conn.: Yale University Press, 2007.

———. "Educating Tat'yana: Manners, Motherhood and Moral Education (*Vospitanie*), 1760–1840." In *Gender in Russian History and Culture,* edited by Linda Edmondson, 1–28. Hampshire, Eng.: Palgrave, 2001.

———. *Refining Russia: Advice Literature, Polite Culture, and Gender from Catherine to Yeltsin.* Oxford: Oxford University Press, 2001.

———. "Shaping the 'Future Race': Regulating the Daily Life of Children in

Early Soviet Russia." In *Everyday Life in Early Soviet Russia,* edited by Christina Kiaer and Eric Naiman, 258–81. Bloomington: Indiana University Press, 2006.

Kharkhordin, Oleg. *The Collective and the Individual in Russia: A Study of Practices.* Berkeley: University of California Press, 1999.

Khomiakov, A. S. *O starom i novom.* Moscow, 1988.

Kiaer, Christina. "Delivered from Capitalism: Nostalgia, Alienation, and the Future of Reproduction in Tretiakov's *I Want a Child!*" In *Everyday Life in Early Soviet Russia,* edited by Christina Kiaer and Eric Naiman, 183–216. Bloomington: Indiana University Press, 2006.

Kirshchenbaum, Lisa A. "'Our City, Our Hearths, Our Families': Local Loyalties and Private Life in Soviet World War II Propaganda." *Slavic Review* 59, no. 4 (2000): 825–47.

———. *Small Comrades: Revolutionizing Childhood in Soviet Russia, 1917–1932.* New York: RoutledgeFalmer, 2001.

Knibiehler, Yvonne, and Catherine Fouquet. *L'histoire des mères du moyen-âge à nos jours.* Paris: Éditions Montalba, 1980.

Kollontai, Alexandra. "Communism and the Family." In *Alexandra Kollontai: Selected Writings,* translated and edited by Alix Holt, 250–60. New York: W. W. Norton, 1977.

———. "Tezisy o kommunisticheskoi morali v oblasti brachnykh otnoshenii." *Kommunistka* 12–13 (1921): 28–34.

Komissar. Dir. A. Askoldov. Perf. N. Mordiukova, R. Bykov, and R. Nedashkovskaia. Mosfil'm, 1967.

Kornblatt, Judith Deutsch. *Divine Sophia: The Wisdom Writings of Vladimir Solovlyov.* Ithaca, N.Y.: Cornell University Press, 2009.

Koven, Seth, and Sonya Michel, eds. *Mothers of a New World: Maternalist Politics and the Origins of Welfare States.* New York: Routledge, 1993.

Kowalsky, Sharon. *Deviant Women: Female Crime and Criminology in Revolutionary Russia, 1880–1930.* DeKalb: Northern Illinois University Press, 2009.

Kramer, Karl D. "Satiric Form in Saltykov's *Gospoda Golovlevy.*" In *Saltykov-Shchedrin's "The Golovlyovs": A Critical Companion,* edited by I. P. Foote, 119–35. Evanston, Ill.: Northwestern University Press, 1997.

Kriuchnikovaia, A. "Zadacha russkoi materi." *Sem'ia i shkola* 2, no. 1 (1874): 24–31.

Krupskaia, N. K. "Kollektivnaia mat'." *O nashikh detiakh* 3 (1930): 1–2.

———. *Zhenshchina-Rabotnitsa.* 2nd edition. Moscow-Leningrad, 1926.

Krylova, Anna. "Beyond the Spontaneity-Consciousness Paradigm: 'Class Instinct' as a Promising Category of Historical Analysis." *Slavic Review* 62, no. 1 (2003): 1–23.

Kudriashev, P. "Mat' i syn." *Rabotnitsa* 2 (1925): 17.

Kunin, Vladimir. *Rebro Adama: Povesti.* St. Petersburg: Novyi Gelikon, 1994.

Kurchatkin, Anatolii. "Babii dom." *Oktiabr'* 6 (1986): 3–55.

Kuznetsova, Tatiana. "Mat' soldata." *Argumenty i fakty,* September 5, 2001, Moscow edition. http://www.moskva.aif.ru/issues/426/06_06.

Laursen, Eric. "'A New Enigmatic Language': The Spontaneity-Consciousness Paradigm and the Case of Gladkov's *Cement.*" *Slavic Review* 65, no. 1 (2006): 66–89.

Lipovetskii, M. N. *"Svobody chernaia rabota": Stat'i o literature.* Sverdlovsk: Sredne-Ural'skoe knizhnoe izdatel'stvo, 1991.

"Liudi, bud'te bditel'ny: Desant materei v Nazrane." *Moskvichka* 17 (1996): 6–7.

Livers, Keith A. *Constructing the Stalinist Body.* Lanham, Md.: Lexington Books, 2004.

Livingston, Sally. "Owning Property, Being Property: Medieval and Modern Women Shape the Narratives of Marriage." Diss., Harvard University, 2008.

Makarenko, A. S. *The Collective Family: A Handbook for Russian Parents.* Translated by Robert Daglish. Garden City, N.Y.: Anchor Books, 1967.

Makashin, Sergei. *Saltykov-Shchedrin: Biografiia.* Moscow: Khudozhestvennaia literatura, 1951.

———. *Saltykov-Shchedrin: Seredina puti, 1860e–1870e gody.* Moscow: Khudozhestvennaia literatura, 1984.

Malen'kaia Vera. Dir. V. Pichul. Perf. N. Negoda, A. Sokolov, and Y. Nazarov. Gorky Film Studios, 1988.

Mandelker, Amy. *Framing Anna Karenina.* Columbus: Ohio State University Press, 1993.

Manning, Roberta Thompson. *The Crisis of the Old Order in Russia.* Princeton, N.J.: Princeton University Press, 1982.

Marker, Gary. *Imperial Saint: The Cult of St. Catherine and the Dawn of Female Rule in Russia.* DeKalb: Northern Illinois University Press, 2007.

Markova, T. "Vzgliad iz zazerkal'ia: zhenshchiny i muzhchiny v proze Liudmily Petrushevskoi." In *Tolerantnost' v kontekste mnogokladnosti rossiiskoi kul'tury,* edited by O. L. Deviatova, A. V. Medvedev, and S. L. Kropotov, 138–44. Ekaterinburg: Izdatel'stvo Ural'skogo Universiteta, 2001.

Marrese, Michelle. *A Woman's Kingdom: Noblewomen and the Control of Property in Russia, 1700–1861.* Ithaca, N.Y.: Cornell University Press, 2002.

"Materi idut v ataku." *Za rubezhom,* March 2, 2000, Moscow edition.

Mat' i ditia: Pribavlenie k "Khoziaike," no. 53. St. Petersburg, 1902.

McReynolds, Susan. "'You Can Buy the Whole World': The Problem of Redemption in *The Brothers Karamazov.*" *Slavic and East European Journal* 52, no. 1 (2008): 87–111.

Meyer, Priscilla. *How the Russians Read the French: Lermontov, Dostoevsky, Tolstoy.* Madison: University of Wisconsin Press, 2008.

Miller, Marlyn L. "Russian Motherhood Discourse in *Zhenskii vestnik,* 1904–14." Master's thesis, Brandeis University, 2002.

Mironov, Boris. *The Social History of Imperial Russia, 1700–1917,* vol. 1. Translated by Ben Eklof. Boulder, Colo.: Westview, 1999.

Molodtsova, Viktoriia. "U terrorizma zhenskoe litso?" *Uchitel'skaia gazeta,* November 13, 2002. http://www.ug.ru/02.46/t28.htm.

Morson, Gary Saul. *Anna Karenina in Our Time.* New Haven, Conn.: Yale University Press, 2007.

———. "Prosaics and *Anna Karenina.*" *Tolstoy Studies Journal* 1 (1988): 1–12.

Moss, Anne Eakin. "Tolstoy's Politics of Love: 'That Passionate and Tender Friendship That Exists Only Among Women.'" *Slavic and East European Journal* 53, no. 4 (2009): 566–86.

Murav, Harriet. *Russia's Legal Fictions.* Ann Arbor: University of Michigan Press, 1998.

Murzina, Marina. "Andrei Konchalovskii: 'My vse v avtomobile bez tormozov.'" *Argumenty i fakty,* February 16, 2000. http://www.aif.ru/oldsite/1008/.

Naiman, Eric. "Historectimies: On the Metaphysics of Reproduction in a Utopian Age." In *Sexuality and the Body in Russian Culture,* edited by Jane T. Costlow, Stephanie Sandler, and Judith Vowles, 255–76. Palo Alto, Calif.: Stanford University Press, 1993.

———. *Sex in Public.* Princeton, N.J.: Princeton University Press, 1997.

Nakachi, Mie. "Population, Politics and Reproduction. Late Stalinism and Its Legacy." In *Late Stalinist Russia,* edited by Juliane Fürst, 23–45. New York: Routledge, 2006.

Nivat, Anne. "The Black Widows: Chechen Women Join the Fight for Independence—and Allah." *Studies in Conflict and Terrorism* 28 (2005): 413–19.

Olson, Laura J. "Russianness, Femininity and Romantic Aesthetics in *War and Peace.*" *Russian Review* 56, no. 4 (1997): 515–31.

Orwin, Donna. *Tolstoy's Art and Thought, 1847–1880.* Princeton, N.J.: Princeton University Press, 1993.

"Otkliki chitatel'nits." *Zhenskii zhurnal* 2 (1927): 12.

Oushakine, Serguei. *The Patriotism of Despair.* Ithaca, N.Y.: Cornell University Press, 2009.

Ouspensky, Leonid, and Vladimir Lossky. *The Meaning of Icons.* Translated by G. E. H. Palmer and E. Kadloubovsky. Crestwood, N.Y.: St. Vladimir's Seminary, 1982.

Owen, Thomas C. *Capitalism and Politics in Russia.* Cambridge: Cambridge University Press, 1981.

Pavlova, I. B. *Tema sem'i i roda u Saltykova-Shchedrina v literaturnom kontekste epokhi.* Moscow: IMLI RAN, "Nasledie," 1999.

Petrushevskaia, Liudmila. "Ditia." In *Sobranie sochinenii* 1:41–44. Moscow: TKO AST, 1996.

———. "Medea." In *Sobranie sochinenii* 2:41–48. Moscow: TKO AST, 1996.

———. "Otets i mat'." In *Sobranie sochinenii* 1:31–35. Moscow: TKO AST, 1996.

———. "Our Circle." Translated by Sally Laird. In *Immortal Love,* 312–48. London: Virago, 1995.

———. "Svoi krug." In *Sobranie sochinenii* 1:45–67. Moscow: TKO AST, 1996.

———. *The Time: Night.* Translated by Sally Laird. Evanston, Ill.: Northwestern University Press, 1994.

———. "Vremia noch'." In *Sobranie sochinenii* 1:311–98. Moscow: TKO AST, 1996.

Pinnick, Kathryn. "When the Fighting Is Over: The Soldiers' Mothers and the Afghan Madonnas." In *Post-Soviet Women: From the Baltic to Central Asia,* edited by Mary Buckley, 143–56. Cambridge: Cambridge University Press, 1997.

Plant, Rebecca Jo. *Mom: The Transformation of Motherhood in Modern America.* Chicago: University of Chicago Press, 2010.

Poliakov, L.V. "Women's Emancipation and the Theology of Sex in Nineteenth-Century Russia." *Philosophy East and West* 42, no. 2 (1992): 297–309.

Politkovskaia, Anna. "Nord-Ost: 6-i riad, 30-e mesto." *Novaia Gazeta,* November 14, 2002. http: //2002.novayagazeta.ru/nomer/2002/84n/n84n-s14.shtml.

Pomperi, Eduard. *Zhenshchina po otnosheniiu k muzhchinam v ispolnenii ee materinskikh, sestrinskikh i supruzheskikh obiazannostei.* Moscow: Ia. F. Bogdanov, 1866.

Popova, A. V. "Zhenskii vopros v russkikh zhurnalakh 60-x godov XIX veka." In *Vzaimodeistvie tvorcheskikh individual'nostei russkikh pisatelei,* edited by V. N. Aniushkina, 151–60. Moscow: Moscow Pedagogical Institute, 1994.

Pouncy, Carolyn Johnston. "Introduction." In *The Domostroi,* edited and translated by Carolyn Johnston Pouncy, 1–53. Ithaca, N.Y.: Cornell University Press, 1994.

Powell, David E. *Antireligious Propaganda in the Soviet Union: A Study of Mass Persuasion.* Cambridge, Mass.: MIT Press, 1975.

Prokhorova, T. "Rasshirenie vozmozhnostei kak avtorskaia strategiia: Liudmila Petrushevskaia." *Voprosy literatury* 3 (2009). http://magazines.russ.ru/voplit/2009/3/pro7-pr.html.

Pushkareva, Natalia. *Chastnaia zhizn' russkoi zhenshchiny: Nevesta, zhena, liubovnitsa.* Moscow: Ladomir, 1997.

———. *Women in Russian History,* translated and edited by Eve Levin. New York: M. E. Sharpe, 1997.

Ramikh, Vera. *Materinstvo i kul'tura (Filosofsko-kul'turologicheskii analiz).* Rostov-na-Donu: Izdatel'skii tsentr DGTU, 1997.

———. *Materinstvo kak sotsiokul'turnyi fenomen.* Rostov-na-Donu: Izdatel'skii tsentr DGTU, 1995.

Rancour-LaFerriere, Daniel. *The Joy of All Who Sorrow: Icons of the Mother of God in Russia.* Moscow: Ladomir, 2005.

Randall, Amy E. "'Abortion Will Deprive You of Happiness!': Soviet Reproductive Politics in the Post-Stalin Era." *Journal of Women's History* 23, no. 3 (2011): 13–38.

Ransel, David L. *Village Mothers.* Bloomington: Indiana University Press, 2000.

Rebro Adama. Dir. V. Krishtofovich. Perf. I. Churikova, E. Bogdanova, S. Riabova, and M. Golubkina. Mosfil'm, 1990.

Reid, Susan E. "The Khrushchev Kitchen: Domesticating the Scientific-Technological Revolution." *Journal of Contemporary History* 40, no. 2 (2005): 289–316.

Rents, Il'ia. "Ekskursiia v 'sviatye mesta.'" *Zhenskii zhurnal* 6 (1926): 9–10.

Riabov, O. V. *Matushka-Rus'.* Moscow: Nauchnyi-isdatel'skii tsentr Ladomir, 2001.

———. *"Rossiia-matushka": Natsionalizm, gender, i voina v Rossii XX veka.* Stuttgart: Ibidem-Verlag, 2007.

———. *Russkaia filosofiia zhenstvennosti.* Ivanovo: Isdatel'skii tsentr 'Iunona,' 1999.

Rich, Adrienne. *Of Woman Born: Motherhood as Experience and Institution.* New York: Norton, 1995.

Rieber, Alfred J. *Merchants and Entrepreneurs in Imperial Russia.* Chapel Hill: University of North Carolina Press, 1982.

Ries, Nancy. "The Burden of Mythic Identity: Russian Women at Odds with Themselves." In *Feminist Nightmares,* edited by Susan Ostrov Weisser and Jennifer Fleischner, 242–68. New York: NYU Press, 1994.

Rit. "Mat'." *Rabotnitsa* 12 (1923): 14–15.

Rivkin-Fish, Michele. "From Demographic Crisis to Dying Nation: The Politics of Language and Reproduction in Russia." In *Gender and National Identity in Twentieth-Century Russian Culture,* edited by Helena Goscilo and Andrea Lanoux, 151–73. DeKalb: Northern Illinois University Press, 2006.

Rogger, Hans. *Russia in the Age of Modernisation and Revolution 1881–1917.* Essex, Eng.: Longman Group, 1983.

Romanov, P. V., V. V. Shcheblanova, and E. R. Iarskaia-Smirnova. "Politicheskii diskurs: Zhenshchiny-terroristki v interpretativnikh modeliakh rossiiskikh SMI (Diskurs-analiz gazetnikh publikatsii)." *Politicheskie issledovaniia* 6 (2003): 144–54.

Roosevelt, Priscilla. *Life on the Russian Country Estate.* New Haven, Conn.: Yale University Press, 1995.

Rotkirch, Anna. "'Coming to Stand on Firm Ground': The Making of a Soviet Working Mother." In *On Living Through Soviet Russia,* edited by Daniel Bertaux, Paul Thompson, and Anna Rotkirch, 146–75. New Brunswick, N.J.: Transaction, 2005.

Rowley, Alison. "Where Are All the Mother-Heroines? Images of Maternity in Soviet Films of the 1930s." *Canadian Journal of History* 44 (2009): 25–38.

Rozanov, Vasily. "Opavshie list'ia: Korob vtoroi." In *Sobranie sochinenii v dvukh tomakh,* vol. 2. Moscow: Pravda, 1990.

———. *Religiia, Filosofiia, Kul'tura.* Moscow: "Respublika," 1992.

Rubchak, Marian J. "Christian Virgin or Pagan Goddess: Feminism versus the Eternally Feminine in Ukraine." In *Women in Russia and Ukraine,* edited by Rosalind Marsh, 315–30. Cambridge: Cambridge University Press, 1996.

Rykov, Sergei. "Mama, otnimaiushchaia zhizn'." *Rabochaia tribuna,* May 18, 1999, Moscow edition.

Saltykov-Shchedrin, M. E. "Dnevnik provintsiala v Peterburge." In *Sobranie sochinenii* 10:271–553. Moscow: Khudozhestvennaia literatura, 1970.

———. *The Golovlyov Family,* translated by Ronald Wilks. London: Penguin Books, 1988.

———. *Gospoda Golovlevy.* In *Sobranie sochinenii* 13:7–262. Moscow: Khudozhestvennaia literatura, 1972.

———. *Gospoda Tashkentsy.* In *Sobranie sochinenii* 10:7–267. Moscow: Khudozhestvennaia literatura, 1970.

———. "Sovremennye prizraki." In *Sobranie sochinenii* 6:381–406. Moscow: Khudozhestvennaia literatura, 1968.

Salys, Rimgaila. "Three-Rib Circus: Women and Historical Discourse in *Rebro Adama." Russian Review* 60, no. 4 (2001): 614–30.

Samarina, Aleksandra. "Nikto ne khotel umirat'." *Vremia-MN,* November 2, 2002.

Sandomirskaia, Irina. *Kniga o rodine: Opyt analiza diskursivnikh praktik.* Vienna: Wiener Slawistischer Almanach, 2001.

Sanine, Kyra. *Saltykov-Chtchédrine: Sa vie et ses oeuvres.* Paris: Institut d'Études Slaves, 1955.

Schulz, Bruno. "The Mythologization of Reality." Translated by John M. Bates. http://www.babelmatrix.org/works/pl/Schulz,_Bruno/Mityzacja_rzeczywisto%C5%9Bci/en/1455-The_Mythologization_of_Reality.

Sergo, I. "Siuzhet antichnogo i khristianskogo v zhenskom prochtenii ('Teshcha Edipa' i 'Ditia' Liudmily Petrushevskoi)." In *Tolerantnost' v kontekste mnogokladnosti russkoi kul'tury,* edited by O. L. Deviatova, A. V. Medvedev, and S. L. Kropotov, 170–72. Ekaterinburg: Izdatel'stvo Ural'skogo Universiteta, 2001.

Shchepanskaia, T. "Mat'." In *Muzhiki i baby: Muzhskoe i zhenskoe v russkoi traditsionnoi kul'ture,* 339–44. St. Petersburg: Iskusstvo-SPB, 2005.

———. "Materinskoe prokliatie." In *Muzhiki i baby: Muzhskoe i zhenskoe v russkoi traditsionnoi kul'ture,* 337–39. St. Petersburg: Iskusstvo-SPB, 2005.

———. "Mat'-zemlia." In *Muzhiki i baby: Muzhskoe i zhenskoe v russkoi traditsionnoi kul'ture,* 344–50. St. Petersburg: Iskusstvo-SPB, 2005.

Shevchenko, Olga. *Crisis and the Everyday in Postsocialist Moscow.* Bloomington: Indiana University Press, 2009.

Shevzov, Vera. *Russian Orthodoxy on the Eve of Revolution.* New York: Oxford University Press, 2004.

Shubaeva, Svetlana. "Ukus chernoi vdovy." *Nasha obshcheregional'naia gazeta,* September 11, 2003.

Sigal, Dr. B. *Sud nad mater'iu po obvineniiu v nevezhestvennom ukhode za det'mi i neprivitii ospy, povlekshem za soboi smert' rebenka.* Omsk, 1925 or 1926.

———. *Sud nad mater'iu vinovnoi v rasprostranenii skarlatiny.* Moscow, 1925.

Skaine, Rosemarie. *Female Suicide Bombers.* Jefferson, N.C.: McFarland, 2006.

Smith, G. S. "Mothers and Sons in Russian Literature." *Journal of European Studies* 34, no. 4 (2004): 291–307.

S. N. "Despotizm materinskoi liubvi." *Zhurnal dlia vospitaniia* 3 (1859): 125–46; 4 (1859): 184–206.

Sofenov, I. "Problema sinteza v metro." *Iskusstvo* 2 (1938): 40.

Solov'ev, Nikolai. *Zhenshchina i deti.* Moscow, 1869.

Sperling, Valerie. "The Last Refuge of a Scoundrel: Patriotism, Militarism and the Russian National Idea." *Nations and Nationalism* 9, no. 2 (2003): 235–53.

Starks, Tricia. *The Body Soviet: Propaganda, Hygiene, and the Revolutionary State.* Madison: University of Wisconsin Press, 2008.

———. "A Fertile Mother Russia: Pronatalist Propaganda in Revolutionary Russia." *Journal of Family History* 28, no. 3 (2003): 411–42.

Stepanov, I. S. "Deti—nashe budushchee (K kontseptu 'Otsy i deti')." *Voprosy filologii* 1 (2001): 5–11.

Stishova, Elena. "The Mythologization of Soviet Woman: *The Commissar* and Other Cases." In *Red Women on the Silver Screen,* edited by Lynne Attwood, 175–85. London: Pandora, 1993.

Stites, Richard. "M. L. Mikhailov and the Emergence of the Woman Question in Russia." *Canadian Slavic Studies* 3, no. 2 (1969): 178–99.

Sutcliffe, Benjamin M. *The Prose of Life: Russian Women Writers from Khrushchev to Putin.* Madison: University of Wisconsin Press, 2009.

Tait, Arch. "Russian Women in Anatoly Kurchatkin." In *Women and Russian Culture,* edited by Rosalind Marsh, 275–80. New York: Berghahn Books, 1998.

Tereb, Natal'ia. "Sestra nasha zhizn'." *Parlamentskaia gazeta,* November 22, 2002.

Thurer, Shari L. *The Myths of Motherhood.* Boston: Houghton Mifflin, 1994.

Tigountsova, Inna. *The Ugly in Russian Literature.* Saarbruecken, Ger.: Lambert Academic, 2010.

Todd, William Mills, III. "The Anti-Hero with a Thousand Faces: Saltykov-Shchedrin's Porfiry Golovlev." *Studies in the Literary Imagination* 9, no. 1 (1976): 87–105.

Tolstoi, L. N. *Anna Karenina.* Moscow: Eksmo, 2010.

———. *Anna Karenina,* translated by Constance Garnett, edited by Leonard J. Kent and Nina Berberova. New York: Modern Library, 2000.

———. "Detstvo." In *Polnoe sobranie sochinenii* 1:11–90. Moscow: 'Nauka', 2000.

Tovrov, Jessica. "Mother-Child Relationships Among the Russian Nobility." In *The Family in Imperial Russia,* edited by David Ransel, 15–43. Urbana: University of Illinois Press, 1978.

———. *The Russian Noble Family: Structure and Change.* New York: Garland, 1987.

Uspenskii, Vasilii. *K. S. Petrov-Vodkin: Materinstvo.* St. Petersburg: Arka, 2010.

Utrata, Jennifer Marie. "Counting on Motherhood, Not Men: Single Motherhood and Social Change in the New Russia." Diss., University of California-Berkeley, 2008.

Vallance, Brenda. *The Rule of Law and Russian Military Reform: The Role of Soldiers' Mothers in Russian Society.* Pittsburgh: Center for Russian and East European Studies, 2000.

Vavra, Nancy Glick. "Rabotnitsa, Constructing a Bolshevik Ideal: Women and the New Soviet State." Diss., University of Colorado, 2002.

Veselá, Pavla. "The Hardening of Cement: Russian Women and Modernization." *NWSA Journal* 15, no. 3 (2003): 104–23.

Vorsheva, Raisa. "Pis'mo Raisy Vorshevoi." *Zhenskii zhurnal* 3 (1927): 13.

Vvedenskii, A. I. "Literaturnye kharakteristiki." In *Saltykov-Shchedrin's "The Golovlyovs": A Critical Companion,* edited by I. P. Foote, 59–62. Evanston, Ill.: Northwestern University Press, 1997.

Wachtel, Andrew. *The Battle for Childhood: Creation of a Russian Myth.* Palo Alto, Calif.: Stanford University Press, 1990.

———. "Death and Resurrection in *Anna Karenina.*" In *In the Shade of the Giant: Essays on Tolstoy,* edited by Hugh McLean, 100–114. Berkeley: University of California Press, 1989.

Wagner, William. *Marriage, Property and Law in Late Imperial Russia.* New York: Oxford University Press, 1994.

———. "Orthodox Domesticity: Creating a Social Role for Women." In *Sacred Stories: Religion and Spirituality in Modern Russia,* edited by Mark D. Steinberg and Heather J. Coleman, 119–45. Bloomington: Indiana University Press, 2007.

———. "The Trojan Mare: Women's Rights and Civil Rights in Late Imperial Russia." In *Civil Rights in Imperial Russia,* edited by Olga Crisp and Linda Edmondson, 65–84. Oxford: Clarendon, 1989.

Walicki, Andrzej. *A History of Russian Thought.* Palo Alto, Calif.: Stanford University Press, 1979.

Wampuszyc, Eva V. "The Narrative of Noble Decline and the Discourse of

Money in Late 19th C. Russia and the Kingdom of Poland: M. E. Saltykov-Shchedrin and B. Prus." Diss., University of Michigan, 2004.

Wasiolek, Edward. *Tolstoy's Major Fiction.* Chicago: University of Chicago Press, 1978.

Waters, Elisabeth. "The Modernisation of Russian Motherhood, 1917–37." *Soviet Studies* 44, no. 1 (1992): 123–35.

Weir, Justin. "Anna Incommunicada: Language and Consciousness in *Anna Karenina.*" *Tolstoy Studies Journal* 8 (1995–96): 99–111.

Woll, Josephine. "The Minotaur in the Maze: Remarks on Lyudmila Petrushevskaya." *World Literature Today* 67, no. 1 (1993): 125–31.

The Woman Question: Selections from the Writings of Karl Marx, Frederick Engels, V. I. Lenin, Joseph Stalin. New York: International, 1972.

Wood, Elizabeth A. *The Baba and the Comrade: Gender and Politics in Revolutionary Russia.* Bloomington: Indiana University Press, 1997.

———. *Performing Justice: Agitation Trials in Early Soviet Russia.* Ithaca, N.Y.: Cornell University Press, 2005.

Wortman, Richard. "The Russian Empress as Mother." In *The Family in Imperial Russia,* edited by David Ransel, 60–74. Urbana: University of Illinois Press, 1978.

Zenkovsky, Serge A. "The Descent of the Virgin into Hell." In *Medieval Russia's Epics, Chronicles and Tales,* 153–60. New York: E. P. Dutton, 1974.

"Zhenshchin-kamikadze v Chechne gotoviat araby." *Komsomol'skaia Pravda,* October 25, 2002. http://www.kp.ru/daily/22662/21453/.

Zhuk, V. N. *Mat' i ditia: Gigiena v obshchedostupnom izlozhenii.* St. Petersburg: Izdatel'stvo Gubinskogo, 1911.

Index

About the Author

Jenny Kaminer is an assistant professor of Russian at the University of California–Davis.